P9-ELH-483

12-26-63

Theology and Race Relations

JOSEPH T. LEONARD, S.S.J.

With a Foreword by
MOST REV. PATRICK A. O'BOYLE
Archbishop of Washington

THE BRUCE PUBLISHING COMPANY
MILWAUKEE

IMPRIMI POTEST:

    VERY REV. GEORGE F. O'DEA, S.S.J.
    Superior General

NIHIL OBSTAT:

    REVEREND HARRY A. ECHLE
    Censor librorum

IMPRIMATUR:

    ✠ PATRICK A. O'BOYLE
    Archbishop of Washington

July 26, 1963

FOREWORD

Almost daily, the front pages of our newspapers are carrying accounts and stories of racial disturbances, demonstrations, and protests occurring in various parts of the United States. During the past few months, the eagerness and expectation of the American Negro to secure recognition of his constitutionally guaranteed rights as a full citizen have been raised to new heights, and the increased protests have assumed a new urgency indicated by the participation of white citizens, including clergymen of all denominations, who are anxious to see the end of injustice which has been long inflicted on Negro citizens.

In 1958, the Bishops of the United States, in their statement on *Discrimination and the Christian Conscience*, made it clear that the heart of the race problem was moral and religious. Since that time, the religious and moral nature of the problem and its solution has become more apparent and widely accepted, and recently President Kennedy reminded the nation of the importance of the moral and religious implications contained in this problem.

It is not sufficient that Christians be merely aware of the legal, political, economic, or social issues involved in this present-day conflict. They must also know and become keenly sensitive to the moral issues at stake.

As I finish reading the manuscript of Father Leonard's book, I find that it is a stark and undramatic presentation of the basic principles of Catholic moral theology involved and an application of these principles to areas of interracial behavior. I am quite pleased with the stress it places on the function and necessity of charity in resolving this problem. The depth of our Catholicism is going to be tested in the crucible of race relations, and the touchstone of our racial attitudes and actions will reveal to the world whether our claim to adhere to Christ's law of charity is true gold or base metal. The sincerity and reality of our Catholicism, our ideals, our virtues, our

iii

preaching, and our teaching is being daily exposed by our acceptance or rejection of the legitimate demands of our Negro brothers. If we reject them, all our high-sounding utterances and well-meaning professions of being followers and disciples of Jesus Christ are shown as counterfeit. St. John tells us: "My dear children, let us not love in word, neither with the tongue, but in deed and in truth" (1 Jn 3:18).

The racial unrest and uneasiness so prevalent today is a clear indication that many Christians have failed to apprehend the scope and significance of Christ's command to love our neighbor. This spiritual blindness is not only a scandal to those whom we are supposed to love but whom we reject, but it is devastating the moral integrity and soundness of all our people and weakening the moral fiber of American life.

THEOLOGY AND RACE RELATIONS makes explicit the moral and religious questions and the obligations entailed, not only in the racial problem in general, but also most usefully in specific and personal areas. Of particular value and interest to Catholics are the sections on the relationship of Catholic Negroes to their parish church and to Catholic schools, as well as the theological examination of the objections which some Catholics have raised to the teaching of their bishop that racial segregation was immoral and sinful. A thorough understanding and appreciation of these moral issues and obligations will go far in helping our people shoulder their moral responsibilities of justice and charity, so that their actions, deeds, words, and thoughts will spring from hearts and minds informed with the deep knowledge of Christian truth and burning with Christian charity.

I was happy to learn that The Bruce Publishing Company is going to make Father Leonard's book available to the public and it is my sincere hope that it will be widely read not only by priests and religious, but by all our Catholic people; that it will be carefully studied in our schools, colleges, and seminaries; and that all men of goodwill will read it and be influenced and moved by these useful and timely applications of sound Catholic moral theology.

PATRICK A. O'BOYLE
Archbishop of Washington

July 26, 1963
Washington, D.C.

ACKNOWLEDGMENTS

The author would like to take this opportunity to make public acknowledgment of his deep gratitude and appreciation to the Reverend John C. Ford, S.J., professor of Moral Theology at the Catholic University of America, for his guidance, encouragement, understanding, and suggestions, invariably reflective of his theological acumen and insight, which were most helpful in formulating what must be considered the better parts of this book. Also extremely helpful and appreciated are the suggestions, criticisms, and corrections so kindly given by the Rev. John C. Selner, S.S., and the Rev. Ernest E. Larkin, O.Carm.

Expressions of thanks are also due to Rev. William J. Kenealy, S.J., Visiting Professor of Law at Loyola University in Chicago, who graciously agreed to read and criticize the legal presentation in Chapter 15 on the right to education, and to Very Rev. James F. Didas, S.S.J., Rector of St. Joseph's Seminary, Washington, D. C., who faithfully and with infinite patience read and checked manuscript, galley sheets, and proofs. His experienced editorial eye rarely passed over a clumsy or ungrammatical construction or sentence format.

A debt of gratitude is owed to Archbishop Patrick A. O'Boyle, not only for the gracious foreword which he has given, but also for his personal interest in this work, and for the time which he devoted to reading it twice in spite of an extraordinarily busy schedule as Archbishop of the Nation's Capitol. And a word of personal thanks should also be given to Very Rev. George F. O'Dea, S.S.J., Superior General of the Josephite Fathers, who helped not only with interest and kindness, but also in a very material and practical way by supplying the necessary permissions and physical requirements for the materialization of this book.

My personal debt to all these, as well as to others who in less immediate, but not less real, ways gave kind cooperation during the past years, can only be expressed and declared — the debt cannot be fully repaid.

Recognition should be made of the kindness of the following for permission to quote from copyrighted books:

Columbia University Press, for quotations from J. Greenberg, *Race Relations and the American Law*; University of Chicago Press for J. Fichter, *Sociology*; W. Stanton, *The Leopard's Spots*; and Newton Edwards, *The Courts and the Public Schools*; Oxford Press (New York) for C. Vann Woodward, *Strange Career of Jim Crow*; Southern Regional Council for *The Segregation Decisions*; S.C.M. Press, Ltd., for *Church and Race in South Africa*; Weston College Press for A. C. Potter, *Humani Generis with Commentary*; Helicon Press for K. Rahner, *Theological Investigations*; Macmillan Co., for Joseph O'Neill, *Catholic Case Against Segregation*; T. B. Maston, *Segregation and Desegregation*; and E. Franklin Frazier, *The Negro in the U.S.*; Pantheon Books for J. Pieper, *Justice*; Chas. Scribner's Sons for J. Maritain, *Person and the Common Good*; B. Herder for J. Messner, *Social Ethics*; and J. Abbo and J. Hannon, *The Sacred Canons*; Benziger Bros. for copyrighted article in *Summa Theologia*; Harper and Row for G. Myrdal, *An American Dilemma*; Chas. Johnson, *Patterns of Negro Segregation*; Martin Luther King, Jr., *Stride Toward Freedom*; C. Abrams, *Forbidden Neighbors*; and J. H. Moynihan, *Life of Archbishop John Ireland*; UNESCO for J. Comas, *Racial Myths*; and Yves Congar, *The Catholic Church and the Race Question*; Catholic University of America Press for F. Gilligan, *Morality of the Color Line*; J. Brokhage, *Francis Patrick Kenrick's Opinion on Slavery*; and Richard Roche, *Catholic Colleges and the Negro Student*; America Press for J. LaFarge, *Interracial Justice*; Loyola University Press for *Social Orientations*; Fides Publishing for Mathew Ahman, *The New Negro*; University of North Carolina Press for M. Proudfoot, *Diary of a Sit-In*; and A. Miller, *Racial Discrimination and Private Education*; Henry Regnery Co. for Calvez and Perrin, *The Church and Social Justice*; Rinehart & Co. for W. Dykeman and J. Stokely, *Neither Black Nor White*; University of California Press for D. McEntire, *Residence and Race*; Rutgers University Press for A. Blaustein and C. C. Ferguson, Jr., *Desegregation and the Law*;

Springer Publishing for B. Karon, for *The Negro Personality*; Oxford University Press (London) for quotation from *Race and Intelligence*; Association Press for F. Loescher, *The Protestant Church and the Negro*; University of Michigan Press for D. Dumond, *Anti-Slavery*; Newman Press for G. Kelly, *Guidance for Religious*; V. Yzermans, *All Things in Christ*; P. Guilday, *National Pastorals*; Geoffrey Bles for J. Maritain, *Anti-Semitism*; Sheed and Ward for C. Journet, *The Church of the Word Incarnate*; Houghton Mifflin for John Griffin, *Black Like Me*; Catholic Theological Society of America for quotations from its proceedings; Dr. Audrey Shuey for permission to quote her *Testing of Negro Intelligence*; Dr. Waldo Beach for quotations from *Theological Analysis of Race Relations*; and Msgr. Joseph Doherty for quotations from his *Moral Problems of Interracial Marriage*.

Also, I wish to express appreciation for permission to quote from copyrighted material which appeared in the following periodicals and newspapers: *The Catholic Mind, America, American Ecclesiastical Review, Social Order, The New York Times, Interracial Review, Review for Religious, The Pope Speaks, Ave Maria, Homiletic and Pastoral Review, Jet Magazine, Michigan Catholic,* as well as to the N.C.W.C. for quotations from its translations of papal encyclicals.

Quotation from *Dusk at the Mountain* by Haynes Johnson. Copyright 1963, by Haynes Johnson. Reprinted by permission of Doubleday and Company, Inc.

Quotation from *Nought for Your Comfort* by Trevor Huddleston. Copyright 1956, by Ernest Urban Trevor Huddleston. Reprinted by permission of Doubleday and Company, Inc.

Quotation from *Catholic Viewpoint on Race Relations* by John LaFarge. Copyright 1956, by Doubleday and Company, Inc. Reprinted by permission of the publisher.

Quotation from *Church and the Reconstruction of the Modern World* by Terence McLaughlin. Copyright 1957, by Terence P. McLaughlin. Reprinted by permission of Doubleday and Company, Inc.

CONTENTS

x   CONTENTS

THEOLOGY AND RACE RELATIONS

CHAPTER 1

RACE RELATIONS —
A THEOLOGICAL PROBLEM

Since the Civil War, many domestic problems have occupied the attention of the American people — the questions of prohibition, woman suffrage, tariff, unemployment, labor and unions, economic depression, etc. But none of these has ever attained the far-reaching importance that the problem of race relations has had in the past one hundred years. In recent years questions of segregation and integration have often overshadowed problems and issues of international scope and import. Indeed, public opinion has been divided on this issue into various camps, each with its own firm adherents. Little wonder, then, that these race-relation problems, which have at times been magnified beyond their actual difficulty, have resulted in emotional, political, and civic disturbances and strife in various parts of the country, both North and South. A mere glance at the almost frightening quantity of studies of this situation, published by sociologists in recent years, is ample proof of interest in this question. However, theologians have not kept pace with the social scientists in their study and consideration of this problem. With a few notable exceptions, there has been a scarcity of ethical, moral, or theological studies of the problem of race relations, resulting in a great disproportion between the theological contributions and the massive quantity of contributions by both Catholic and non-Catholic social scientists.

This lack of theological literature has caused Waldo Beach to complain of the tendency to separate completely religious truth and secular truth. This trend has resulted in theology being held in disrepute and suspect by the natural scientists:

> . . . the issue of racial relations . . . has been, at least in America, the special province of social science. Christian theologians have given relatively little attention to this problem, while sociologists have produced many detailed studies, in apparent independence of Christian inspiration. The spirit underlying the extensive literature by the students of interracial tension and cooperation, as with most social science, seems entirely quantitative, "scientific," naturalistic, positivistic. If theology was ever the queen of the sciences, for the major number of social scientists today she has long since been dethroned.[1]

This disproportion is all the more disturbing in view of the fact that the social scientists themselves realize, and recently have become more articulate in stating, that the entire problem must be solved on a moral or ethical basis. Gunnar Myrdal, whose study of the American race problem first appeared in 1944 and is still considered a sociological *locus classicus*, emphasizes that when considered practically, the problem is a moral or ethical issue:

> When we thus choose to view the Negro problem as primarily a moral issue, we are in line with popular thinking. It is as a moral issue that this problem presents itself in the daily life of the ordinary people; it is as a moral issue that they brood over it in their thoughtful moments. It is in terms of conflicting moral valuations that it is discussed in church and school, in the family circle, in the workshop, on the street corner, as well as in the press, over the radio, in trade union meetings, in the state legislatures, the Congress and the Supreme Court. The social scientist, in his effort to lay bare concealed truths and to become maximally useful in guiding practical and political action, is prudent when, in the approach to a problem, he sticks as closely as possible to the common man's ideas and formulations, even though he knows that further investigation will carry him into tracts uncharted in the popular consciousness.[2]

In a more recent analysis of prejudice and discrimination, sociologists Simpson and Yinger also indicate the role of ethical and moral values in a solution of the race problem. They establish complete social equality and integration as the goal which must be sought for

---

[1] Waldo Beach, "A Theological Analysis of Race Relations," *Faith and Ethics: The Theology of H. Richard Niebuhr*, Paul Ramsey (ed.) (New York: Harper & Bros., 1957), p. 206.

[2] Gunnar Myrdal, *An American Dilemma: The Negro Problem and Modern Democracy* (New York: Harper & Bros., 1944), p. 1.

its ultimate solution, and hold that it must be adjudged as a *moral first principle* that no one is to be considered merely as a member of a useless group.[3]

Of great significance in this problem is the conflict which arises between those basic principles of American democracy and Judeo-Christian ethics, which are held and believed by an overwhelming majority of American citizens, and the denial of these principles implied in their reactions to daily relations with members of other races and minority groups. In other words, a conflict arises because the average citizen, who actually holds high principles, such as the equality of all men, the brotherhood of man, and the classic rights to life, liberty, and the pursuit of happiness, is subjected to an interior struggle when he either denies them himself or tolerates their denial by others. To resolve this inner conflict, of course, he must do quite a bit of rationalization. This conflict represents the "American Dilemma," to which Myrdal refers in the title of his book, and which he describes as:

> . . . the ever-raging conflict between, on one hand, the valuations, preserved on the general plane which we shall call the "American Creed," where the American thinks, talks, and acts under the influence of high national and Christian precepts, and, on the other hand, the valuations on specific planes of individual and group living, where personal and local interests; economic, social, and sexual jealousies; considerations of community prestige and conformity; group prejudice against particular persons or types of people; and all sorts of miscellaneous wants, impulses, and habits dominate his outlook.[4]

This conflict or dilemma has produced in our people, not only a moral struggle among themselves, but also a struggle within themselves. The contrast between their beliefs and their actions causes their average daily behavior to become a moral compromise. This moral compromise, which Myrdal calls the "American Dilemma," is precisely that which takes the problem beyond the field and scope of the social scientist and places it squarely within the domain of the ethician or moralist. Recognition of the moral nature of the question has forced the sociologist, despite his admission that ethics and morals

---

[3] George Eaton Simpson and J. Milton Yinger, *Racial and Cultural Minorities: An Analysis of Prejudice and Discrimination* (New York: Harper & Bros., 1953), p. 649.

[4] Gunnar Myrdal, op. cit., p. xlvii.

are outside his science and competence, to adopt moral viewpoints and enunciate moral principles in his approach to the problem, while at the same time, he renounces responsibility for the validity of these moral valuations and principles. This can readily be seen in the admonition which Myrdal makes in the introduction to his book:

> In approaching the Negro problem as primarily a moral issue of conflicting valuations, it is not implied, of course, that ours is the prerogative of pronouncing on a priori grounds which values are "right" and which are "wrong." In fact, such judgments are out of the realm of social sciences, and will not be attempted in this inquiry. Our investigation will naturally be an analysis of morals and not in morals. In so far as we make our judgments of value, they will be based on explicitly stated value premises, selected from among those valuations actually observed as existing in the minds of the white and Negro Americans and tested as to their social and political relevance and significance. Our value judgments are thus derived and have no greater validity than the value premises postulated.[5]

Thus, despite renunciation of responsibility for the validity of moral values and principles, the sociologist is forced to take them into consideration in his studies of the race question. He does not make or construct these principles, but seeks to find them in some other source.

Admitting the moral nature of the problem, it is evident that Catholic theology should have, and in fact, does have much to offer in the way of presenting principles to help effect a solution of the problem of race relations. The science of ethics, because it is founded solely on a natural approach and does not utilize the great supernatural realities of revelation, such as the Incarnation, Redemption, Grace, and the Church, can give only a partial answer. It cannot extend itself or its answers beyond the nature of man and a natural end. Hence the answers which ethics can give, while they are valid and true, nevertheless only answer part of the question. Man is destined for a supernatural end, and for the attainment of that end, he has been raised to the supernatural by habitual grace. He must direct all his actions, through the help of actual graces, to the attainment of that supernatural end. Any attempt toward a solution of the race problem must take these facts into consideration if the answer is to be adequate. Thus it can be seen that this is a theological task.

This does not mean, however, that the theologian is free to dis-

---

[5] Ibid., Introduction, pp. l–li.

regard data supplied by the extensive scientific work and research of sociologists. A proper theological consideration must be made in the light of these data. To study the problem properly, the theologian must look to theology for the principles, guides, and values; and to social science for the data regarding patterns and effects of interracial relations.

In utilizing these sociological data, the theologian is acting within his competency, for he has both the right and the obligation to use and interpret these findings. At the same time, it must be remembered that it is not the sociological data which shape or establish the theological principles, but rather that the theological principles, which are unchanging, are applied to findings offered by the social scientist, just as the theological solution of a moral-medical problem utilizes the data of medicine. In this way, theology will once again play her proper role as the queen of the sciences, employing, as her handmaids, all the inferior disciplines.

CHAPTER 2

COMPETENCE OF THE CHURCH
AND THEOLOGY IN SOCIAL QUESTIONS

Since a purely natural ethics can give only a partial solution, theology and the Church must enter into the problems of race relations. Indeed, even if only the question of social justice, which is so intimately connected with the matter of discrimination, were considered, this alone would suffice to cause the Church and the theologians to take cognizance of the problem. But even outside the matter of social justice, the Church would have to enter the question, if only for her own defense. Basic to the question are certain matters of human relations which the Church must perforce enter under penalty, not merely of loss of leadership and influence, but even of loss of her identity. There is a question here of a vital principle, essential to the religious position of the Church. Because she is the guardian and teacher of the revelation entrusted to her by her divine Founder, Jesus Christ, she has the duty and the right to demand that the conduct of her members be in accord with that revelation. Her authority, teachings, and admonitions must extend beyond the limit of questions that are purely religious or dogmatic, and they must, if she is to fulfill her divine mission, influence many problems which may, at first glance, appear purely secular. Pope Pius XII, in his address to the Catholic Associations of Italian Workers, made clear that Christ's teachings cannot be excluded from social problems, and because of this, the Church not only treats of these problems in a general way, but also indicates the fundamental principles:

Jesus Christ does not wait for such social systems as "lay-humanitarianism," "non-materialistic socialism," or others not derived from Him to grant Him entrance into the world of social problems. His divine kingdom, the kingdom of truth and justice, is already present, even in the areas of the world where the threat of class warfare is constantly increasing. For this reason the Church does not limit itself to appeals for a more just social order, but points out clearly the fundamental principles on which it must be based.[1]

Since the appearance of the great social encyclicals of Leo XIII, we have grown accustomed to the exercise of this authority of the Church, especially in matters of economics, capital-labor relations, and social conditions of the working classes. In 1954, Pius XII affirmed the right of the Church to extend its teachings beyond these economic subjects and to treat directly of political problems which belong to and have a relation to the moral order, since these could harm or hinder the attainment of man's final end. As examples of these areas, the Pope mentioned: the purpose and extent of temporal, political power; relations between individuals and society; totalitarianism; morality of war, etc. For Catholics, any doubt as to the Church's right to extend her teaching beyond the purely religious and to treat of social and political matters should be dissipated when they consider these words of Pius XII:

The power of the Church is not bound by the limits of "matters strictly religious," as they say, but the whole matter of the natural law, its foundations, its interpretation, its application, so far as their moral aspects extend, are within the Church's power. For the keeping of the Natural Law, by God's appointment, has reference to the road by which man has to approach his supernatural end. But, on this road, the Church is man's guide and guardian in what concerns his supreme end. . . . Many and serious are the problems in the social field — whether they be merely social or socio-political, they pertain to the moral order, are of concern to the conscience and the salvation of men; thus they cannot be declared outside the authority and care of the Church. Indeed there are problems outside the social field, not strictly "religious," political problems, of concern either to individual nations, or to all nations, which belong to the moral order, weigh on the conscience, and can, and very often do, hinder the attainment of man's last end. . . . Common sense, and truth as well, are contradicted by whoever asserts that these and like problems are outside the field of

---

[1] *Poco piu di dieci anni*, address of Pius XII on the Tenth Anniversary of the Catholic Associations of Italian Workers (A.C.L.I.), May 1, 1955, English translation, *The Pope Speaks*, II (Summer, 1955), 149–150.

morals, and hence are, or at least can be, beyond the influence of that authority established by God to see to a just order and to direct the consciences and actions of men along the path to their true and final destiny. This she is certainly to do not only "in secret," within the walls of the Church and sacristy, but also in the open, crying "from the rooftops" (to use the Lord's words, [Mt. 10:27]), in the front line in the midst of the struggle that rages between the "world" and the kingdom of God, between the prince of this world and Christ its Savior.[2]

However, granting the authority of the Church's magisterium in the field of race relations which certainly represent problems of the moral order, it is unfortunate that the older theologians in their writings did not treat explicitly of this matter. This lack can perhaps be understood when we realize the relatively late appearance of racial prejudice or racism as such. Juan Comas, in his study of racism, states that real racial prejudice did not appear on the European scene before the fifteenth century, and that before that time, the distinction of men was always into categories of "Christian" or "infidel." This he calls a more humane basis because the abyss produced by religious differentiation can be spanned by conversion while biological differences can never be equalized.[3]

If we accept Comas' late dating of the appearance of racial prejudice, we can see that it is contemporaneous with the age of exploration and colonization in the New World, and the rise of strong nationalistic movements in the Old World. With this period of colonization, the world saw the revival of slavery by the Spanish and Portuguese who forced into slavery the Indians whom they found in the New World, and who later imported Negroes from Africa for that purpose when they realized that the Indians did not adjust satisfactorily to slave status. It was only later, when it became necessary to rationalize and justify the existence of slavery as a de facto institution that recourse was had to the explanation that the Indian and Negro were substandard, inferior, and retarded races, destined by nature, because of their inherent limitations and defects, to a lowly or servile status. The humanist, Juan Gines de Sepulveda, in a public debate at Valladolid, 1550–1551, held that Aristotle's theory

---

[2] Magnificate Dominum, address of Pius XII to the Hierarchy on the Eve of the Proclamation of the Feast of Mary, Queen of Heaven and Earth, November 2, 1954. English translation, The Pope Speaks, I (1954), 375–385.

[3] Juan Comas, Racial Myths (Paris: UNESCO, 1951), p. 9.

of "natural slavery" applied to the American Indians and argued that "Indians are as different from Spaniards as cruelty is from kindness and as monkeys are from men," while his opponent, Bartolome de las Casas, the famous "Apostle of the Indies," maintained that there was no such thing as "submen."

The older theologians treated of questions pertinent in their day to this field, hence we find treatises on slavery in many of their works in which they discussed the nature of slavery, rights of the slave, his dignity as a person, his right to religious instruction and reception of the sacraments, his right to marry, the indissolubility of his marriage, and the like. However, the absence of explicit treatment of race relations does not mean that the theologian lacks the tools, namely the principles of moral theology and the analogous applications of these to formulate a theological treatment of this specific problem.

In this book we will attempt to fashion a unified theological treatment of the problem of race relations, utilizing the theological tools required for the accomplishment of this, and which we believe are available. In this way perhaps, we can make available an instrument for the instruction of our Catholic people regarding their obligations, the attitudes they should adopt, and the example they should give. Monsignor Francis J. Gilligan, in a theological dissertation presented to the Catholic University in 1929, and which unfortunately has been out of print for many years, commented on the evils produced by racial prejudice and segregation, and stated that although Catholics did not cause all of these evils, nevertheless, many of them did exist simply because well-intentioned Catholics failed to recognize their obligations. Many of these had never received detailed instruction. Religious teachers had preached and taught only the most general and broadest principles, assuming that their people would be capable of applying the principles to concrete cases. Their assumption was ill-founded, the required applications to particular cases were never made. This deficiency in instructional method must be remedied and repaired. Consequently there is a serious and grave obligation for the religious teachers and leaders of the United States to indicate the sinfulness and evil of many of the particular actions against the Negro. And it is to the Catholic Church that men must look for the answers to these moral problems. The Church, as the protector of morals and the teacher of truth, must be a beacon light in the darkness, pointing out the truth and revealing the hazards:

> There is one influence for good in these United States which has never lost sight of the true worth, common destiny and essential unity of all men. It is the Catholic Church. This is the Church which has always maintained personal rights when they are threatened by the totalitarian State, be it of racist, imperialistic, or whatever ideology. It is a Church identified with lawful authority when order is threatened by unbridled anarchy. This same Church has been graced with a dazzling array of brilliant thinkers who have set forth her teachings. Unfortunately they have left no legacy specifically on the point in question. Nevertheless they have enunciated principles in light of which modern problems can be solved. One such brilliant thinker is Francis Suarez whose treatise on law remains till this day the classic work of its kind. Modern theologians and canonists are also safe guides to follow when they reflect the teaching of the Church in their pages.[4]

Thus the work of the theologian is to apply revealed truths, the teaching of the *magisterium* of the Church, as well as the theological principles to the problem of race relations, and simultaneously to utilize and interpret the data supplied to him by the social scientists, and thus to produce a solid theological and doctrinal approach to the question. This theological and doctrinal approach should augment the knowledge and the realization, both of ourselves and of our neighbors, of what it means to be a Catholic and what relationship this bears to the race question. It will also effect the actual implementation of that knowledge to the realities of everyday life and will apply these principles to concrete situations. And in accomplishing his task, the theologian, without fear, can work within the framework of the traditional and well-founded moral and political principles of Thomism. He can use all the sociological data, and should not fear them, or attempt to avoid them. This use of the data will actually place them in proper perspective so that their most profound meaning can be apprehended and utilized.

Although this book will primarily be concerned with race relations precisely as manifested between Negro and white, we believe that the principles, as well as the concrete applications, will be and are pertinent to various other racial problems, namely those concerning

---

[4] Joseph F. Doherty, *Moral Problems of Interracial Marriage* (Washington, D. C.: The Catholic University of America Press, 1949), pp. 208–209.

Mexicans, Orientals, and Jews. We have limited our consideration principally to the Negro racial problem because in it there is a permanency which is not found in the others. Further, it has a more acute and urgent importance at the present time, and is the more universal problem while the others are more regional. Thus, for example, the problem of discrimination and prejudice against Jews or Puerto Ricans is actually limited to those urban sections with large concentrations of these groups; the problem of prejudice against Indians and Mexicans is limited to a few areas. On the other hand, the Negro problem exists in most states, North and South, especially since the heavy migrations of the Negro workers to Northern states since the end of World War II.

CHAPTER 3

BACKGROUND OF THE PROBLEM

Popular usage and understanding of the terms *prejudice,* *discrimination,* and *segregation* are often inaccurate and inexact. Frequently, in common parlance, *segregation* refers to a legalized form of separation regulated and required by statute or custom which has attained the force of law, while *discrimination* refers to separation effected without sanction of law. On the other hand, *prejudice* is considered to refer to personal attitudes and to be the actual cause of *discrimination*. Inasmuch as these terms are used throughout this work, it is important to clarify their meaning and to indicate the sense in which they will be used.

Myrdal has given the following explanation of the common use of *prejudice:*

> The popular term "race prejudice," as it is commonly used, embraces the whole complex of valuations and beliefs which are behind discriminatory behavior on the part of the majority group (or, sometimes, also on the part of the minority group) and which are contrary to the equalitarian ideals in the American creed.[1]

As stated above, the popular conception of prejudice is of a mental attitude which is causative of external acts of discrimination. However, while this notion has a valid foundation and certain elements of truth, it is, nevertheless, not completely accurate. The correct foundation in this popular concept is that prejudice is a judgment, while its inaccuracy consists in the notion that it is merely a simple judgment causative of discrimination.

---

[1] Gunnar Myrdal, op. cit., p. 52 n.

12

Actually, race prejudice is a judgment formed without sufficient motive, consideration, or reason. It is a rash judgment not that a person has sinned, but a rash judgment of the intrinsic inferiority of either an individual or of an entire group because of racial origin. Race prejudice draws the conclusion that an individual is inferior morally, intellectually, physically, or socially simply because he is a member of a particular racial group. Father John LaFarge, S.J., in his book, Interracial Justice, written in 1937, has given this definition of race prejudice:

> Race prejudice, in its gravest and most typical form, is the passing judgment of criminality or of essential inferiority upon all the members of a racial or ethnic group, with no sufficient intellectual motive for such a judgment. If such a judgment is passed upon an individual, it is race prejudice, if it is passed upon him as a member of that racial group. [p. 128]

Although prejudice consists essentially in a rash judgment, it is not a simply or easily understood phenomenon. It involves not merely the actual rash judgment enunciated by the intellect, but behind this formulation there lies a complex network of perverse dispositions of will and emotional and psychological vagaries and conceits. Father Albert Foley, S.J., writing from the sociological viewpoint, has described the complexity of racial prejudice:

> Of itself, prejudice is any preconceived judgment or opinion. It takes sides without due consideration, or because of irrelevant or even unreasonable likes or dislikes, preferences or antipathies, predilections or objections. Prejudice involves usually three elements: mistaken judgment, deviant will attitudes, and concomitant emotional complexes. It is therefore not a unitary phenomenon. It is quite complicated, and each of its elements leads to further complications.[2]

Thus the rash judgment in racial prejudice, when we attempt to unravel its complexity, is discovered to involve many previous and erroneous judgments which have been founded on gossip, hearsay, rumors, and generalities. Usually, it is worded in the form of a cliché, or catchword, which has been so widely and frequently repeated that it has now come to represent group attitude. It will also be found

---

[2] Albert Foley, "Minorities in American Society," Social Orientations, by Staff Members of the Institute of Social Order of St. Louis University (Chicago: Loyola University Press, 1954), pp. 620–621.

to involve a variety of will attitudes which range from carefully rehearsed indifference, disregard, and coldness of disposition toward members of the rejected racial group, all the way to violent hostility shading into real hatred. Despite the fact that prejudice is essentially an intellectual defect, it will always reflect these volitional factors.

In addition to the intellectual and volitional components, prejudice is also accompanied by emotional disturbances. Basic emotional fears find their externalization and expression in prejudicial attitudes, whether they be fears of competition, of insufficiency or insecurity, or any other type of fear. Thus prejudice can have degrees of intensity ranging from a mild and negative attitude to a violent and positive hatred. Prejudice may be restricted to existence in a single individual, or can multiply, and often does so, to become the attitude of a large group.

Closely associated with the notion of racial prejudice is racism, which is the formalization of the rash judgment. Since revelation of the atrocities in the Nazi concentration camps in the attempted genocide executed by Aryan racists, and the consequent horror and repugnance aroused in the civilized world, the term "racist" has acquired a pejorative meaning, and men shy away from the application of "racist" or "racism" to their pattern of thinking. However, abandonment of the term does not mean abandonment of the theory. Actually, a euphemism has been substituted. This is the term "blood," which has a certain mystical connotation. A drop of Negro blood, according to the "mystique of blood," represents a potential for moral dereliction, and no matter how good, how moral, or how well educated, religious, or urbane such a man may be, if he has a drop of "Negro blood," he has within himself the seed and potentiality for the most heinous crimes, which will, sooner or later, be actualized either in him or his descendants.

Racism cloaks itself with the garb and appearance of a systematic scientific proposition, creating and utilizing its own nomenclature, apparatus, and principles. The pioneer among modern classic racists is Joseph Arthur de Gobineau (1816–1882), who was a dilettante sociologist, in addition to being an Orientalist and a diplomat. His theory, which has been called Gobinism, was proposed in his book which appeared in 1854 under the title *Essai sur l'Inegalite des Races*

Humaines. Gobineau maintained that the blond Aryan, or Teuton, is the superior race among all races of men. This theory was molded by Houston Stewart Chamberlain (1855-1927) into what appeared as the Nazi theory of the superior Aryan race. Chamberlain, born in England, lived most of his life in Germany and Austria. In 1908, he married Eva Wagner, the daughter of Richard Wagner. His presentation of Gobinism appeared in 1899 in his book *Die Grundlagen des Neunzehnten Jahrhunderts.* This book was translated into English in 1911 and published under the title, *The Foundations of the Nineteenth Century.* In the United States, Madison Grant (1865-1937) popularized racism in his book, *The Passing of a Great Race: or the Racial Basis of European History,* published in 1916. In this work, Grant leaned heavily on de Gobineau and Chamberlain.

The racist classifies large segments or groups of mankind because of hereditary traits. Father Doherty has defined racism as:

a way of thinking that has dogmatized the notion that one ethnic group is condemned by the laws of nature to hereditary inferiority and another group is marked off as hereditarily superior. Its corollary maintains that the hope of civilization is in keeping the one race pure and eliminating the inferior group, or keeping it segregated.[3]

Thus, while prejudice is essentially a complex rash judgment, involving roots of perverse will attitudes and emotional disturbances, it is by its nature internal and personal. In fact, it is not even necessary that prejudice be externalized, manifested, or made effective. We have stated that the *popular concept* of discrimination is that it consists in the practice of forms of racial separation which lack legal sanction or approval. However, it would appear that the correct notion of discrimination is that it consists in the external and practical applications of prejudice, with or without the sanction of law. Discrimination includes the laws and customs which have acquired legal status, but it also includes those practices which are undertaken by private initiative, and which might even involve a violation of justice. This does not follow, however, that all discrimination is the product of prejudice. It may often be that the person who discriminates against a Negro actually has no prejudice against him either as a person or as a group member, but rather his action is the result of a

[3] Joseph F. Doherty, *op. cit.,* pp. 121-122.

necessity on his part to conform to an accepted pattern of behavior which has become conventional, or because there are economic advantages accruing to him for acting in this way. For instance, a store owner may be forced to purchase and install separate drinking fountains, even though he personally would prefer to install only one and thus avoid the added expense. So, too, white persons may refuse to sit next to a colored person on a bus or streetcar not because they are actually prejudiced, but in order to preclude and avoid any appearance of nonconformity and to prevent disparaging criticism from other white persons. Father Fichter has stressed the internal, conceptual nature of prejudice, considering it as a "way of thinking accompanied by emotional overtones." Discrimination is stressed as an external pattern of conduct, and he indicates that while they are closely related, "it is difficult to say in any particular case whether prejudice causes discrimination or discrimination causes prejudice."[4]

Since discrimination frequently represents an objective aspect of prejudice, it is observable, and its manifestations can be objectively examined and measured. Prejudice, on the other hand, being subjective, is a more personal and controversial subject. In fact, there are many persons who, while they protest their lack of racial prejudice, consciously or unconsciously practice racial discrimination.

We have also stated that the popular concept of racial segregation usually considers it to be a mere correlative of integration. In this concept, discrimination is considered to lack legal approval; segregation, on the other hand, is understood to have the approval of law or statute.

However, we can distinguish a strict meaning of segregation and a broad meaning. Taken strictly, segregation is a social separation, based on racial origin, whereby there is a mutual exclusion of both races from associating with each other or from entering upon joint enterprises or exchanges. If segregation is understood in this meaning, it is, in theory at least, as restrictive of the white race as it is of the Negro, since both are enjoined from association in many, if not all, areas of mutual activity. This meaning of segregation has been the foundation

---

[4] Joseph H. Fichter, S.J., Sociology (Chicago: University of Chicago Press, 1957), pp. 197–198.

of the "separate but equal" principle which, since 1896, has been a canonized principle of American law in decisions involving race relations.

But in practice, segregation in the United States does not conform to this strict meaning. Rather, segregation in practice has worked to exclude associations in which social equality would be implied rather than to prevent all racial associations.

In its broader meaning, and as it is in practice, *segregation is synonymous with discrimination*. Understood in this way, it embraces the entire complexus of discriminatory techniques, practices, and patterns, and includes the whole system of racial discrimination. It is in this meaning that *segregation* is often used by sociologists, and with this significance, Myrdal wrote that "social segregation and discrimination is a system of deprivation forced upon the Negro by the white group."

The identity of segregation and discrimination, in practice, is indicated by Charles Johnson who points out the inevitability of discrimination whenever there is compulsory segregation:

It is obvious that the policy of segregation which the American system of values proposes, merely to separate and to maintain two distinct but substantially equal worlds, is a difficult ideal to achieve. Any limitation of free competition inevitably imposes unequal burdens and confers unequal advantages. Thus, segregation or any other distinction that is imposed from without almost invariably involves some element of social discrimination as we have defined it. Residential segregation enforced by law is an obvious instance.[5]

However, it must be kept in mind that *segregation*, understood either in its strict or broad meaning, must always have a public or at least semipublic character. The term *segregation* should not be applied to private exclusions which may be made on the basis of race. This type of exclusion even when based solely on race and racial prejudice, if it obtains between private individuals or involves a private home or private association, cannot be termed *segregation*. If a man refuses to invite a Negro co-worker to go to lunch with him,

---

[5] Charles S. Johnson, *Patterns of Negro Segregation* (New York: Harper & Bros., 1943), p. 4.

his exclusion of the Negro co-worker is not segregation, because his act lacks the public or semipublic character which must always be found in segregation.

ORDER OF DISCRIMINATIONS

Gunnar Myrdal has made a study of the logic motivating the discriminatory system in the matter of race relations with which we are so familiar in the United States. The logic behind the entire pattern of segregation and discrimination is, of course, subject to and patient of scientific criticism. Nevertheless, no scientific disproval of the logic can change the basic fact that it does represent the de facto motivation of popular beliefs and actions. Myrdal calls this logic: "the white man's theory of color caste."

This "theory of color caste" is dominated by the notion of racial purity. The prevention of racial amalgamation is the primary concern and goal, and to accomplish this, the whites are committed to the use of any means. Secondarily, and as a subsidiary feature, is the rejection of "social equality" between the races as a necessary means to prevent pollution of racial purity through avoidance of occasions which might lead to miscegenation and intermarriage. And this denial of equality is extended to various areas of daily life — religion, education, voting, housing, jobs, recreation, and stores.

This logic, of course, when applied to the practical order is productive of definite patterns of discrimination, and it is directive of the entire system. As a result, there is an order of discriminations considered by the white group as necessitated and demanded by this "theory of color caste." Briefly, this order of discrimination can be distributed into six classifications, which are listed here in descending order of importance to the white group:

1. Ban against miscegenation and intermarriage.
2. Patterns regulative of social behavior, e.g., bans against socialization and fraternization, and regulations of such activities as eating, bathing or swimming, dancing, working, handshaking, use of titles of respect, etc.
3. Segregation by race in use of public facilities, e.g., transportation, schools, churches, etc.
4. Political disfranchisement.

5. Discriminations before the law, by police or public officials, in the administration of public services.

6. Discriminations in regard to purchase of property, obtaining employment, securing credit, and in social welfare participation.[6]

These six classifications represent approximately the entire pattern of racial discrimination as it exists today, varying, of course, in degree and intensity according to locale. However, the order of importance of these classifications is universal for the white group, and it is in descending order of importance so that if concessions are required, they will be more readily and easily made in the lower classifications than in the higher. In other words, concessions or ameliorations of discrimination will be easier to secure in matters concerning social welfare participation than they will be in reference to voting rights or social fraternization.

The Negro group which is subject to these discriminations, of course, resents them. But although their resentment is parallel to the six classifications listed above, it is in inverse order of importance. The result is that the Negro resents least the discriminations in regard to intermarriage, and resents most those in the sixth classification. Hence, he is much more anxious to secure equality of job opportunity than he is to obtain an end of discrimination in the use of public facilities. Obviously this is because the lower classifications are more urgent and of more immediate and practical need than the others. Personally, the Negro is more in need of a job than he is of a vote or juridical equality, and intermarriage is of the least importance to him, and indeed is only doubtfully of any interest to him.

These "rank orders" are those evolved by Myrdal, and they form the cornerstone of his hypotheses. He readily admits that he cannot prove them a priori, but has established and based them on his observations as a social scientist. A study made by W. S. M. Banks, Jr., in which he empirically tested the "orders of discrimination" in regard to Negro sensitivity revealed that within the tested area, Myrdal's order was substantially correct, and that variations from it consisted merely in reversal of a few contingent ranks.[7]

---

[6] Cf. Gunnar Myrdal, op. cit., pp. 57–67.

[7] W. S. M. Banks, Jr., "Rank Order of Sensitivity to Discrimination," American Sociological Review, XV (August, 1950), 529–534.

SEPARATE BUT EQUAL

This is the legal principle which maintains that segregation of the races will entail no deprivation or violation of legal rights so long as the facilities which are provided for each group are equal qualitatively and quantitatively. As a working legal principle, its authoritative enunciation is attributed to the decision rendered by the United States Supreme Court in the case of Plessy v. Ferguson in 1896. Homer Plessy, an octoroon, was arrested when he refused to ride in a "colored" railway coach as required by the Louisiana statutes. He instituted a restraining action against Judge Ferguson who was scheduled to conduct his trial. The restraining action was denied in the Louisiana state courts, and Plessy appealed the case to the United States Supreme Court. The Supreme Court affirmed denial of the restraint. Plessy had argued that the Louisiana state statutes violated the Thirteenth and Fourteenth Amendments. The Supreme Court decision upheld the segregation statute on the grounds that it was a reasonable law since it was founded on existing traditions, customs, and usages.

"Separate but equal" became axiomatic in the handling of racial relations and in the use of public facilities in practically all the states with legislated segregation, and it was implemented not only by court decisions, but even by private initiative in the establishment of segregation patterns beyond those actually required by statute. It continued to play this important role for over a half century, and only received its deathblow as an official legal principle when the Supreme Court handed down its now famous School Segregation Cases in 1954 and 1955.

Speculatively, and in theory, separation does not necessarily indicate discrimination. Even in practice, groups can be separated and yet suffer no infringement of their rights. In the practical order, however, a distinction must be made. If the basis of the separation is not some quality which is opposed to the operational or functional end of the group, but rather is an unreasonable and arbitrary motive, then inevitably the enforcement of separation will result in a violation of either the dignity of the person or the loss of some of his rights. For example, in practice, we have various types of separation in which no rights of those excluded are violated. A Catholic society, e.g., the Knights of Columbus or the Catholic Daughters of America, may exclude from membership those who are not Catholic; our parochial schools in many instances exclude non-Catholics, and indeed, even Catholics who are members of other parishes. The American Legion or Veterans of Foreign Wars may exclude those who have not served in the armed forces; a building trade union, e.g., the bricklayers or carpenters, may exclude those not engaged at those trades. Yet, in all these exclusions, no one who is denied participation or membership feels that he is being discriminated against since the basis for exclusion is a realistic one, namely that this person lacks a quality or qualification for proper interest in and securement of the operational end of the entire group.

Again, a passenger who has a first-class ticket on a steamship line or Pullman accommodations on a train has the right to use those special facilities provided for him. On the other hand, if he has a third-class ticket on the steamship or a coach ticket on the railroad train, then he is not allowed to use those higher-fare facilities, and indeed is excluded from them. Yet here the one excluded does not feel that he is being discriminated against. Indeed, in this case, the basis for the separation and exclusion is reasonable, namely, he has not paid the extra charge which will entitle him to use the more comfortable, spacious, convenient, or luxurious accommodations.

However, when the basis for separation is unreasonable, then it is certain to be detrimental to one group and this especially where it involves large numbers of peoples, in many and varied situations, and over a long period of time. This is precisely the situation obtaining where the basis for separation is race or color.

In striking down the "separate but equal" principle, the Supreme Court, in the opinion delivered by Chief Justice Warren, on May 17, 1954, declared:

> We conclude that in the field of public education the doctrine of "separate but equal" has no place. Separate educational facilities are inherently inequal. Therefore, we hold that the plaintiffs and others similarly situated for whom the actions have been brought are, by reason of the segregation complained of, deprived of the equal protection of the laws guaranteed by the Fourteenth Amendment.[8]

---

[8] *Brown, et al., v. Board of Education of Topeka, et al.,* 347 U.S. 483 (1954).

This was finally an official recognition that no matter how "equal" separate facilities may be quantitatively or qualitatively, they are intrinsically unequal when one group is forced to use them by reason of race or color. This was also the finding of the Committee established in 1946 by President Truman to investigate the civil-rights situation. The report of this committee, published under the title *To Secure These Rights*, stated that the policy of "separate but equal" as practiced in some states was a failure:

> The theory behind this policy is complex. On one hand, it recognizes Negroes as citizens and as intelligent human beings entitled to enjoy the status accorded the individual in our American heritage of freedom. It theoretically gives them access to all the rights, privileges, and services of a civilized, democratic society. On the other hand, it brands the Negro with the mark of inferiority and asserts that he is not fit to associate with white people.

Moreover, the principle of "separate but equal," even if its intrinsically discriminatory character is overlooked, actually was seldom carried out in practice. In its application, in most instances, the facilities provided for Negro use were separate but they were not equal. This was also the finding of the Committee on Civil Rights who reported that in education, as well as in other public services, the "equal" part of the formula was very often disregarded. This inequality, they stated, could be discovered by a comparison between white and Negro schools of expenditures per pupil, salaries of teachers, ratio of students to teacher, school transportation, school buildings and equipment, length of school terms, and even curricula content. In all these areas, "Negro students are invariably at a disadvantage."

CHAPTER 4

RATIONALIZATION OF
DISCRIMINATION AND SEGREGATION

The contradiction which arises between principles of Christianity and equalitarian ideals basic to American democracy, which at least in theory are held by the vast majority of Americans, and their overt violation in practice, is responsible, as we have said, for an inner conflict in our people. Two remedies are on hand for the solution of this conflict. Americans can either recognize the situation and attempt to correct it or else they can defend and excuse it. The continuation of the racial problem is witness to the fact that too many have adopted the latter solution. They defend and excuse it by means of rationalizations.

Essential to the defense of the system is the claim that it was not instituted by modern-day members of society, but rather came to them as a sacred and ancient tradition from their forefathers; an inherited way of life. Hence what is done is de facto right. In the grip of such a tradition, which received tangible form in personal relations, individuals or groups proclaim their impotence to alter the situation or to defy the tradition.

However, the claim of the support of tradition, while it has a certain validity must nevertheless be understood with certain reservations and distinctions. Previous to the Civil War, the common relation between the races was that of slave and master. From the time of the legal closing of African slave trading, in 1807, the institution of

23

slavery in the United States continued and was maintained with a minimum of force. Its continuation was more by persuasion and custom. That is, most slave owners were born into their class status and most of the slaves were born into their slave status. The result was that after the turn of the nineteenth century, slavery became a way of life not only for the owners, but even for the slaves. Neither had known any other way of life except to be either slave or slaveholder.

On the other hand, and almost in contradiction, it was about this time that increasingly restrictive legislation was enacted in various states to prevent any improvement of the status of the slaves. Indeed these laws were not only restrictive of the slave, but many of them were directed against the free Negro. Litwack reports that, during this period of seventy years (1790–1860), there was no clarification of the status of the freeman. The federal government and various states defined his legal status in different ways. In many instances, this resulted in disfranchisement, immigration restrictions, and school segregation. Congress, in 1790, restricted naturalization to aliens who were white; in 1792, the newly organized militia restricted enrollment to "each and every free, able-bodied white male citizen." In 1810, Negroes were prohibited from carrying U. S. mail, and in 1820, the District of Columbia was authorized by the federal government to elect white city officials and to establish a code governing all Negroes, slave and free. Free Negroes were refused passports, and in 1847, Buchanan, then Secretary of State, declared that it was usual to give free Negroes "not a passport, in the ordinary form, recognizing them as citizens, but a certificate suited to the nature of the case." At the height of the abolition movement, many free Negro leaders requested passports so they could lecture in England and raise money for the abolitionist movement. In 1858, Secretary of State Lewis Cass rejected a request for a passport for a free Negro and stated that a passport which was a certificate of citizenship has "never since the foundation of the Government been granted to persons of color."

In other areas, free Negroes were prohibited from associating with slaves because of the fear that their presence would be a cause of discontent among the slaves. In fact, this fear led to the enactment of laws which required a manumitted slave to leave the state within a certain number of days or else be returned to slave status.[1]

Under the slave system practiced in the United States and in most instances legally approved, the slave was regarded as a chattel. Rights possessed by a slave constituted the issue in the famous *Dred Scott* case. In 1857, when Chief Justice Taney handed down the decision in this case, he stated that the history of the nation, the legislation of the original colonies and the language of the Declaration of Independence indicate that "a Negro has no rights which a white man need respect." He further explained that the expression "people of the United States" as used in the Constitution did not include Negroes. This decision crystallized and formalized a century of tradition which had regarded Negroes as members of an inferior order, totally unfit to associate with the white race either politically or socially. Hence the Negro could be reduced to a state of slavery for the benefit of the white race. This became axiomatic in practice, and men of all classes acted daily on it and very few of them ever thought of questioning its validity.

Among the state laws prohibiting certain attempts to alleviate the status of the Negro were laws placing various restrictions on manumission, education, and in some cases, religious instruction. Other state laws deprived the slave of the right to marry, denied him the right to testify in court, and established the fact of color as a presumption of slave status. If a man was a Negro, he had to prove that he was not a slave. If he could not do this, he could be taken by the sheriff and sold at auction as a slave — his purchase price going to the county or township. Illustrative of the pattern of these laws and the rationalization of the situation which accompanied it is the decision in the Douglas case in 1853. A Virginia state law prohibited anyone from teaching Negroes to read or write. Mrs. Douglas of Norfolk was found guilty of violation of this statute and

---

[1] Leon Litwack, "The Federal Government and the Free Negro, 1790–1860," *Journal of Negro History*, XLIII (1958), 261–278. Litwack indicates that although there were many such laws, there were relatively few attempts to enforce them. However, it is necessary to remember that possibility of enforcement was always a club held over the head of the free Negro.

sentenced to one-month imprisonment in the Norfolk city jail. In the decision in the case, the judge stated:

> . . . and while the Negroes of our town and State are known to be surrounded by most of the substantial comforts of life, and invited both by precept and example to participate in proper moral and religious duties, it argues, it seems to me, a sickly sensibility towards them to say their persons, and feelings, and interests are not sufficiently respected by our laws, which in effect, tends to nullify the act of our Legislature passed for the security and protection of their masters.

The decision continues and explains the origin of these restrictions, citing their cause as the propaganda of the antislavery groups who have distributed documents and pamphlets to Negroes to induce them "to cut our throats." Because of this antislavery agitation, the Court concluded "there was but one measure of protection for the South, and that was adopted."[2]

Simultaneous with enactment of legal restrictions was a second movement which aimed to justify slavery. The need for a well-articulated justification of slavery was felt more and more in face of the increasing moral attacks of the Abolitionists, as well as the personal need which individual slave owners felt for a moral justification for the continuance of slavery. As a result, during this period, and particularly in the years between 1830 and 1860, when antislavery tracts and pamphlets were so numerous, we find a great number of writings which have for their purpose the vindication and justification of the existence of slavery. The authors of these works sought to justify its continuance from various sources, but chief among them were (a) the benefits the Negro received from slavery, and (b) the destination of the Negro by God and by nature to a condition of servility.[3]

In fact some of these authors went so far in defense of slavery that they present in idyllic terms the life of the slave and almost make it appealing. George Sawyer is a good example of this. In his book, written in 1858, he states:

---

[2] Henry Steel Commager (ed.), Documents of American History, 5 ed., I, pp. 327–329.
[3] There was also an extensive antislavery literature. Cf. Dwight Lowell Dumond, A Bibliography of Antislavery in America (Ann Arbor: The University of Michigan Press, 1961).

The slave is relieved from all this oppressive burden of troubles; he is comforted by the pleasing consolation, if he has any thought for his family, that they have a sure support, in sickness and health, in infancy and old age. He is relieved of all those dark fore-bodings of the future that so weigh down and depress the spirits of the poor laborer of the free States. All that the slave makes is his own; he has nothing to pay out for the necessaries of life, though in strictness of law all that he has belongs to his master; yet this is but a nominal provision; it is all included, like a wheel within a wheel, in his possessions. But he is the proprietor of his slave's *peculium* only as his representative, guardian and protector, to see that he is not wronged, and that he does not apply his means inconsistent with his duties as a servant. It is given in charge by the law to the master for the same reason that the slave's person is, and that is because he is incapable of managing it himself.[4]

Yet behind all the presentations of benefits and happy, carefree existence of slaves, there lurks the argument basic and conclusive for all contemporaneous defenders of slavery. That is the basic racist argument maintaining that the Negro belongs to a race which is separate and distinct from the white race, that he is by nature inferior to the white man and thereby incapable of any social, economic, or political equality. When all other arguments fail to convince or fall apart in face of contradictory evidence, there always remains the firm argument of racial inferiority. Even Sawyer, after affirming the benefits of slavery accruing to the Negro, states with more firmness and conviction:

This all goes to show that the Negro race, by universal consent of the civilized world, are considered a separate and distinct race of beings, suited only to their own peculiar state and condition. Their freedom is but a name, an unmeaning sound; they are by nature totally incapacitated to enjoy the rights and privileges of freemen, except in secluded communities of their own kindred blood, which ever have been, and ever will be, sooner or later, when left to themselves, in a state of barbarism. Their condition among the whites is necessarily that of pupilage and dependence.[5]

Nor does Sawyer overlook the benefits of slavery that accrue to the white man, especially feelings of superiority and well-being which are produced in him by the very sight of an inferior group, and who, even though he be poor, can be proud of the fact that he belongs to

---

[4] George S. Sawyer, *Southern Institutes: or An Inquiry into the Origin and Early Prevalence of Slavery and the Slave-Trade* (Philadelphia: J. B. Lippincott & Co., 1858), pp. 201–202.
[5] *Ibid.*

the right race. It is extremely interesting to see presented these psychological effects of racial discrimination in so early a writing:

> Not only does Negro slavery elevate the character of the master, and where the master is free, render his devotion to liberty a high and holy feeling, but where, as in our own country, the slave is of a different and inferior race, marked and set apart by his color, physical and mental characteristics, it elevates the character, not only of the master, the actual owner of the slaves, but of all the individuals of his own race who wear the color and distinguishing characteristics of freemen. With us color, not money, marks the class: black is the badge of slavery, white the color of freemen; and the white man, however poor, whatever be his occupation, is inspired with the just pride of a freeman, a sovereign.[6]

While this type of literature in defense of slavery may seem devastating enough both in derogation of the Negro as a person and as a member of a particular race, and in false exaltation of the white race, yet there is another type of literature which appeared at this time in defense of slavery, which because of its vicious character, had far more injurious effects. These works defended the *status quo* by means of an extremely rabid racism. They carried the racist theory to such an extent that they actually denied the human nature of the Negro, maintaining that he did not possess a soul. We might mention at this point that Bishop Augustine Verot, Vicar-Apostolic of Florida, was keenly aware of and disturbed by these books, their wide circulation, and the harm they were doing. In 1870, while at the Vatican Council, during a discussion of the agenda of the Council, he protested that Chapter XV was only concerned with very obscure German philosophical errors which few persons even knew about, let alone understood, while it passed over in silence more important and practical errors which were widespread in America, England, and France in regard to the unity of the human race. In his speech, Bishop Verot mentioned two books which openly denied the unity of the human race. The first book, which he identified as *Ariel*, was published in America and maintained that there were two creations, one of the white race in the person of Adam, and a second creation of Negroes who were midway between men and beasts. *Ariel* was a pseudonym for Buckner H. Payne (1799–

---

[6] *Ibid.*

1883), and the book mentioned by Bishop Verot was *The Negro: What is his ethnological status? Is He the Progeny of Ham? Is he a descendant of Adam and Eve — What is his relation to the white race?* published in 1867. Bishop Verot also complained to the Council that there were Protestant ministers in his diocese who were teaching that the Negro had no soul. The second book he identified simply as *Vestigia creationis*, and said that it was published in England. Most probably this is the work of Robert Chambers (1802–1871), *Vestiges of the Natural History of Creation*, published in London in 1844, anonymously because Chambers feared that his ideas were so radical that they would shock his readers and injure his publishing business financially. Later, several American editions of this work appeared. This book taught that all things tend to come to perfection and that apes are rude and imperfect men who only after centuries will become men. Chambers can be identified as a pre-Darwinian evolutionist. In this work he denied the fixity of species and maintained that creation was accomplished by progressive evolutions. These he explained by a divinely bestowed impulse to advance through grades of perfection and to modify the structure as required by circumstances.

Disturbed by these teachings, Bishop Verot proposed that the Council define that the Negro does have a soul and also that it define the unity of the human race. His proposal to cover these points which he desired included in Chapter XV read as follows:

> We especially condemn the inept error of those who dare to assert that Negroes do not belong to the human family nor are they endowed with a spiritual and immortal soul. Indeed, in this condemnation, we include those who do not hesitate to state that in the necessary and natural progress of all things to perfection, apes are as yet crude and imperfect men, and the human race, living a jungle life for many ages, not only found gradually all sciences and arts, but even speech. . . . We declare, however, that the accidental differences of color or conformity which exist in various tribes of the human family, if they could not have arisen by various accidental causes of place, time, way of living, and education, can be attributed to the omnipotence of God Who confused the languages at Babel, and established the various human tribes when he made men forget the first language and suddenly learn a new one.[7]

---

[7] Mansi, L, 166.

The *Ariel* pamphlet which so disturbed Verot can be seen, upon examination, to be a particularly dangerous work because of its appearance and claim of scholarly research in history, Scripture, Hebrew, Greek, anthropology, and social science. It is particularly vicious in its attempt to show, from Scripture, that the Negro did not have a soul. In this work, Payne says that the usual assertion that the Negro is a descendant of Cham, who had been cursed by Noah, is not true. The Negro, he writes, is not a descendant of any of the sons of Noah. Since the Negro is present in the world then we have to admit that he was on the ark and was saved from the flood, but not as a member of Noah's family, but rather as one of the cattle and animals who were on the ark. The Negro is not a descendant of Adam and Eve, but was actually created before them and is actually the highest of the animals because he could make imitable sounds which other animals could not do, and hence was able to communicate with Adam and Eve. In fact, Payne declares, the serpent in the garden who tempted Eve was not a reptile, but was a Negro who was the only animal that could speak. Having established these points of his theory, Payne proceeds to attempt to prove from Scripture that the Negro does not have a soul:

> . . . now let us read the Bible, the divine record and see whether or not the Negro has a soul. It reads thus: "When the long suffering of God waited, in the days of Noah, while the ark was preparing, wherein few, that is eight souls were saved," the Negro being in the ark, was not one of those eight souls and consequently he has *no soul to be saved*. . . . But God only promised to save eight — Noah and his wife and his three sons and their wives. These *had souls* as the Apostle (Peter) testifies, and *all that were in the ark that did have souls*. The Negro was in the ark and God thus testifies that he has no soul.[8]

With the end of slavery at the close of the Civil War, a legalized Jim Crow system applying to all possible phases of life was not the immediate common practice. Rather, there came first the Reconstruction Period which has become so obnoxious a term to the South. With the closing of the Civil War, the crucial and immediate Southern problem was not a race problem, but an economic and labor problem. The ravages of a war which had been largely waged in

---

[8] Buckner H. Payne, *The Negro: What is his ethnological status? Is He the Progeny of Ham? Is he a descendant of Adam and Eve — What is his relation to the white race?* (Cincinnati: published for the proprietor, 1867), p. 44.

Southern territory produced vast devastation in most areas. The problem of food supply was crucial, plantations and farms were in ruins, crops had been destroyed, and most of the South was deeply in debt. Meanwhile, with the granting of citizenship to the newly freed slaves, they were able to, and did, enjoy civil and legal rights, even though they were often used as pawns by unscrupulous politicians. Jim Crow, as we know it, as a legalized system with economic and social restrictions and disfranchisement only grew into a full system in the years between 1896 and 1904. An explanation of the reasons why this system appeared is beyond the scope of this work. Whether it can be attributed to economic, social, political, or racist ideas, or even to psychological motivations such as a search for a substitute for punishment, or a scapegoat for defeat is a field properly belonging to the historian and social scientist. All we can do is present the fact, and leave to others the explanation of the causes of the fact.

At any rate, Jim Crow made a discernible appearance as an organized system by 1896 and was full grown by 1904. The period of slavery, as we have seen, had many instances of legal enactments based on the principles of chattel slavery, but the period of genuine racial segregation, deliberately applied and extended to all possible areas of life, was to come later. In fact, its firm establishment was not until forty years after the Civil War, and while this new system was physically milder than slavery, paradoxically, it was harsher spiritually.

C. Vann Woodward is one of the leading proponents of the theory that Jim Crow is not of as long a tradition as its defenders claim, but is of more recent origin. He summarizes his position thus:

My only purpose has been to indicate that things have not always been the same in the South. In a time when the Negroes formed a much larger proportion of the population than they did later, when slavery was a live memory in the minds of both races, and when the memory of the hardships and bitterness of Reconstruction was still fresh, the race policies accepted and pursued in the South were sometimes milder than they became later. The policies of proscription, segregation, and disfranchisement that are often described as the immutable "folkways" of the South, impervious alike to legislative reform and armed intervention, are of a more recent origin. The effort to justify them as a consequence of Reconstruction and a necessity of the times is embarrassed by the fact that they did not originate in those times. And the belief that they are immutable and unchangeable is not supported by history.[9]

Woodward offers as an indication of this late appearance of political disfranchisement the fact that in Louisiana, in 1896, there were 130,334 registered Negro voters. At that time, literacy, property, and poll-tax requirements were enacted to exclude Negro voters, and, by 1904, the Negro voters in the state had been reduced to 1342.

Restoration of white supremacy in the South in 1876 brought with it the appearance of a new middle class. It should not be thought that the restoration of white supremacy was merely as a corrective of Reconstruction abuses since many of the state constitutions which were adopted during Reconstruction, and which were claimed to be mere instruments for the maintenance of Negro power, were actually retained for decades after 1876, when the whites could have easily changed them had they been disadvantageous to them. Their retention for such a long period was actually due to the fact that these constitutions were in reality expressions of middle-class interests and actually suited the goals of the newly established Southern middle class. Frazier maintains that Southern demagogues, assisted by the propertied classes, spent twenty-five years in a campaign to demonstrate that the Negro was degenerate and intellectually inferior and that their campaign finally culminated in the establishment of Jim Crow.[10]

A rationalization of prejudice must be brought to bear for the defense of the system, and this acts also as a basis for objections to alleviation of the racial system. Dollard, in his study *Caste and Class in a Southern Town*, states and describes this white rationalization of the white community. He claims that the notion of the Negro as a mere animal was more easily accepted during slavery when there were cultural as well as physical differences between the races. Today,

---

[9] C. Vann Woodward, *The Strange Career of Jim Crow*, new and rev. ed. (New York: Oxford University Press, 1957), p. 47. Cf. Charles E. Wynes, *Race Relations in Virginia, 1870–1902* (Charlottesville: University of Virginia Press, 1961), p. 149, where the author concludes that Woodward's thesis is basically correct, and though certain qualifications should be made, these qualifications would not substantially alter the validity of the thesis.

[10] E. Franklin Frazier, *Black Bourgeoisie* (Glencoe: Free Press and Falcon's Wing Press, 1957), pp. 17–18; cf. also E. Franklin Frazier, *The Negro in the United States* (New York: Macmillan, 1949), pp. 155–164.

in many instances, this cultural lag has been taken up and there remain only the physical differences. Americans do not believe or act on the axiom that the Negro is a mere animal, but they do say it and use it to justify their actions.

The vehemence of the objection to removal of discrimination will, to a large degree, depend on the type of discrimination under discussion. There are certain formulae of objections. Dependent on the type of discrimination, the objector will utilize some form of rationalization and claim that the Negro is incredibly stupid; that he lacks normal social perception; that he is incapable of even realizing that he is being misused; that he is a savage, hence placed outside the pale of American mores. Indeed, behind all these rationalizations is the fact that the Negro is more or less denied a personality. It is not actually understood by many whites that the Negro has personal relationships, friends, memories, grudges, and preferences; that he feels pain, has immediate needs, wants, or desires.

The social rejection of the Negro is rationalized and justified by blaming his lower caste on himself, and his present position in society merely proves his permanent inferiority and incapability of being civilized. He must be rejected because he lacks initiative and is shiftless; he has no sense of time or desire to better himself. Implied in all these objections is the idea that these qualities are permanent and universal features of all Negro personality.

Rejection of the Negro on a personal level is excused by the claim that he is emotionally unstable, capricious and changeable, and untrustworthy; he is immoral, a liar, and a thief. Indeed all these are summarized by the rationalization that he is culturally inferior and hence unable to share on an equal basis in social privileges.

Rationalization against any friendly association with the Negro is also varied. He uses language poorly; violates rules of grammar; speaks improperly, and this is a sign of his social inferiority. The crushing argument against any possibility of personal association with the Negro is that "he smells."

The Negro is considered to be carefree, comical, happy-go-lucky, and amusing. If he is happy, why do anything to change his situation. He likes it. Because he is happy with his status, there should be no consideration of situations of poverty, disease, hunger, humiliation, lack of opportunities or education. And if he is not content with his position, then someone has put ideas in his head and he is now getting "uppity."

Rationalization and racial beliefs have a close correlation with the actual practices of discrimination. Some instances of this dovetailing of rationalization and discrimination have been described by Father Albert Foley, S.J.:

Discrimination or Exclusion	Rationalization and Racial Belief
Keep the Negro out of industrial jobs.	*Negro gets sleepy at machines, is lacking in mechanical aptitudes.*
Deprive the Negro of civic rights, of the vote.	*Negro is immature, childish, servile, lacking in initiative.*
Exclude the Negro from technical schools and jobs.	*Negro has inborn lack of ability for sustained mental activity, a lower intelligence, and so forth.*
Deprive the Negro of educational facilities.	*Mind of Negro cannot be improved beyond a certain level; they work better with their hands, and so forth.*
Confine the Negro to slum sections.	*Negro is lazy, shiftless, immoral, happy-go-lucky, likes to be with his own, and so forth.*
Deprive the Negro of health and hospital services.	*Negro is more susceptible to diseases, infant mortality, and so forth.*
Keep the Negro in a lower and disprivileged caste.	*Negro is happy, contented, satisfied with little pay, and so forth.*[11]

This correlation clearly shows the interplay between the intellectual prejudice and the practical discrimination. However, it is useful once again to call to mind that we should not regard prejudice as being univocally causative of the discrimination since, in some instances, it is the prejudice that is caused by experiencing existent discrimination.

The rationalization for a solution of inner conflicts between principle and practice, as can be seen, need not be logical. For example, we can see the inconsistency in refusing health or hospital services to a Negro and the corresponding rationalization that this refusal is right because the Negro is more susceptible to disease. Another instance of lack of logic can be seen in the racial policies of South Africa. A free lunch program for schoolchildren had been established.

---

[11] Albert Foley, op. cit., pp. 623–624.

However, the allotment granted by the government for each lunch given to white children was three times the allotment for each lunch to be given to colored children. White schoolchildren were given lunches worth 6 pence whereas, colored children were given lunches worth only 2 pence, and later this was reduced further to 1½ pence. When the injustice which would seem to be apparent in this was protested, a speaker in the House of Assembly of Transvaal publicly justified the practice by stating that Negro children needed less food than white children because Negroes sleep more.

To justify rationalization, all that is required is that it have the appearance of applying logically, and, more important, that psychologically it helps to dispel and resolve the inner conflict.

1247546

CHAPTER 5

EVIL EFFECTS OF
SEGREGATION AND DISCRIMINATION

The very patterns of racial discrimination and segregation make immediately apparent the main disadvantages of the system to the Negro. His preclusion from industrial employment and technical jobs necessitates his seeking employment outside these fields and accepting jobs where there is less remuneration and a minimum of advancement opportunity. Exclusion from the polls results in his being deprived of a voice in the government and election of its officials; the venal politician has no regard or care for the Negro's interests or needs if he lacks the weapon of a vote. Substandard educational opportunities produce poorly educated groups, and restriction to slum areas with their inferior housing and facilities produces numerous threats and dangers to health, both physical and moral. Finally, there is the psychological trauma of inferiority inflicted on the Negro when the constant assertion, both in word and deed, that he is naturally inferior has produced a sense or belief of inferiority in him, which is often a deterrent to any efforts of self-advancement. Indeed, this psychological factor played a role, though not an exclusive one, in the formulation of the decision of the Supreme Court in the *School Segregation* cases in 1954. The Court stated that separation of school students from others solely because of race "generates a feeling of inferiority as to their status in the community that may affect their hearts and minds in a way unlikely ever to be undone."

Though any practice productive of such heinous effects as these merits reprehension and condemnation, discrimination produces further deleterious effects. Besides the harm inflicted on the Negro who is victimized by discrimination, there are evil effects which redound to the very group which does the discriminating.

So too, the effects of discrimination today are not limited to the Negro, but also extend to the white race. In many instances, these effects are as grave and serious as those inflicted on the Negro and indeed, very frequently, are more serious morally and spiritually. In a paper read at a meeting of the Southern Historical Association in 1955, Benjamin E. Mays summed up these twofold effects of discrimination:

> The chief sin of segregation is the distortion of human personality. It damages the soul of both the segregator and the segregated. It gives the segregated a feeling of inherent inferiority which is not based on facts, and it gives the segregator a feeling of superiority which is not based on facts. It is difficult to know who is damaged more — the segregated or the segregator.[1]

One of the most immediate and most personal losses to the white race because of discrimination is psychological. This psychological conflict has its origin, as we have seen, in the contradiction on the one hand between basic Christian ethics and the belief in the brotherhood and equality of all men (which has received legal formulation in the Declaration of Independence) and on the other hand the actual practices of enmity, superiority, and segregation. The contradiction is a source of inner feelings of guilt, conflict, and tension in the individual. Rabid racial prejudice is frequently the result of frustrations and the resentment of situations which the individual is unable to cope with. The frustration is shifted to a weaker and inferior group which is unable to retaliate, and this group is made a substitute object of hatred and revenge. In this way, the rabid racist is victimized by his own prejudices and prevented from facing his real problems and attempting to solve them in a positive manner or, at least, from adjusting himself to his situation if it is irremediable.

Arnold Rose has listed ten ways in which racial prejudice is harmful to the prejudiced persons themselves. These are (1) economic waste; (2) increased cost of social services; (3) time wasted in the handling of racial problems; (4) international results particularly on

---

[1] Benjamin E. Mays, "The Moral Aspects of Segregation," *The Segregation Decisions* (Atlanta: Southern Regional Council, 1956), pp. 13–18.

nonwhite nations; (5) barriers to intercommunication; (6) psychological effects; (7) closing of minds to anything new and an inability
to reciprocate fully in human relationships; (8) fear of and anxiety
regarding the racial group discriminated against; (9) facility with
which such prejudice may be shifted to make another minority group
its target, so that no group is safe; (10) disrespect for law and order
and an unwillingness to settle disputes peacefully.[2]

Repercussions of discrimination on the white race are also felt in
the field of morality. Violations of the principles of Christian ethics
and morality which occur in discrimination produce a general weakening of moral fiber in all other areas of morality, just as defects
in the practice of one moral virtue mean that the other virtues are
less than perfect.

The economic life of the nation also has to sustain and carry an
extra economic burden as a result of discrimination. First, there is a
loss to the general national economy of a source of manpower because
of restrictions in the training and employment of the Negro labor
potential. This in turn reduces the actualization of that group's production with a concomitant reduction of purchasing power. Discrimination practices against the Negro, who constitutes 10 percent
of the entire population in the United States, have resulted in the
establishment of a large underprivileged class with undeveloped abilities and potentialities. The earning power of this group is curtailed
and so too is its purchasing power. The nondevelopment of a tenth
of the population's potentiality is a prodigality of national resources
which demands, even if only in the name of good economics, remedial
action. It is not right to waste such valuable potentialities by nondevelopment.

Another serious economic by-product of discrimination is the extra
tax burden placed on the citizen. The presence of large segregated
slum areas in a city represents a much lower real-estate evaluation,
with a corresponding lower tax return for that area than would be
the case if the area were developed and a normal one. Tax returns
from slum properties seldom cover the cost to the community of the
social services required in that area. Gordon and Roche relate that
in Cleveland, the city received $225,000 in tax monies from a slum

---

[2] Arnold Rose, The Roots of Prejudice (Paris: UNESCO, 1951), pp. 18–22.

area. But at the same time it had to provide social services, including family relief, extra fire and police protection, and handling of juvenile offenders, which cost $1,360,000 — an amount six times greater than the tax receipts.[3] In addition, in communities where separate educational and recreational facilities must be provided, the duplication of these places an extra tax burden on the individual taxpayers of the community even where the facilities are "separate but not equal." If they are "equal," this places a correspondingly higher tax burden on the citizen.

In the struggle against the threats of Communism in which the free nations of the world are engaged today, the task is made more difficult by the fact that racial discrimination is practiced. The ideals of freedom and equality and the dignity of man as antitheses and antidotes to Communism are compromised by the contradiction between these ideals and our practices. We are not practicing what we preach! Discrimination in the United States is offering a fertile field to the Communist propagandists for their assertions that offers of freedom made by Democracy are nothing but empty promises and lies, and that the real policy of the United States is one of imperialistic conquest and aggrandizement. The propaganda value of racial discrimination to the Communists was indicated in the report of President Truman's Committee on Civil Rights, *To Secure These Rights.* Here it was stated that discrimination and prejudice in the United States contradict the democratic ideals we are preaching to other nations, and that this conflict was embarrassing our foreign policy. Racial prejudice and discrimination in the United States was causing suspicion and resentment in foreign countries, especially those with large non-white populations.

C. Vann Woodward has described the use that Communist propaganda experts have made of discrimination to discredit American sincerity:

> The issue gained tremendously in poignancy when the two powers faced each other in an ideological struggle for world leadership. It came near the focus of antagonism when the center of rivalry between Russia and America shifted to Asia and the two systems began to contend

[3] Milton M. Gordon and John P. Roche, "Segregation — A Two-Edged Sword," *New York Times Magazine* (April 25, 1954); reprinted, Gordon C. Zahn, *Readings in Sociology* (Westminster: Newman Press, 1958), pp. 230–235.

desperately for the friendship of the great colored races of the Orient. In this struggle the issue of segregation, far from being confined to regional boundaries, became international in scope. The daily press of Tokyo, Delhi, Peiping, and Saigon was diligently searched in our State Department for reactions to the latest outburst of interracial violence in Florida or Detroit, or the latest Supreme Court decision on segregation.[4]

In addition, at various times, officials of the State Department have expressed the handicap which racial discrimination was imposing on the government in the conduct of its foreign policy. In May, 1963, Secretary of State Dean Rusk remarked that discrimination was compelling this country to run with one leg in a cast in its race against Communism.

The mission which Christ gave to His Church to teach all nations is also being impeded by racial discrimination. Just as the lag between the teaching and practice of the United States causes suspicion and distrust in other nations, so too the difference between the teaching of the Church and the practices of many Catholics raises doubts and difficulties for the Negro. Father LaFarge describes the stumbling block created by Catholics who discriminate against Negroes:

> . . . for the person who looks upon the Church from the outside . . . this gap between Catholic teaching and Catholic practice, has long been a solid roadblock to a generalized embracing by the American Negro of the Catholic faith . . . Here is the Negro's perplexity. He would like to identify himself first and foremost with the universal Church. The Church herself places no obstacle. Nor does her Supreme Pontiff nor her hierarchy create any problem, yet so many of her members continue to identify him above all other considerations — divine or human — with a mere accident of racial origin . . . This, as I said, gives rise to a basic spiritual problem. The problem of a man who finds evasiveness where he is entitled to love. He is perplexed that the one Church of Christ claims his soul with absolute authority, yet at the same time so many of its members warn him not to take her teachings too universally, too seriously.[5]

The divine command to bring the Gospel to all nations and races is being rendered difficult of fulfillment. Not only is the non-Catholic Negro confused by the contradiction between the teaching of the Church and the practices of some of her members, but also the

---

[4] C. Vann Woodward, op. cit., pp. 120–121.

[5] John LaFarge, S.J., The Catholic Viewpoint on Race Relations (New York: Hanover House, 1956), pp. 41–42.

Catholic who is prejudiced is himself indifferent, or even antagonistic, to the conversion of the Negro. Thus the teaching mission of the Church is retarded, and the indifference engendered by prejudice is depriving her of missionaries needed to carry out the task. The spiritual ministry of the Church to the Negroes of America is being frustrated and her goal of training souls and developing a Christian people who will be a credit to the Church and to the nation is being defeated because of prejudice and discrimination.

CHAPTER 6

THE UNITY
AND SOCIAL NATURE OF MAN

In the present order, bonds of a natural union as well as of a supernatural union form a double foundation for the unity of men. The natural unity is established primarily by reason of men's descent from the first parents as a common ancestor, as well as by the common end and the obligation to procure that end. The supernatural unity is founded on the revealed fact that God has established a supernatural end for man, while the universality of redemption unites men since they are co-sharers in graces merited by Christ.

The sharing of a common goal will frequently lead men to a unity necessitated by the nature of the problems to be solved in order to attain that mutual goal. Four or five men whose lives are threatened, because of their mutual desire for self-preservation, can very easily overcome difficulties in uniting. At times, they may disagree over means or methods, but they are united and in agreement about their goal. They must settle their differences prudently and quickly, and compromises must be made in order to secure unity of action in pursuing that mutual goal. If they fail to suppress differences, they splinter into small groups, or end up working as individuals. As such, they cannot do those things which can be accomplished only when a number work together. Instead, unknowingly, they may even work at cross-purposes, canceling out the accomplishments of other groups, thus rendering all efforts fruitless. Unity is required for difficult and venturesome exploits which in ordinary life may rarely eventualize. But common necessity and the need that all pursue and obtain their end also demand unity between men.

Man's dignity and all his rights flow from the fact that he is a person. The quality of personality places man at the pinnacle of creation, with the right to utilize lower creatures and to exert superiority over them. This superiority comes not because he possesses superior powers or the ability to perform complex operations which the lower creatures can not, but from the fact that he is a rational being. Rationality bestows upon man a dignity and worth preeminently surpassing that of any other creature.

Besides this superiority, man's dignity involves a relationship to his Creator since he is an image of God in intellect and will, and a child of God by sanctifying grace. He is a reflection of God in these faculties and their operations, and particularly so when these have the same object as God's intellect and will, namely God himself. Man can direct his rational powers toward God, and in this way is not only intelligent as God is, but can, with grace and charity, love as God loves. This imaging of the divine activity is also a reason of man's dignity and worth.

The worth of man derives also from the fact that he was created by God and for God. God is to be his end in this life and in the life to come. All his faculties and endowments, natural and supernatural, have been bestowed so that he can freely direct himself to his end. Not only internal endowments, but also all material creation was established by God to be utilized by man to help him realize his ultimate end. Perhaps the most succinct formulation of the dignity of man and its implications was given by Pius XI in his encyclical on atheistic Communism:

> Man has a spiritual and immortal soul. He is a person marvelously endowed by his Creator with gifts of body and mind. He is a true "microcosm," as the ancients said, with a value far surpassing that of the vast inanimate cosmos. God alone is his last end, in this life and the next. By sanctifying grace he is raised to the dignity of a son of God, and incorporated into the kingdom of God in the Mystical Body of Christ. In consequence he has been endowed by God with many varied prerogatives: the right to life, to bodily integrity, to the necessary means of existence; the right to tend toward his ultimate goal in the path marked out for him by God; the right of association and the right to possess and use property.[1]

---

[1] *Divini Redemptoris*, Eng. translation, Terence P. McLaughlin, C.S.B., *The Church and the Reconstruction of the Modern World: The Social Encyclicals of Pius XI* (Garden City: Image Books, 1957), No. 27.

And the dignity of man deriving from his personality and the rights and duties which flow from his nature have been enumerated and explained in great detail in Pope John's encyclical, Pacem in Terris.[2]

All men, because of their endowment of personality, are joined by a bond founded on the unity of origin, the unity of nature, and especially on their common destiny and the common means to be utilized in order to secure that end. They all have a right to attain their temporal and eternal goals. This right entails certain prerogatives belonging to every man by reason of human dignity and which cannot be denied or refused him. The Church, even though it admits that there are differences in individuals, and even in groups or races, has always insisted that these differences, whether they be cultural, social, economic, or racial, are not intended by God to give rise to or excuse for the denial of any basic right. It was consideration of this constant teaching of the Church on the dignity of man and its implications which caused Monsignor Gilligan to write that when this doctrine of Christianity was applied to the race question, all Christians would be compelled to admit that the Negro possessed natural rights which were identical in number and sacredness and inviolability with those of the white man.[3]

Every properly directed and oriented political body, no matter what form it may assume, if it is to be of value and fulfill its essential mission, will measure its value and worth in terms of its success in protecting these basic rights for all its citizens. All good government, it is true, must look to the establishment of order, but order is not an end in itself, but is merely a means to justice. Justice, in turn, is a means to liberty or the ability of the members of the political society to cooperate with each other in peace, attain happiness, and achieve perfection in the fulfillment of their ends. A rightly ordered and just liberty is the aim of a good government. Jacques Maritain states that it would be a degradation of government if its activities were restricted to those which are inferior to the improvement of human life and the protection of these basic rights. This restriction to inferior activities, however, occurs frequently in totalitarian states:

[2] Pacem in Terris, Eng. translation, Paulist Press edition, edited by William J. Gibbons, S.J., Nos. 8–34.

[3] Francis J. Gilligan, Morality of the Color Line (Washington, D. C.: The Catholic University of America Press, 1929), pp. 41–42.

. . . in the individualist-bourgeois notion, there is, properly speaking no common task, but the function of the state is merely to assure the material commodities of a handful of individuals, each of whom is busy seeking his own well-being and his own enrichment. In the totalitarian-communist concept, the essential and prime task of the social whole is the industrial domination of nature. In the racist-totalitarian concept, the essential and primary task of the social whole, or rather the way in which "communion" inevitably is affirmed is the political domination of other men. In these three conceptions, *and the third is certainly the worst* — political society is degraded, and the human person is sacrificed. . . . In the communist concept, and in the racist concept, the dignity of the human person is unknown, and the human person is sacrificed to the titanism of industry which is the economic community's god, or to the demon of race and blood which is the god of the racial community.[4]

The protection, cultivation, and defense of these natural rights is a principal end of government. These rights include moral powers and opportunities as well as those freedoms required to lead a good life and obtain man's end. These rights are founded on man's nature, and not on race or nationality. His personality and his needs, not his race or color, or even the will of the majority, are their source. If he, as a rational being, is to fulfill his ultimate destiny, he must have the free exercise of all these rights. J. Messner, in speaking of the ends of man toward which these rights are directed, calls them "existential," to indicate that they are not dependent on the will, desire, or intention of man, or any subjective purposes, but are objective ends founded on human nature. These rights, of course, also involve obligations. They imply not only an obligation to respect them in others, but also require the possessor to utilize them to fulfill his end. If they are not respected and granted, or if man refuses to utilize them, the fulfillment of man's ends are excluded effectively, and he can never attain that perfection which his nature demands.[5]

Pope Pius XII stressed the obligation of man, from the time he reaches the use of reason, to direct himself toward his end.

From the moment in which a human person feels the first stirring of human reason until the time when that light is finally extinguished, man has a multitude of individual duties to carry out, and at the

---

[4] Jacques Maritain, *Les Droits de l'Homme et le Loi Naturelle* (Paris: Paul Hartmann, 1947), pp. 45–46.

[5] J. Messner, *Social Ethics*, trans. by J. J. Doherty (St. Louis: B. Herder Book Co., 1949), p. 34.

root of all of them lies his obligation to direct himself toward what is right and good. . . . Man learns the rule that will direct him toward his end from his own nature, from the teachings of others and from God's revelations to men. If you cut man off from this law, you make him incapable of carrying out his basic mission, just as you would paralyze him if you cut the tendons and ligaments which join together and support the limbs and parts of his body.[6]

But any enumeration of rights will be valid only when the true human nature with all its implications are taken into consideration. Among these fundamental rights, Maritain has included the right to life, personal liberty, and the pursuit of happiness, as well as the "right of association, the respect for the human dignity of each one whether or not he represents an economic worth for society — all these rights are rooted in the vocation of person, a free and spiritual agent, in the order of absolute values and of a destiny superior to time."[7]

The right of association, which Messner also includes in his enumeration of rights, although usually considered as applying to the right of the workingman to associate and unite in organizations, should not be restricted to this field. The right allows men to come together for the securement of religious, intellectual, or social goals which are not opposed to the rights of others or injurious to the common good. It is founded on the social nature of man and his dependence on cooperation to accomplish self-development. Although man, as a person, is an individual and separate, yet paradoxically, he is also a social being. His nature as an individual person cannot be developed without social fellowship and association with his fellowmen. Nor can he acquire this fellowship and association if his personality is not recognized by them. The need for social association by nature can be seen from a threefold aspect. Physically, man must depend on association with the family more than any other animal in order to sustain and maintain life. Compared with man, animals are more capable of self-development and feeding from babyhood by reason of certain factors, such as instinct, means of self-defense, and protective covering. Spiritually, the arousing, stimulating, and training

---

[6] Ci torna sommamente, address by Pius XII to Representatives of the Italian Film Industry, June 22, 1955, English translation, The Pope Speaks, II (Summer, 1955), 101–112.

[7] Jacques Maritain, Les Droits de l'Homme et le Loi Naturelle, pp. 81–82.

of man's spiritual faculties depend on association with others, especially in the family and in the state. If he is to make any progress in science, literature, art, and culture, he must depend on social life. Finally, for the attainment of his end as an individual, or the realization of God's image in him, this can only be obtained through social union. The fact of the necessity of the Church as the indispensable means for the perfection of man as the image of God and for divine adoptive sonship indicates that the social nature of man reaches to the very core of his being.

This need for social intercommunication and exchange is even more basic than the need of human nature for things required for material, intellectual, and moral life. There is in man a radical generosity requiring communication of intellect and of love which can be secure only when he is admitted to communication with others. Maritain expresses this fundamental spiritual need of communication:

> Speaking absolutely, a person cannot be alone. That which he knows, he wishes to speak, and to express himself — to whom, if not to other persons? It can be said with Jean-Jacques Rousseau that the breath of man is fatal for man; and it can be said with Seneca: "Every time that I have gone among men, I have returned less a man." That is true — but by a fundamental paradox, we cannot, however, be men, and become men without going among men. We cannot have the life and activity within us increase without breathing with those like ourselves. Thus, society is formed as a thing required by nature, and since this nature is human nature, as a work accomplished by the labor of reason and of will, and freely agreed to. Man is a political animal, which means that man needs political life, life in society, not only a family society, but also a civil society.[8]

Deprivation of the right of association with his fellowmen is the basic and fundamental reason for the immorality of racial segregation. This explains why segregation fosters and augments those social, cultural, intellectual, and economic deficiencies which are in turn used as a basis to justify racial segregation. It explains why the Supreme Court had to decide that the very fact that schools are segregated means that they can never be equal regardless of their material or physical excellence. It is the metaphysical explanation of the psychological harm done by segregation, as well as of the personality traumata and the derogation of the human person inflicted by racial segrega-

---

[8] *Op. cit.,* p. 12.

tion. Racial segregation takes away from the Negro the opportunity and ability to associate with many, and sometimes most, of his fellowmen. His very nature demands and requires this freedom to associate in order to develop and actualize his potentialities as man. The scope of this isolation can be realized when it is recognized that racial segregation effectively precludes Negroes from association with almost 90 percent of their fellow citizens. Restriction of communication is effective in all areas except the most basic and essential material requirements. Under segregation, the Negro is excluded from communication with the white race except where he is permitted to supply labor or services needed by the whites, and to render to them essential services and public utilities. Even these are often rendered in minimal quantities because their complete refusal could threaten the welfare or health of the white community. In regard to communication in the fields of political, social, cultural, educational, and even religious endeavors and development, segregation prevents almost every opportunity for the Negro to develop his potentialities through social communication.

Frequently we hear it said that a distinction should be made between compulsory and voluntary segregation. It is stated that while compulsory segregation is wrong, there is nothing wrong with voluntary segregation. In the light of what has been said above, let us examine whether voluntary segregation is as harmless as claimed. By voluntary segregation is meant the practice whereby large groups freely disassociate themselves from their fellowmen either in extensive areas or even in all areas of communication. But if man's nature requires and needs association in order to achieve actualization of potentialities, it would seem that even voluntary segregation or separation is per se illicit because man is placing himself in a position whereby he renders fulfillment of his perfection more difficult, if not impossible. We say per se because there can be instances where this would be allowable, viz., where the common good requires it and where attainment of the end, at the same time, is not rendered impossible. The fact that voluntary segregation or separation is opposed to human nature can be seen from the fact that often well-meaning, but misunderstanding, men are shocked and repelled when someone embraces a cloistered life, separated from family, friends, and worldly interests. Of course, this abhorrence is caused because they misunderstand the nature of the religious life, and consider it as motivated by disinterest in one's fellowmen. Although such repugnance is incorrect, nevertheless, its existence is indication of an almost automatic repulsion of the separation of man from his fellowmen and a realization of the need of social association.

It can be said that racial segregation, whether it is voluntary or involuntary, is per se illicit for it opposes the very nature of man and renders attainment of his end at least more difficult. Father Gerald Kelly, S.J., reasoning along similar lines, states that discrimination, considered as unequal treatment, is unjust, and adds:

> . . . also unjust is compulsory segregation, first, because it implies a stigma imposed on one race by the other, and secondly because it inevitably leads to unequal treatment. The only form of segregation that might conceivably be morally justifiable is segregation by mutual agreement and with equal rights. *Even this, it seems to me, is per se contrary to the bond of union that should exist between people of the same nation and contrary to the common good of the nation itself.*[9] (Italics added.)

Segregation, because it violates the bond of unity between men which is established by their common origin, common nature, and common destiny, is immoral. This unity requires per se association of men with each other, and this association is what is primarily prevented by racial segregation, especially when involuntary.

---

[9] Gerald Kelly, S.J., "Notes on Current Moral Theology," *Theological Studies,* XIII (1952), 68.

CHAPTER 7

NATURAL
AND SUPERNATURAL UNITY

Advocates of compulsory racial segregation, who act from conviction or prejudice (in contrast to those who merely react to various pressures, human respect, or custom) are basically motivated by some form of racism. Rarely is their adherence to racism explicit, or do they advert to it. If charged with it, they can be convinced only with the greatest difficulty, if at all. But the very patterns of segregation and the motives of prejudice reveal racist foundations. They take no cognizance of the individual or his attributes. The fact that he is a member of that race is all that is required to place him outside the pale of normal interrelations, and he must conform to the racial restrictions. All the base and dishonorable characteristics of a racial stereotype are attributed to him personally. This aspect of segregation is common to its practice not only in the United States, but also in *apartheid* in South Africa. The refusal to consider the individual and his qualities is, according to Ambrose Reeves, Anglican Bishop of Johannesburg, the fundamental reason of the immorality of *apartheid*. Bishop Reeves has stated:

The cardinal error of apartheid is that it never regards human beings as individuals. It persists in ignoring their personal worth because it always treats them as members of a particular ethnic group, and in so doing personifies the racial group, the tribe, the race. Indeed, it declares in effect that the individual has worth only as he has a value to the racial group to which he happens to belong. Such a theory must be condemned as unethical. It is at this point that *apartheid* demon-

50

strates most clearly that it is immoral, because it seeks to deal with people not as persons, but as members of a particular racial group.[1]

A similar observation of the racism involved in segregation was made by the Catholic bishops of South Africa, and they indicated quite clearly that the motive behind *apartheid* was white supremacy.

> The basic principle of *apartheid* is the preservation of what is called white civilization. This is identified with white supremacy, which means the enjoyment by white men only of full political, social, economic, and cultural rights. Persons of other races must be satisfied with what the white man judges can be conceded to them without endangering his privileged position. White supremacy is an absolute. It overrides justice. It transcends the teaching of Christ. It is a purpose dwarfing every other purpose, an end justifying any means.[2]

Judgment of the inferiority of the entire Negro race in compulsory segregation in this country was mentioned by the American Bishops in their statement on race relations in 1958. They declared that this judgment that an entire race, merely because of race, is unfit to associate with white people cannot be reconciled with the Christian teaching on the nature of man and his rights.

Bishop Albert Fletcher of Little Rock has written that segregation is founded on racism, teaching that certain races and nationalities are inherently and naturally superior to other races, implying that the other races or nationalities are inherently and naturally inferior.[3]

The segregationist may be reluctant to admit that racism is implicit in his beliefs and practices, but he cannot escape its reality. The fears of intermarriage or of "mongrelization" of the white race so frequently offered as motives for segregation only make sense when the unstated premise is that the white race, by its very nature, so surpasses any other race that any contamination by racial intermingling would result in a loss of that superiority. Racism as an abstract set of philosophical principles adapted to certain environmental situations can reflect varying degrees of moderation or excess. It can range from

---

[1] Rt. Rev. Ambrose Reeves, "Charge to Diocesan Synod, 1957," *Church and Race in South Africa*, David M. Paton (ed.), (London: SCM Press, Ltd., 1958), p. 47.

[2] Statement of the Catholic Bishops of the Union of South Africa, July, 1957, Eugene McManus, S.S.J., *Studies in Race Relations* (Baltimore: Josephite Press, 1961), p. 84.

[3] Most Rev. Albert L. Fletcher, *An Elementary Catholic Catechism on the Morality of Segregation and Racial Discrimination*, 1960, p. 3.

the attitude that one race is naturally superior on the plane of the intellectual, cultural, moral, and physical, and extend to the extreme where a common human nature is denied to members of another race.

We have previously mentioned the great debate at Valladolid in 1550 in which the jurist, Juan Gines de Sepulveda, in defending Conquistador treatment of the Indians, maintained that they were "natural slaves" fit only to obey their natural masters, in this case, of course, the Spaniards. If they refused subjection, they could be forced to obey. War may be waged against them with as much justice as wild beasts are hunted, and the survivors of such a war may be enslaved. This position was opposed by the Dominican friar, Bartolome de las Casas, who maintained that such a position contradicted the teachings of Christ, the laws of the Church, and his personal experience in the New World.

Some Catholics went further and maintained that the Indians were not human, but were merely animals. This can be seen in the necessity which led Pope Paul III to issue the Bull, Sublimis Deus, in 1537. In this document, he castigated, as being diabolically inspired, the notion that Indians were animals and he explicitly affirmed their human nature:

> The enemy of the human race, who opposes all good deeds in order to bring men to destruction, beholding and envying this, invented a means never before heard of, by which he might hinder the preaching of God's word of Salvation to the people: he inspired his satellites who, to please him, have not hesitated to publish abroad that the Indians of the West and the South, and other people of whom We have recent knowledge should be treated as dumb brutes created for our service, pretending that they are incapable of receiving the Catholic faith. We . . . consider, however, that the Indians are truly men and that they are not only capable of understanding the Catholic faith but according to our information, they desire exceedingly to receive it.[4]

However, the papal pronouncement did not end the notion of the subhuman nature of the Indians. For more than a century afterward, some priests in the New World refused to administer the sacraments to the Indians in the belief that they were incapable of receiving them. In fact, Lewis Hanke in his article on Pope Paul III and his

---

[4] John Tracy Ellis (ed.), Documents of American Catholic History, 2 ed. (Milwaukee: The Bruce Publishing Co., 1962), pp. 7–8.

treatment of the Indians quotes a formal deathbed retraction made in 1549 by a Dominican friar in which he retracts his opinion that the Indians are merely animals.[5]

Mention has already been made of the attempt of some of the American defenders of slavery to justify it on the grounds that the Negro was not human. The influence of racism in American life can be seen in the writings of Orestes Brownson. Even though he became a strong advocate of abolition as a war measure, he believed that all nonwhite races were inferior, not because they were of different origin, or that they were primitive men in a low state of evolution, but because they had fallen below the normal human type. Brownson believed that the Negro was at the lowest point of degeneracy and that even the truths of Christianity could not be taught to him because all he could understand or grasp were the mere external forms, and thus all religion degenerated into superstition among the Negroes.[6]

The attempts of the Nazis in Germany to put into practice their racist philosophy which maintained the superiority of the Aryan race over all other racial groups culminated in genocide. Exaltation of the mystique and myth of blood and race brought about the attempt to overthrow Christianity and replace it with neo-paganism. The Nazi philosophy, including its racism, and the violations of the 1933 Concordat were vigorously condemned by Pope Pius XI in his encyclical, *Mit brennender Sorge* in 1937. Shortly after the appearance of this encyclical, the Sacred Congregation of Seminaries and Universities ordered all seminaries and universities to defend the teaching of the Church against racism and to use all the sciences: biology, history, philosophy, and law, to refute racism. The Congregation listed eight of these racist propositions, the first two of which are:

> 1. The human races, by their natural and unchangeable characteristics, are so different that the lowest of them is farther removed from the highest race of men than from the highest species of animal.

---

[5] Lewis Hanke, "Paul III and the American Indians," *Harvard Theological Review*, XXX (1937), 96–98; cf. also Lewis Hanke, *Aristotle and the American Indians: A Study in Race Prejudice in the Modern World* (Chicago: Henry Regnery Co., 1959), for a thorough account of the debate at Valladolid.

[6] *Works of Orestes A. Brownson*, collected and arranged by Henry F. Brownson (Detroit: Thorndike Nourse, 1885), Vol. 17, pp. 557–559.

2. The vigor of the race and the purity of blood must be preserved by every possible means; whatever conduces to this is *ipso facto* honorable and licit.[7]

Maritain has summarized racism and its evil effects, calling it the most "intrinsically unhuman and hopeless barbarism" threatening civilization today, because it binds permanently to biological categories and necessities from which there can be no escape.[8]

The racist aspect of segregation and prejudice involves an implicit denial of the unity of the human race. According to the constant teaching of the Church, this physical unity is the result of the common origin of all men from the same first parents. Polygenism, denying this common origin, maintains that various racial groups had different origins. The father of polygenism is usually considered to be Isaac de la Peyrere, a French Calvinist, who, in 1655, published a work on pre-Adamites in which he maintained, because of his interpretation of Romans 5:12–14, that there had been two creations of man; the pre-Adamites on the sixth day, and Adam later, after the day of rest. The Jews were descendants of Adam; the Gentiles descendants of the pre-Adamites. Later, when de la Peyrere became a Catholic, he retracted this theory. During the nineteenth century, scientists investigating the origin of man returned to the idea of polygenism as well as pre-Adamite theories. In America, during the controversy over slavery, these explanations found great favor when it was realized that they gave a scientific justification for slavery. But the theological implications soon became apparent in the early 1800's to the religious men who believed in original sin and the fall of man: the theological problem which confronted them formed a dilemma. If all men did not descend from Adam, or were not of the same species, the problem to be answered was: Which species had inherited original sin? Stanton in his study of scientific explanations of race in the 1800's describes the problems which confronted the religious man who accepted these scientific explanations:

> If they had always inhabited distinct provinces, as Agassiz believed, how many Resurrections were there? Of course the pious who ac-

---

[7] T. Lincoln Bouscaren, S.J., *The Canon Law Digest* (Milwaukee: The Bruce Publishing Co., 1949), Vol. II, pp. 395–396.

[8] Jacques Maritain, "Menace of Racialism," *Interracial Review*, X (May, 1937), p. 70.

cepted the new theory blandly assumed that Adam and Eve were the progenitors of the Caucasian species, but even they had to face the theological implications of hybridization. Was the mulatto half-saved, half-damned? And the theological problems presented by the quinteroon and octoroon led one into higher mathematics. There was too . . . the first parents of Caucasians, then why send missionaries to carry the blessings of grace to heathens whose own first parents had never fallen from grace? The theory of the specific diversity of man tossed the religious into a theological bramble patch.[9]

Typical of this American anthropology and a proponent of polygenism is the work of J. C. Nott and George R. Gliddon, first published in 1855, and entitled *Types of Mankind.* Despite the fact that it was an 800-page volume and cost over $7 (a considerable price in 1855), it had a large sale and went through ten editions before 1871. John C. Calhoun, Secretary of State, in 1844, because he feared French support of the British desire to see the abolition of slavery in America, and particularly in the recently annexed Texas, prepared a defense of slavery predicated on polygenist theories expounded to him by Samuel Morton and George Gliddon, which defense he forwarded to the American Minister to France, William R. King. In his letter to King, Calhoun stated that he feared that the abolition movement would be used by England as a means of economic control, and that if the abolitionists were successful, it would mean a race war in America which would only result in the "ascendancy of the lowest and most savage of the races and a return to barbarism." And he authorized King to spend up to $500 to publish, in the French press, American defenses of slavery.[10]

Polygenism, advocated by American scientists as well as by European scientists, especially in France and England, received consideration at the Vatican Council. It is interesting to note that in the original schema for a dogmatic constitution, polygenism was condemned as heretical. Franzelin, who is chiefly responsible for the entire theological schema, believed that the physical unity of the human race was the strongest argument against all forms of racism. A dogmatic canon was prepared which read: "If any one denies that

---

[9] William Stanton, *The Leopard's Spots: Scientific Attitudes toward Race in America, 1815–1859* (Chicago: University of Chicago Press, 1960), p. 112.

[10] "Letters of John C. Calhoun," *American Historical Association Report* (1899),Vol. II, pp. 631–633.

the entire human race has come from one protoparent, let him be anathema."[11] Bishop Verot, who was the chief opponent of English and American polygenistic slavery defenses, objected to the annotation in the schema that monogenism was being doubted by many "*ex levissimis rationibus geologicis et ethnographicis.*" He maintained that these reasons were not light, but were very serious and that only the scriptural account of creation kept him from assenting to their scientific reasonings.

However, discontinuation of the Council because of war prevented this canon on polygenism, as well as many others, from reaching the General Congregation of the Council or being voted upon. Proposed canons which are not put to a vote at a Council and approved cannot be considered to have any conciliar authority or force. But the great care and consideration which have been used in their formulation give them a worth and value as representative of the common teaching of theologians at the particular time they were worked out. And this proposed canon on polygenism enjoys no higher status or authority than this.

The only official statement by the Church treating *ex professo* of polygenism is in the encyclical *Humani Generis* of Pius XII, when he states:

> When, however, there is question of another conjectural opinion, namely polygenism, the children of the Church by no means enjoy such liberty. For the faithful cannot embrace that opinion which maintains either that after Adam there existed on this earth true men who did not take their origin through natural generation from him as from the first parent of all, or that Adam represents a certain number of first parents. For it is in no way apparent how such an opinion can be reconciled with that which the sources of revealed truth and the documents of the Teaching Authority of the Church propose with regard to original sin, which proceeds from a sin actually committed by an individual Adam and which through generation is passed on to all and is in everyone as his own.[12]

This teaching of Pius XII on polygenism was foreshadowed in his previous encyclical, *Summi Pontificatus*, written in 1939, when racism was rampant in Germany and Italy, and which should be considered

---

[11] *Coll. Lacensis,* VII, cols. 1637; 515; 544; 555; and 566.

[12] A. C. Cotter, S.J., *The Encyclical "Humani Generis" with a Commentary,* 2 ed. (Weston: Weston College Press, 1952).

in the light of that circumstance. In condemning various errors, he lists as the first, the forgetfulness of the law of human solidarity and charity which is imposed because of common origin and the equal possession of rational nature by all men, and by the Redemption. Pius XII cites Genesis' account of the creation of Adam and Eve and the descent of other men from this first couple as indicative of the solidarity and unity of all men:

> In fact, the first page of the Scripture, with magnificent simplicity tells how God, as a culmination to His creative work, made man in His own image and likeness. . . . It shows us besides how other men took their origin from the first couple and then goes on in unsurpassed vividness of language to recount their division into different groups and their dispersion to various parts of the world. . . . A marvelous vision, which makes us see the human race in the unity of one common origin in God "One God and Father of all, Who is above all, and through all, and in us all"; in the unity of nature which in every man is equally composed of material body and spiritual, immortal soul.[13]

Some controversy among theologians over the theological note which should be given to monogenism in view of the teaching of *Humani Generis* has arisen. This does not mean that theologians are in disagreement as to whether this is the official teaching of the Church or whether they must accept it. There is no disagreement on these points. The question rather is whether it can now be said that monogenism is a part of revelation. Sagüès believes that it is at least proximate to faith.[14] Muldoon states that monogenism is of divine faith since it is clearly contained in revelation,[15] and Ott maintains that it is certain.[16]

The question has also arisen whether the Pope in *Humani Generis* left the door open for a different decision on polygenism in the future. Father Cotter, in his commentary on the encyclical, emphatically denies that this is so and believes that monogenism is Catholic doctrine:

---

[13] *Summi Pontificatus*, N.C.W.C. edition, No. 31.
[14] J. F. Sagüès, S.J., "De Deo Creante et Elevante," *Sacrae Theologiae Summa* (Madrid: Biblioteca de Autores Cristianos, 1955), II, No. 545.
[15] Thomas Muldoon, *Theologiae Dogmaticae Praelectiones* (Rome: Catholic Book Agency, 1959), III, p. 138.
[16] Ludwig Ott, *Fundamentals of Catholic Dogma*, edited in English by James Bastible (St. Louis: B. Herder Book Co., 1954), p. 94.

Some die-hards might wish to see a loophole in the words "for it is unintelligible" (*cum nequaquam appareat*) as if they left the door open for a different decision in the future. This would be an illusion. Polygenism is definitely banned; it should not even be put forward as a hypothesis. Monogenism is the Catholic doctrine, though the Encyclical does not settle the further question what precise theological note is to be assigned to it.[17]

Others, however, believe that the encyclical neither approves nor excludes any possible theory which may be reconciled with Catholic dogma. Father Karl Rahner summarizes his own position on these questions and attributes the note of "theologically certain" to monogenism, stating that it cannot be said that the door is open positively for some polygenistic theory, but on the other hand there is no positive statement that something of the sort will always be impossible. "Thus the attitude adopted is precisely that which theology describes with respect to the propositions which it calls theologically certain."[18]

Racial prejudice and segregation are also injurious to the supernatural unity which exists between men. This unity can derive from different sources, and hence there can be degrees in the closeness of such unity. The primary supernatural unity derives, however, from the fact that in the present divine economy, the ultimate end established by God for man is a supernatural one — the intuitive vision of God. Just as the physical unity derives from the origin of all men from the same first parents, so too all inherit the debt of original sin by reason of this physical descent. And the redemption of Christ, which was required because of the inheritance of the sin of Adam by all men, as well as by personal sin, is extended to all who have shared in this sin of Adam. "Therefore, as by the offence of one, unto all men to condemnation: so also by the justice of one, unto all men to justification of life" (Rom 5:18).

But to perceive a fellowman as one who is also called by God to attain eternal beatitude and co-sharer in the merits of Christ's sacrifice, or to desire that he obtain his ultimate end and aid him in doing so, cannot be accomplished if he is rejected and repulsed from association, if he is regarded as inferior and unworthy of consideration or respect

---

[17] A. C. Cotter, S.J., *op. cit.*, p. 105.
[18] Karl Rahner, S.J., *Theological Investigations*, translated by Cornelius Ernst, O.P. (Baltimore: Helicon Press, 1961), Vol. 1, p. 237.

or love. When his value as a human person is denied, there can be no appreciation of his value as one who is coredeemed by Christ.

An even more intimate supernatural unity is present between those who are members of the Mystical Body. The very notion of parts of a body conveys the necessity of unity between these parts. This unity also exists between the members of the Church which is the Mystical Body of Christ. Unfortunately, before the issuance of *Mystici Corporis Christi*, in 1943, there was confusion as to the nature of the Mystical Body. In this encyclical, Pius XII identified the Catholic Church as the Mystical Body of Christ.

This identity of the Catholic Church as the Mystical Body of Christ was repeated in *Humani Generis* when Pius XII corrected those who claimed that they were not bound by the doctrine that "the Mystical Body of Christ and the Roman Catholic Church are one and the same thing."

The doctrine of the Mystical Body implies a union between the various members of the Church establishing them in a relationship to each other as parts of a living body, as well as to the head of that body, who is Christ. In an application of the doctrine of the Mystical Body to the racial situation, incorrect notions were occasionally used which beclouded the special unity which exists between the members of the Church. And often the treatment meted out to members of the Mystical Body because they are Negroes is a denial of that unity and relationship. When white Catholics refuse to allow a fellow Catholic, for no other reason than race, to kneel beside them at Mass, to receive the sacraments with them, or will not worship God with them or will even, shamefully, refuse to administer the sacraments to them, they implicitly deny and attack the unity of the Mystical Body. Unity requires that they be concerned for the needs of their fellow members, whether these be spiritual or material needs.

Especially divisive of the unity of the Mystical Body is the action of some Catholics who insist that if Negroes are permitted to attend their church, they receive Communion only after all the whites have left the Communion rail, or who, as has actually happened, leave the rail without receiving Communion because a Negro kneels beside them. One of the effects of the Eucharist is to unite one in a mystical union with Christ and with His members through a bond of charity.

St. Thomas calls the Eucharist the "sacrament of ecclesiastical unity," because from it many are made one in Christ.[19] There is a tendency to emphasize the Eucharist as a strictly personal and private communion between the individual and Christ and to overlook and forget completely the bonds of union which it produces between the individual worshipers. Father John Connery, S.J., has been among those who have tried to remind us of the social aspect of the whole of Catholic dogma and especially of the Eucharist. He states that this social aspect is most pronounced in the Holy Eucharist which is the sacrament of unity — involving unity with the sacramental body of Christ and the Mystical Body of Christ.[20]

The priest through his ordination is established as another Christ, endowed with the power to offer the sacrifice of the Mass and to forgive sins. Pius XI has described him as the minister of Christ and as an instrument in His hands for the continuation of His work. This teaching was repeated several times, particularly by Pius XII, who calls the priest the representative of Christ and applies the words of the Gospel to this relationship: "As the Father has sent me, I also send you"; "He who hears you, hears me." But racial prejudice causes the union and relationship between Christ and His priest as minister frequently to be disregarded by Catholics who do not want to attend Mass said by a Negro priest or to receive the sacraments from his hands. The incident at Jesuit Bend, Louisiana, when Catholics refused to permit a Negro priest in their mission chapel, gives evidence of what extremes of prejudice can do to this union between Christ and His priest as well as to the unity of the Mystical Body. An Osservatore Romano editorial condemned this action at Jesuit Bend in very strong terms:

> It is a sacrilege to show racial animosity against a priest by preventing him from ascending the altar to say the words of consecration taught and commanded by Christ for all His people of every race and nation at all times. . . . To prevent a priest from repeating that sacrifice . . . is a sacrilege concerning which we can only pray with the prayer of the crucified Christ for his crucifiers, "Father, forgive them, for they know not what they do."

---

[19] Summa Theologiae, III, q. 82, a. 2; q. 67, a. 2; q. 85, a. 5.

[20] John R. Connery, S.J., "Social Aspects of Catholic Dogma," Catholic Mind, L (1952), 486.

Because of the implicit denials of the physical and supernatural unity in racial prejudice and segregation, Father Yves Congar, O.P., was led to the conclusion that all forms of racism struck at the main truths of Christianity, particularly the truth of charity. Racism, he states, attacks the very notion of love or charity for our neighbor.[21]

---

[21] Yves M.-J. Congar, O.P., *The Catholic Church and the Race Question* (Paris: UNESCO, 1953), p. 24.

CHAPTER 8

JUSTICE AND RACE RELATIONS

In discussing problems involving race relations, the frequent, and almost exclusive, use of the expression "interracial justice" is likely to give the impression that the solution of these problems is merely a matter of the fulfillment of obligations of justice. It would be unfortunate if this impression were to become current and the role of the other virtues in these problems neglected or passed over. This does not imply, however, a belittling or disparagement of the function of justice in interracial matters. But overemphasis on justice is likely to result in a distorted theological presentation. In fact, it could easily lead to an intensification of the awareness of separateness between races since justice always stresses the *alteritas* or "otherness" of the person to whom something is due.

The virtues of charity and prudence also deserve attention in a theological consideration of these problems. Racial prejudice is basically a rash judgment and, therefore, is of the speculative order, while racial discrimination, which involves deliberate acts usually motivated by prejudice, is of the practical order. But both must be corrected by acts of justice and charity. These two virtues are particularly useful for the correction of racial prejudice and discrimination because they are virtues having the neighbor as their object. They primarily perfect the will, but in different ways. The object of justice is the right of our neighbor, while the object of charity is God and our neighbor insofar as he is related to God.

The distinction between justice and charity, beside their essential distinction as moral and theological virtues, consists in this that justice in considering the neighbor stresses his "otherness," since for the application of justice, there must be separateness of persons. No one is said to be unjust to himself. In fact, this separateness or distinction is so necessary to the virtue of justice that in areas where it diminishes sufficiently, e.g., those relations of father and son, as such, in which the son is an *alter ego* of the father, the virtue of piety applies rather than justice. Vermeersch describes this:

> An accurate distinction must be made between those things which are done to a conjoined person, e.g., father-son, insofar as they are conjoined, and those things which are due insofar as they are persons. In the example given of the father and son, the former are obligations of piety, and only the latter are controlled by justice, or by justice accompanied by piety. To express it in a more general way: What I owe to my neighbor insofar as he is an "alter ego" pertains to charity; what is owed to him as a distinct person is the province of justice.[1]

Thus, the overstressing of justice in the field of race relations may produce the opposite of the desired effect, namely an emphasis and greater awareness of separateness of the races evidenced by the existence of separate rights and obligations. Charity, on the other hand, seeks an identification of the beloved with the lover, and strives to accomplish this identity. In cases where there is inequality, love will move to the bestowal of those things which are lacking so that equality can be established. This proportionality is effected in us when God, in order to span the difference between us, as creatures, and Himself, so that we may be objects of Divine Love, bestows on us the habit of grace, thereby elevating us to a supernatural level. Describing the difference between justice and charity in regarding their object, Pieper expresses it:

> What distinguishes justice from love is just this: in the relationship of justice, men confront each other as separate "others," almost as strangers. . . . Because the loved one is not properly "someone else," there is no formal justice between those who love. To be just means to recognize the other *as other*; it means to acknowledge there where one cannot love. Justice says: This is another person, who is other than I, and who nevertheless has his own peculiar due. A just man is just, therefore, because he sanctions another person in his very separateness and helps him to receive his due.[2]

---

[1] Vermeersch, II, No. 318.
[2] Josef Pieper, *Justice*, translated by Lawrence E. Lynch (New York: Pantheon Books, 1955), pp. 25–26.

Charity, since it is a *theological* virtue, beholds the "other" as he is related to God, either as a creature of God, or redeemed by Christ. Justice, being a *moral* virtue, regards him, not in terms of a relationship to God, but as a separate person possessing rights. Even the operative and perfective qualities of these two virtues differ. As habits, they perfect the faculty in which they reside, but this perfection of the faculty is not accomplished in isolation and without regard to the other faculties. When the will is perfected, it is in a position to command acts of the other faculties, including the intellect. This corelationship can be illustrated by the example of the formulation of an act of faith. The virtue of faith is an intellectual habit. Its act is the formulation of a *credo* by the intellect. But before this *credo* can be uttered, the intellect must receive a command of the will. When this command has been received, then, and only then, can the act of faith be made. To correct racial prejudice, which, as we have said, is basically a rash judgment, the act of the will must be taken into consideration. Before a rash judgment can be corrected and revised by the intellect, the will must give the command. The racially prejudiced person will not correct his prejudices unless he first wills to do something about them. At the same time, defects of the will in racial matters will have to be corrected by justice and charity. In this way, both charity and justice play an important role in removing both racial prejudice and racial discrimination.

When one speaks of justice, it is usually commutative or strict justice which is first thought of. Violations of strict justice are frequently involved in race relations because often there is a racial basis which either occasions the injustice or makes it feasible, e.g., when a Negro is denied a right due him in strict justice and this denial is made because he is a Negro, or when it is possible to make this denial because of the patterns of racial discrimination. Restriction to segregated housing is very often coupled with noticeably higher rents. A Negro family, because of its limited selection of housing, is often victimized by unscrupulous landlords charging more for rent than could be obtained from a white family. In most instances, the rent paid by a white family will represent what the housing is actually worth, but the Negro because he has little choice is forced to pay more. This overcharge of rent made possible by segregation is an example of a violation of justice. A similar situation obtains when the Negro attempts to purchase a home. When the seller realizes that a Negro family is seeking to purchase the house, he will demand a higher price than he would ask from a white family. Premium prices for houses, especially where the premium represents an appreciable increase over the normal value of the property, violate strict justice. Recently Haynes Johnson, a reporter for the Washington *Evening Star*, indicated the increased prices which Negro families have to pay for housing in Washington. He reported an incident where the rent for an apartment occupied by a white family was $65 a month, but when Negro tenants were accepted into that apartment house, the rent for the apartment was increased to $85 a month. He also indicated that in Washington, Negroes have to pay from $3,000 to $7,000 more for a house than a white purchaser.[3]

Frequently stores operating in segregated areas charge excessive prices for inferior merchandise. They depend on the ignorance and need of their customers, glib talk and high pressure salesmanship, and the extension of "easy credit." Often usurious interest rates are charged for credit, disguised as charges for credit investigation, service charges, etc. Some of these store owners, knowing the inexperience of their Negro customers, descend to fraud and trickery, obtaining customer signatures on sales contracts or chattel mortgages under the pretense that the customer is just signing a receipt so that he may take the merchandise home on trial.

Ignorance of the nature of his rights or inability to enforce these rights because of lack of police protection or inability to obtain justice in court against a white man is the occasion for the Negro's being robbed of wages, property, and insurance benefits. Surely this is the modern sin which cries to heaven for vengeance. "Behold the hire of the laborers who have reaped down your fields, which by fraud has been kept back by you, crieth, and the cry of them hath entered into the ears of the Lord of Sabaoth" (Jas 5:4).

Right-thinking people will condemn these more flagrant violations of justice, especially when they involve outright fraud and deceit. But

---

[3] Haynes Johnson, *Dusk at the Mountain: The Negro, the Nation, and the Capital* — *A Report on Problems and Progress* (Garden City: Doubleday & Co., 1963), Chap. IV, "The Two-Price System."

too often injustices are "winked at," or considered shrewd business practices. Often this latter toleration of injustice does not stem from racial prejudice but is rather reflective of a more general relaxation of moral standards in the field of business practices and a false conception of the nature of prudence.

Frequently in considering commutative justice, we tend to restrict our notion to these open violations, disregarding more common violations of strict justice involved in daily speech. St. Thomas, discussing violations of justice, devotes five questions to backbiting, reviling, tale-bearing, derision, and cursing.[4] His enumeration of these as violations of strict justice may surprise some, especially since we so often regard them solely as related to charity, disregarding completely their relation to justice. We shall treat briefly of these violations of justice since they do have an important bearing on race relations.

Reviling or Contumely: Reviling injures the honor of our neighbor. By honor we understand an external acknowledgment of the excellence and worth of another, manifested either by words of praise, actions, or material objects. The basis of honor may be qualities or endowments of any sort, internal or external, natural or supernatural. This honor or recognition is injured by reviling or contumely when something deleterious or harmful to the honor of another is publicized and made known, not only to others, but also to the person dishonored. Contumely is defined as the unjust dishonoring of a man while he is present.

It is important to note that contumely occurs not only by a denial of honor, but also by acts which are expressive of contempt. In its strict meaning, contumely is verbal, but in its broad meaning it also extends to actions or deeds, e.g., a gesture indicative of contempt, a slap in the face, etc. The mere omission of honor which is due does not necessarily constitute contumely, unless circumstances are such that it is equivalent to and indicative of contempt, as when a person is deliberately excluded from a general greeting or welcome. The requirement of the presence of the person is also to be understood in a broad sense. It does not demand physical presence, but can be through his representative or by later making the injury known to him. And while contumely is usually in the presence of others, it

---

[4] *Summa Theol.,* II–II, qq. 72–76.

does not require their presence; the mere presence of the one reviled is sufficient. However, the guilt will be greater in proportion to the number of witnesses.

Establishing the gravity of the sin of contumely, St. Thomas states that where the purpose is to dishonor or to manifest contempt, then it will be a sin against justice *ex genere suo grave* — i.e., grave of its very nature. The reason is that contumely deprives a man of something to which he has a strict right, viz., honor, which men value no less than material possessions. However, if the intent of the act is merely to correct a defect or fault, it may be no sin, or at most, a venial sin. But even in such a case, St. Thomas cautions that great care and discretion are required lest the action really injure the one who is being corrected.

Contumely differs from mockery, which is wittiness without intent to dishonor or hold in contempt, but merely to entertain and amuse. It is possible that this may not be sinful, but if injury or pain is inflicted on the person who is made a butt of the mockery, then it would not be lacking in moral fault even though the injury was not directly intended.

It would be impossible to enumerate all instances in which contumely enters into race relations. In practically all instances of the so-called "racial etiquette" practiced especially in those localities having legalized segregation, there is a derogation of the honor due to the Negro. For example, "racial etiquette" requires that the Negro, entering a white home, do so by the back door, unless, paradoxically, he is a servant close to the family or has been specifically invited to use the front door.

But when a white man goes to a Negro home, no matter for what purpose, he will choose either entrance, and it cannot be insisted that he enter by the rear door. White salesmen often expect to sell goods or make deliveries through the front door of middle-class Negro homes. However, the problem is not so much to prevent the use of the front entrance by such persons, but to avoid positive signs of disrespect after they are in the house. Some will insist on keeping on their hats while in the Negro's house. And the only control the Negro has over this situation is to refuse to buy, but frequently he has need of that merchandise and must tolerate those practices.

In some localities, insurance agents have been compelled to abandon many of these disrespectful practices because of competition from Negro insurance companies, or because the Negro elected to pay the premiums by mail or at the office which entailed loss of commission to the agent. Increasing awareness that the Negro expects signs of respect to be shown by those entering his home has produced a reluctance on the part of some whites to enter the Negro's home. Instead, they will sit in their car and honk the horn, or stand outside and call until the Negro comes out to talk to them.[5]

"Racial etiquette" also requires that the Negro not be given any sign or title of respect by a white person, regardless of his education or position. "Mr." or "Mrs." is not to be used in speaking or writing to a colored person. If his first name is known, it is used, and if not known, he is simply called "Boy" or "Uncle." Young Negro women are called by their first name, but if that is not known, "you, there" is used. The "etiquette," however, demands that the Negro in return make a display of subservience, removing his hat in the presence of any white person, male or female, and use titles of respect, such as "Mr." or "Sir." These titles of respect must be shown by the Negro regardless of the social status of the white person. While the Negro usually does not object to their use toward a white man who is socially and economically superior, he is irritated when he must use them in addressing a "poor white."

Another common form of dishonor today is the use of the word "nigger." Originally this was simply a slurred pronunciation of "Negro," but today it is a term of contempt, and has been for many years. Variations in its use and pronunciation are common, depending on locality. Southerners pronounce it *niggah*. In Southern urban centers, whites, at least in the presence of the Negro, will avoid it and use "colored," but in the Southern rural areas, it is more widely used. A variation used in the South occasionally is *nigra*, which is considered by its users as slightly more respectful, and is used when talking to someone from whom they may expect criticism about the treatment of the Negro. John Wicklein, in his series of articles on Southern churches in the New York Times, indicated this usage. He

---

[5] Charles S. Johnson, *Patterns of Negro Segregation* (New York: Harper & Bros., 1943), pp. 129–135.

reported that a white cab driver in Atlanta was one of the few persons who used the word "nigger" when talking to him. He also noted that church leaders favoring segregation generally used *nigra*, while those leaders who opposed segregation said *Negro*.[6]

Exclusion from public facilities affords an occasion of contumely to the Negro as when he is ordered to give his seat on a bus to a white person; refused service in a restaurant; forced to stand at soda fountains or lunch counters; denied admittance to theaters or restricted to the upper balcony; told that Negroes are not tolerated, served, or admitted to hotels, etc. Difficulty in arriving at a realization of the existence of contumely in racial segregation is attributable to the fact that most whites have never made a conscious effort to know what the Negro's feeling in a particular situation must be. The excuse is often made that the Negro does not mind this, or prefers to be with other Negroes, or expects this kind of treatment. One fortunate effect of the present racial conflict is the destruction of this myth that the Negro does not resent the treatment he has been receiving. The bus strike in Montgomery, Alabama, as well as the various "Sit-In" demonstrations in the South, must be considered successful protests because they contradicted this myth.

Lack of consideration for the feelings of the Negro and a refusal to consider what one's own feelings would be were the situation reversed are largely responsible for such practices. If a Christian would carefully evaluate and consider what the feelings of the Negro must be in certain situations, how he is dishonored and insulted by various practices and customs, he would become increasingly aware of the fact that the sin of contumely is present in many of his actions.

Detraction or Backbiting: A man's property can be injured in two ways: openly by robbery or violence, or secretly by theft or deceit. So too a man's honor can be injured in two ways: openly by contumely or reviling, and secretly by detraction or backbiting. To speak disparagingly of anyone indicates that you think little of him, hold him in contempt, and thus dishonor him. When this is done in his absence, there is an injury to his good name since the detractor intends that his listeners believe him and form a bad opinion of the

---

[6] John Wicklein, "The Church in the South and Segregation," *New York Times*, July 5–8, 1959.

person against whom he is speaking. Detraction differs in two ways from contumely: (1) in manner: detraction is unknown to the victim, while contumely is in his presence; (2) in intention: detraction intends to injure the person's good name; contumely intends to injure his honor.

Detraction can be defined as the unjust belittling of the good name of another through secret words. It is a sin against justice ex genere suo grave — grave of its very nature. It violates strict justice because it takes from the neighbor that to which he has a strict right — his good name, and to which in ordinary circumstances, he has a right even though it is undeserved. Detraction also impedes the common good which requires that envy, hatred, and quarrels be avoided so that peace, order, and social tranquillity may be preserved. These could not be secured if the faults of others were revealed and publicized without sufficient reason. It is also opposed to charity since a good name facilitates charity and inclines others to friendship, while a bad name inclines them to distrust, enmity, and hatred. By detraction, the law of charity is violated since our neighbor is depicted in such a light that others find it difficult to love him, and easier to detest or hate him. Deprived of his good name, a man is prevented from accomplishing many good works. Since detraction is serious of its nature, it will admit of parvity of matter so that if a neighbor's fault is unnecessarily revealed, but the injury done is not serious, the detraction would usually be venially sinful. Since detraction is a violation of commutative justice, it entails the obligation to repair the injury done.

Because an audience is necessary for the success of detraction, there is an obligation on the part of one to whom the faults of another are being divulged unnecessarily, to try to prevent their revelation if he can do so without grave inconvenience. If he could do something to prevent this, without inconvenience, but does nothing, then he would seem to give consent to the detraction and become a participant. Even more, if he encourages the detractor in any way, or if he takes pleasure in the detraction, then he sins no less than the actual detractor. But, on the other hand, if because of human respect, neglect, or fear, he does not prevent it, it is probable that at most he would sin venially by listening.

The part played by detraction in race relations is obvious to anyone who has a passing acquaintance with discrimination and segregation. How often are stories, rumors, fictions, and even lies regarding the Negro as a race circulated and repeated. These stories are picked up, passed on until their repetition causes them to acquire the appearance of truth, and finally they become incorporated into the vast corpus of Negro myths. These stories sustain, support, and increase prejudice. Their circulation, it is true, is often made without consideration or from a motive of levity, but occasionally, the motive is to secure an economic, political, or social benefit, or from hatred which can only find satisfaction in increasing and spreading itself. An example of the latter type will be found in the rabid racist with whom reason finds no welcome, nor logic any consideration.

It should be said, however, that the detraction of an entire race made by an individual would rarely be of such weight that it could seriously injure the good name of the race, or cause grave injury to the good name of an individual. Therefore, there is less likelihood that detraction of a race in general would be mortally sinful.

But detraction may also extend to the application of these stories and half-truths to individuals, especially those with whom there has been personal contact. It may be a Negro who has just been employed as a co-worker; or one who has recently moved into the neighborhood; or one accused or suspected of a crime; or even, illogically, one suspected of being "uppity" or not "knowing his place." Detraction, in these instances, results not only in the loss of good name, but can even spread fires of hatred and irrationality until such national shames occur as race riots, burning or bombing of Negro homes, lynching of Negro suspects, and dismissal of employees. Obviously not every detraction terminates in these violences, but nevertheless, in practically every instance where these did occur, ringleaders have been able to stir up and fan the fires of prejudice and fanaticism through whispering campaigns of detraction and talebearing.

Closely allied with detraction is talebearing, which differs from it only in the intention of the agent. A detractor wishes to injure the good name; a talebearer wants to sever bonds of friendship existing between his audience and a certain individual. His intention in speaking ill is to stir up the audience against that man so that bonds of friendship will be destroyed. The reason why St. Thomas places talebearing under violations of strict justice is that he considers a friend as the greatest of external goods which a man possesses, since no one can live without friends. Since a friend is a greater good than honor, and since to be loved is a greater good than to be honored, St. Thomas considers talebearing a greater sin than detraction or reviling.

Derision: The next violation of justice considered by St. Thomas is derision, which is an attempt to shame a person. The derider reveals some defect or evil of a person in public to embarrass him. Any evil or defect, if it is serious, ought to be regarded as an evil, but when it is used as a jest, the speaker indicates that he considers this evil either as of no importance in itself or in relation to this person. Where the defect or evil is, in itself, only minor, the derision will usually be venially sinful. However, if the defect is actually serious, but is considered slight merely because this man is inflicted with it and that in him it is a source of amusement and ridicule, the derision will generally be gravely sinful. Thus, if blindness is made a butt of ridicule, no one can seriously consider such a misfortune as a source of laughter. But, in this case, such a defect is regarded as not serious because it is in this particular man. Derision is a more serious sin than reviling because the reviler considers the defects as serious and speaks of them as such, whereas the derider takes them as a joke and dishonors his neighbor more because of them.

Derision and ridicule of the Negro have become common. The stereotype Negro, which is actually a caricature, has been an object of ridicule for a long time. Various stereotypes have become familiar through songs, jokes, and stage or movie presentations. These types have resulted in ridicule for individual Negroes who justly resent these classifications.

In addition to the derision of the Negro as a race, the individual is frequently made the butt of jokes, ridicule, laughter, and mockery, even in his presence, and with no consideration of his feelings. Often those who employ Negroes as domestics are most cruel in their remarks and ridicule. In many instances, the only restraint is the fear that these servants will quit and there will be a consequent difficulty and inconvenience in hiring others.

Educational defects, manifested in mispronunciations, grammatical errors, lack of social polish or nonacquaintance with social etiquette, or physical characteristics are made the object of ridicule. Here also, as in contumely, there is that inability to realize or the neglect to try to understand the feelings of the Negro. Those who claim that they alone really understand the Negro are frequently the ones who have the least understanding of him or the least consideration of his feelings. As in contumely, an awareness of the hurt inflicted on the Negro would make Christians aware of the sin of derision in many of these actions.

Distributive Justice: Differing from strict justice, distributive justice inclines society and its leaders to distribute common burdens and benefits among the individual members of that society according to their abilities and merits. Father John Cronin indicates that when the older theologians treated of distributive justice, they were chiefly concerned with the allotment of public offices and the distribution of tax obligations. He adds, however, that modern examples would be such legislation as that which involves public subsidies, e.g., educational grants, pensions, agricultural subsidies, health and medical assistance, hospital grants, and the like.[7]

Racial prejudice and discrimination frequently give rise to violations of distributive justice. However, when prejudice is involved in these violations, it is usually the distribution of benefits which is involved rather than the distribution of obligations. In other words, except for singular and isolated instances, the distribution of tax burdens is equitable for both races, as is the obligation of military service, although there has been discrimination within the various branches of the armed services against Negro members. The military services were completely segregated at the beginning of World War II. Opportunities of Negro servicemen for training and advancement were limited because they were usually assigned to unskilled jobs in transportation or construction units. The prohibition of racial discrimination contained in the 1940 Selective Service Act was understood in the light of the "separate but equal" principle. In 1946, President Truman issued an executive order to the Armed Forces which had the effect

---

[7] John F. Cronin, S.S., *Social Principles and Economic Life* (Milwaukee: The Bruce Publishing Co., 1959), p. 72.

of nullifying the "separate but equal" policy in training and military service.

Examples of discrimination in public services which violate distributive justice can be found when it is more difficult for a needy Negro to get on the relief rolls, or when after being placed on the relief rolls, his allotment is less than that given to a white man in identical circumstances. The segregated public school system, and practically the entire field of segregated public services give evidence of discrimination in those facilities reserved for the Negro, e.g., public hospitals, library services, recreational facilities, and parks. Paved streets, water and sewage lines, and street lighting often end at the beginning of the Negro section, depriving those who must live within that section of the benefit of those public services.

The outstanding area of violations of distributive justice, however, is that of civil rights, including voting and jury service, which frequently involve violations of strict justice also. The deprivation of the right to vote of qualified Negroes takes from them the opportunity, granted by law to all citizens, of having a voice in the policies and management of the civil government. The 1961 United States Commission of Civil Rights has devoted an entire volume of its report to the matter of discrimination in the exercise of the right to vote. Admitting progress and improvement in the exercise of this right, it indicated that in approximately 100 Southern counties there were serious reasons to believe that a substantial number of Negroes were being disfranchised. The report also indicated that there were many Southern counties where the votes of Negro citizens were being diluted by means of unequal electoral districting, gerrymandering, and malapportionment. An outstanding example of this technique was in the case of the Tuskegee, Alabama, gerrymander.[8] And in speaking of the practice of excluding Negroes from juries, this 1961 Civil Rights Commission reported:

> The practice of racial exclusion from juries persists today even though it has long stood indicted as a serious violation of the 14th amendment. As a result, the bar of race and color is placed at the only gate through

---

[8] *1961 United States Commission on Civil Rights Report*, Book 1, "Voting" (Washington, D. C.: U. S. Government Printing Office, 1961), pp. 5–6, 15–72, 113–132; cf. also Bernard Taper, *Gomillion versus Lightfoot: The Tuskegee Gerrymander Case* (New York: McGraw-Hill Book Co., 1962).

which the average citizen may enter for service in the courts of justice. In some areas at least, only the Federal Government can resolve this grave problem.[9]

Social Justice and Legal Justice: Legal justice and its role in race relations remains to be discussed, but this is somewhat difficult because of the various explanations of the relationship between legal justice and social justice. Some consider social justice as a distinct species of justice, separate and distinct from legal justice. But J. Messner, a leading proponent of this opinion, admits that the discussion is purely speculative since it does not involve any differences as far as the practical order is concerned. On the other hand, Father William Drummond, S.J., claims that the identification of social justice with legal justice is retarding the "evolution of doctrine which the encyclical [*Quadragesimo Anno*] seems to encourage."[10]

All agree, however, that legal justice involves at least the obligations of the individual as determined by positive law whereby he must render to the community those things necessary or useful for the common good. They also agree that legal justice demands that the citizen obey the just laws and pay taxes. But, in speaking of social justice, some extend its notion so that it includes the obligations of both legal and distributive justice, while others identify it with legal justice either in a restricted sense whereby the individual is held to obligations established by positive law, or in a broader sense so that it includes positive and negative norms of law required to advance the common good in any area of social life. Still others, as mentioned, see social justice as a distinct species of justice, and understand it as ordering the various groups among themselves with a view to the advancement of the common good so that the individual orders contribute to the socioeconomic common good.

Father Cronin's definition of social justice sums up its various aspects and stresses the long-range ideal to which the virtue tends:

A virtue which inclines the individual to seek the common good, and particularly directs him to seek in an organized fashion to achieve

---

[9] *1961 United States Commission on Civil Rights Report*, Book 5, "Justice," p. 103, and pp. 89–103 on jury exclusion.

[10] J. Messner, *Social Ethics*, translated by J. J. Doherty (St. Louis: B. Herder Book Co., 1949), pp. 219–220; also William Drummond, S.J., *Social Justice* (Milwaukee: The Bruce Publishing Co., 1955), p. v.

an economic society whose laws, customs, and institutions are directed toward the promotion of the common good.[11]

On the other hand, Father Zalba, who holds that social justice is equivalent to legal justice, stresses the duty of rendering to the community those things necessary for the common good and which are demanded either by positive or natural law.

Despite these different viewpoints, authorities agree that social justice is ordered to the advancement of the common good. Hence it will be useful to demonstrate the nature of the common good and see how it is affected by racial prejudice and discrimination. A statement of what common good is not may be helpful for an understanding of what it is. Common good is not constituted by the totality of private goods, nor is it the personal private good of many persons, even though it does not exclude private goods. St. Thomas states that common good differs from the private good "not only according to the many and the few (quantitatively), but also according to a formal difference (qualitatively and specifically). The nature of the common good is one thing, while the nature of a private good is another, just as the whole is one thing and the part is another.[12]

Common good cannot be discovered by adding up the total of private goods since no such addition can constitute common good. Common good is a superior human good, which is more eminent than private good, though it is of the same order. Common good must be protected and advanced through the cooperation of the social whole, or society as such, and the individual members. Though formally and qualitatively distinct from private good, it redounds to and aids private good.

The temporal common good consists in the well-being of man, embracing the practice of the moral and intellectual virtues. Man, being in potency to act, finds his perfection in his movement to act, or the operation of virtues conformed to rational nature. The essential operations are found in those virtues necessary for perfect human life, and these are further integrated and perfected by operations in the arts and sciences, made possible through the possession of those external goods needed in any well-organized society. The result of

---

[11] John F. Cronin, S.S., op. cit., p. 76.
[12] Summa Theol., II–II, q. 58, a. 5, ad 1.

these various operations is the possession of friendship and peace. Based on a study of the means required by man to obtain his primary end, Father Hyland, O.P., lists four classifications of both means and ends. These include the actual preservation of the species as a physical end, and based on this, means required to preserve individual, family, as well as community life; also the natural rational end, or a life of virtue, including acts of intellect and will which are in accord with natural law; and finally the means to obtain this rational end, or happiness which is fostered by a peaceful and tranquil community.[13]

J. Maritain includes in the notion of common good, not only material and physical goods, e.g., just laws, good customs, wise institutions, and sound fiscal and political policies, but also many spiritual goods. He describes the common good:

> It includes the sum or sociological integration of all the civic conscience, political virtues and sense of right and liberty, of all the activity, material prosperity and spiritual riches, of unconsciously operative hereditary wisdom, of moral rectitude, justice, friendship, happiness, virtue and heroism in the individual lives of its members. For these things all are, in a certain measure *communicable* and so revert to each member helping him to perfect his life and liberty of person. They all constitute the good human life of the multitude.[14]

The correlation between the individual good and the common good is indicated by J. Messner to be such that promotion of the common good will depend, to a large degree, on the ability of the individual members of society to procure individual goods compatible with the common good. Accordingly, institutional organizations, such as legal systems, educational systems, public health services and hospitals, social welfare services, etc., should not be considered as constituting the common good. Actually they are only means to be utilized for the service and advancement of common utility. The common good requires supplementation, through social cooperation, of the individual's powers of self-perfection and development, particularly in

---

[13] Philip Hyland, O.P., "The Field of Social Justice," *The Thomist*, I (1939), 295–330. Cf. also V. Vanghleluwe, "De iustitia sociali," *Collationes Brugenses*, XLIII (1947), 309–321, 383–398, 436–449; XLIV (1948), 306–319, 388–395, for a survey of various opinions on the nature of social justice.

[14] J. Maritain, *The Person and the Common Good*, translated by John L. Fitzgerald (New York: Chas. Scribner's Sons, 1947), pp. 42–43.

areas where this development would be impossible without corporate assistance.[15]

Thus the common good of a community is only being advanced when the powers of the individual members receive, through social cooperation, that supplementation which they require to perfect themselves. Promotion of the common good will guarantee that all members of the community have an equitable participation in all the community facilities so that these members, through self-perfection, are able to attain their existential ends. Among these existential ends, Messner includes self-preservation, social respect or personal honor, spiritual and physical self-development, enlargement of experience, knowledge and appreciation of aesthetic beauty, self-propagation; social fellowship as well as knowledge and worship of the Creator and the ultimate perfection of self in a union with God.[16]

The essential aim of the political community is the common good of the multitude so that each individual, and not merely certain groups or classes, can reach a degree of independence and perfection in the attainment of these ends. It must also protect these goods by guaranteeing property, political and civil rights, natural virtues, and by promoting cultivation of intellectual abilities. But if we examine these goals and the role of the community in promoting and protecting them, it is apparent that racial discrimination not only denies the social assistance and cooperation required to develop these, as required by its obligation to promote the common good, but that discrimination actually places obstacles to their development, thus retarding the common good.

With this general view of the nature of common good constituting the end of social justice, we can more readily appreciate the importance of social justice as a factor in the problems of racial discrimination. Because common good involves the development of the potentialities of all the members, and not of one race alone, the demands of social justice for an equitable and proportionate opportunity for the Negro to share in this development become more apparent. Laws, customs, or actions, either of individuals or groups, must contribute to the common good; but if these actions injure

---

[15] J. Messner, op. cit., pp. 122–123.
[16] Ibid., p. 21.

the common good, they violate social justice, and, in some instances, will also violate strict justice or distributive justice.

The practices of discrimination and segregation, as historical events, represent, in many instances, violations of social justice. Demands for improvement of race relations are often expressed in terms of an appeal for "social justice for the Negro," or, as we have previously indicated, "interracial justice." Obviously, in some instances, it is difficult to demonstrate clearly a violation of strict or distributive justice. But violations in general of social justice are more apparent in the branding of an entire racial group with the stigma of inferiority without consideration of individual character, abilities, or personality, such as is implied by the very existence of segregated facilities. Racial discrimination is retarding a large segment of the American people instead of helping them to develop. In practice, it preserves and saves the best for one group, and forces the other group to accept the inferior. As practiced in the United States today, discrimination also produces in those whites who discriminate against the Negro, evil effects in the economic, political, international, and psychological fields. The production of these effects on the white community also retards the common good, and hence discrimination, considered even from the effects on the white community, is a violation of social justice.

Common good is impeded by any act which hinders the individual in his pursuit of his existential ends. When large groups are so retarded in the exercise of any social function, or are prevented from developing because of restriction of common facilities to privileged classes, then social justice is violated, and existential ends of large numbers of the community remain unfulfilled. It is only necessary to mention a few of these existential ends and parallel them with the effects of segregation and discrimination to realize how they injure and retard. Bodily integrity and social respect are retarded by inferior or inadequate medical and hospital facilities and housing; personal honor is denied in the refusal to bestow the ordinary forms of politeness; development of faculties and improvement of living conditions are hindered by restricting the Negro to slum areas, to low-paying, servile jobs, refusing union membership, economic and financial disadvantages, etc., while the entire pattern of segregation prohibits and restricts social fellowship. The knowledge and worship of God is impeded by discrimination in Churches and by the scandal given by the actions of Christians.

Obviously, the determination of a particular and individual obligation to be imposed solely under social justice is a difficult task. The difficulty of determining obligations of commutative justice fades to a minimum in comparison with the question of the particular and individual obligations of social justice. Father John Connery, S.J., has remarked that the difficulties of determining obligations of strict justice are insignificant when compared with the difficulties in determining obligations of legal or social justice.[17]

Yet, despite this difficulty, there is an obligation in general to seek and work toward a change in imperfect social situations. This is required by the dynamic aspect of social justice. It requires that the individual work and make contributions toward alterations of the status quo so that the common good can be obtained when the social system is retarding it. This struggle looks to a gradual change of the entire socio-economic order; a struggle which is to be continuous even though only gradual or slight improvements seem imminent. Pius XI, in Quadragesimo Anno, speaking of the ideal of a family wage to be paid to the head of a family, said that every effort should be made to pay a wage which would be adequate for the family's need, but that if it cannot be done, social justice demands that changes be made as soon as possible so that such a family wage can be paid.

Social justice, therefore, has a role to play in the perfecting of institutions since it is the concern of social justice to make these institutions good and keep them good. It deals with changes, continually building up the existent institutions so that they can promote common good, or by completely changing these institutions where they are preventing or injuring common good. Social justice demands the continual striving and working for a betterment of race relations, even though there be very slow progress, until the pattern of race relations which today is retarding the common good will be changed to allow all members of the community to achieve their existential ends.

---

[17] John Connery, S.J., "Notes on Moral Theology," *Theological Studies*, XV (1954), 616.

CHAPTER 9

THE VIRTUE OF CHARITY

Despite the extensiveness and scope of the rights and obligations involved in the various species of justice, this virtue never operates in a moral vacuum. If it excludes other virtues, the result will be a sterile and mechanical form of justice which tends to become minimal, looks solely to obligatory fulfillment, and is burdened with distinctions and measurements. Justice must always be preceded by, operate within, and be followed by charity, the greatest of all the virtues. The roots of true and real justice are buried deep in the charity of Christ, and only then is it a fruitful and kind justice. For it is only charity which softens the rigidity of the operations of justice.

The close association of charity with justice is indicated by the fact that "justice" is often used to designate the entire sum of virtue, or charity itself. Lessius, in *De Iustitia et Iure*, indicates this in speaking of the different uses of the word "justice":

> Hence it is that the word "justice" is also used for charity itself, because charity renders the will conformed to the whole divine law so that charity, in a certain way, contains within itself the sum of all virtues.[1]

Justice needs to be informed by charity. They go hand in hand in the living of a true Christian life, and are not opposed to each other. In an address to the Italian Workers, Pius XII warned of the necessity of antecedent charity to make possible real justice:

[1] L. Lessius, *De Iustitia et Iure*, Sec. I, Cap. I, Dub. I, *Theologiae Cursus Completus*, J. P. Migne (ed.) (Paris, 1839), v. 15.

Let other workers' associations say, "Justice is enough for us!" — as though the virtues of justice and charity were opposed to one another. Precisely the contrary is true. There is, in fact, no genuine justice which is not preceded and prepared for by the warmth of charity. Have you ever seen hard-hearted men do justice willingly, sincerely, and completely? Certainly not, for selfishness is like ice which prevents any good seed from germinating and flowering.[2]

Charity must lead the way if there is to be a real effective justice. In *Quadragesimo Anno*, Pius XI warned those social reformers who were overemphasizing and excessively concerned with enforcing commutative justice while they proudly disdained and rejected charity. He admitted that while charity is not, and should not be considered, a substitute for what is due through justice, yet even after justice has been fulfilled, there is still room for charity. Charity alone can produce a union of hearts and minds, and this union is the only foundation of institutions seeking peace and the bestowal of mutual aids and cooperation. He does not, however, intend that charity is to replace justice so that what is due in justice is denied, and in turn bestowed on our neighbor as an alms, as when a worker is denied a just wage and then made the recipient of charity in the bestowal of alms.

The coincidence of justice and charity can be especially seen in those violations of strict justice mentioned above, viz., detraction, derision, contumely, etc. The foundation of the popular concept of these as violations of charity now can be seen by the fact that these violations of strict justice are, under another aspect, violations of charity. Justice regards the person as he is separate; as he is distinct; and as he is the "other"; charity regards him as he is identified with self; as he is united; as he is one. The right in justice is founded on personality which is always incommunicable and distinct, whereas the foundation of charity is the unity established by the relation of the "other" to God. Because of this, some feel that for practical purposes in the education and instruction of Catholics as to proper thinking and acting regarding race relations, justice should not be the prime consideration. Its emphasis on the "other" tends to keep the notion of separateness or segregation uppermost, while its stress

---

[2] *Di gran cuore*, address of Pius XII to the Italian Workers, May 1, 1958, English translation, *The Pope Speaks*, V (Spring, 1959), 209–213.

on the vindication of rights against any encroachment emphasizes the distinction between races. They feel that for more effective instruction the stress should be placed on charity because it underlines the unity and identity of man and because of the difficulty of ascertaining with exactitude obligations and violations of justice in this particular field.

Unfortunately, today many misunderstand charity and replace it with a form of philanthropy or some sentimental "togetherness." Bestowal of alms is often considered the exhaustive fulfillment of the law of charity. In a pastoral letter condemning segregation in South Africa, the hierarchy of Northern Rhodesia commented on this lack of understanding of charity:

> There are few words more misunderstood than the word "charity" or "love." Christian love is not the emotion we feel towards those who are dear to us; it consists in wishing our fellow men well and in taking a genuine and active interest in their spiritual and material welfare. It is not alone hatred which is contrary to the laws of Christian charity, but also indifference to the welfare of our neighbor.[3]

Charity inclines us to love God above all things and our neighbor as ourself. Love consists in wishing well or good. If we consider the object of love or the good itself, we will love it either because it is perfect in itself, or else because it is good for us and benefits us. The former is amor benevolentiae; the latter is amor concupiscentiae. When the object of love is a person, this twofold distinction also obtains: amor benevolentiae when we love the person because he is good in himself; and amor concupiscentiae when we love him and wish good for him, because in some way it will redound to our benefit.

Charity requires an amor benevolentiae, which is brought to its highest perfection in amor amicitiae or friendship. Friendship requires (a) an amor benevolentiae; (b) that it be mutual; and (c) that there be some interchange or communication of good between the lovers. Perfect charity is unselfish and disinterested friendship, for in it we seek nothing for our benefit, but wish good to God and to our neighbor. The law of charity, expressed by Christ, is threefold in object, but actually is one because its formality or motive is the same, viz., God considered as He is perfect goodness. "Thou shalt love

---

[3] "Joint Pastoral Letter of the Hierarchy of Northern Rhodesia," January 6, 1958, Catholic Mind, LVII (Jan.–Feb., 1959), 88–95.

the Lord thy God with thy whole heart and with thy whole soul and with thy whole mind. This is the greatest and the first commandment and the second is like to this: Thou shalt love thy neighbor as thyself. On these two commandments dependeth the whole law and the prophets" (Mt 22:37–40). Thus Christ summed up the law and commandments into the law of charity and placed the obligation of love of neighbor on a par with love of God. St. Paul realizing the singleness of the motive of charity also summed up the law into love of neighbor: "For all the law is fulfilled in one word: Thou shalt love thy neighbor as thyself" (Gal 5:14).

Love of neighbor is an essential part of charity, not merely an integrating part useful for greater perfection. It is not a counsel of perfection, but an absolute necessity for love of God. "If any man say: I love God, and hateth his brother; he is a liar. For he that loveth not his brother whom he seeth, how can he love God whom he seeth not: And this commandment we have from God, that he who loveth God love also his brother" (1 Jn 4:20–21). Love of neighbor must be manifested in a practical way, according to the example of Christ's love for us, who gave His life for us. "In this we have known the charity of God, because he hath laid down his life for us: and we ought to lay down our lives for the brethren" (1 Jn 3:16). St. John did not intend this to be a single heroic act of martyrdom which, for most never materializes, but meant it to be understood of those opportunities in our daily life for the manifestation of love, where charity can find myriad ways of showing itself. St. John adds: "He that hath the substance of this world, and shall see his brother in need and shall shut up his bowels from him: how doth the charity of God abide in him?" (1 Jn 3:17)

Love of neighbor has identifying characteristics. It is in imitation of the love of Christ for us. The first characteristic it possesses, if it is like the charity of Christ, is that it is completely generous. It extends beyond the exigencies of justice, and is a love which is kind and patient; a love which serves. It is gratuitous like God's love for us. God's love is the cause of the goodness in creatures; our love does not cause goodness, but rather is itself caused by preexistent goodness to which we wish good and attempt to supply what is lacking. The gratuitous character can be seen in the requirement that charity extend not only to those who are our friends, but also to those who hate us and who are our enemies. "Love your enemies: do good to them that hate you: and pray for them that persecute and calumniate you" (Mt 5:44). If our love lacks this characteristic and is restricted to those who are pleasing to us, excluding those who offend, where is its Christian character; how does it resemble the love of God for us? "And if you love them that love you, what thanks are to you? For sinners also love those that love them. And if you do good to them who do good to you, what thanks are to you? For sinners also do this. And if you lend to them of whom you hope to receive, what thanks are to you? For sinners also lend to sinners, for to receive as much" (Lk 6:32–34).

Charity is all-embracing and includes those who are beyond the ambit of our social and economic status. It must love with the same love those who cannot or will not reciprocate and those who are outcasts and social rejects. "When thou makest a dinner or a supper, call not thy friends nor thy brethren nor thy kinsmen nor thy neighbors who are rich; lest perhaps they also invite thee again, and a recompense be made to thee. But when thou makest a feast, call the poor, the maimed, the lame and the blind. And thou shalt be blessed, because they have not wherewith to make thee recompense" (Lk 14:12–14).

The Northern Rhodesian hierarchy affirmed that the law of charity obliged Catholics in Africa, even to the point of sacrifice, to aid the Negroes to attain a standard of culture which was equal to their own.[4]

The spirit of generosity in charity will also entail a spirit of pardon and peace which will seek to suppress strife and divisions because the command of charity demands that we forgive our enemies if we, in turn, expect to secure pardon from God. Love of neighbor is not only to be like the love of Christ for us, but is, in a mysterious way, our love for Christ. "Amen I say to you, as long as you did it to one of these my least brethren, you did it to me. . . . Amen I say to you, as long as you did it not to one of these least, neither did you do it to me" (Mt 26:40, 45).

The opposite of love is hatred, and here we find the sin opposed to

---

[4] *Ibid.*

the precept of charity. Hatred can be directed toward any of the three objects of charity: God, ourselves, or our neighbor. Here we can omit consideration of hatred of God or self, and consider only hatred of neighbor. Just as hatred of God is the gravest of sins, its correlative, hatred of neighbor, even when restricted to an internal act, claims parallel primacy among acts committed against our neighbor.

Hatred of the Negro, either as a race or an individual, is a common accompaniment of racial attitudes. As we have stated, this attitude may range all the way from complete indifference and disdain, through various degrees of dislike, reaching the violent hatred of the rabid racist, which may approach the psychotic. The sinfulness of hatred of the Negro as a violation of charity is expressed by Monsignor Gilligan, who also stresses the obligation to suppress and control movements of the passions which eventually lead to this hatred:

> The familiar unbalanced hatred of the Negro race and its individual members is sinful. The failure to repress or to attempt to control prejudice and antipathy against the Negro is just as wrong as the neglect to attempt the repression of the passion of anger or of sloth. From such unbridled prejudices have been born serious injustices.[5]

The obligation to resist temptation to hate the Negro and to resist feelings of dislike of being near or associated with him, which is a common excuse to exonerate or excuse refusal to grant the Negro social courtesies, is clear. Father Yves Congar, O.P., speaking of racial prejudice, believes that the facility with which physical features are associated with or productive of contempt and prejudice makes a slave, psychologically, out of the man who is prejudiced, and it destroys the roots and foundation of charity within him. Father Congar considers that this prejudice and scorn of the Negro is the root of murder, at least internal murder, because hatred of a man will sooner or later, because of the nature of hate and despisal, change into such thoughts as "People like that ought not to be alive!" Such a thought is the source of murder. And for proof, we have merely to look at the genocide of the Jews by the Nazis. Anti-Semitic feelings developed into statements that such people ought not be allowed to live, and this developed into the actual murder of millions.[6]

[5] Francis J. Gilligan, The Morality of the Color Line, p. 49.
[6] Yves M-J. Congar, O.P., The Catholic Church and the Race Question (Paris: UNESCO 1953), pp. 25–26.

It is true that a feeling of dislike or discomfort which many complain of when obliged to associate with a Negro, may in some instances represent a psychological problem. But more frequently it is exaggerated and made too much of. This is particularly so when the person feels no discomfort from the proximity of a Negro *if he is not there as a social equal*. The reality of this discomfort would be more credible if it were present in all instances. But it is difficult to understand how no uneasiness is experienced when they are being waited on or served by a Negro when they claim to be uneasy in the presence of a Negro. It is more than possible that this is a mere rationalization for the prejudicial attitude that no Negro could possibly be equal.

Initial passions of dislike or hatred toward the Negro must, like any disordered passion, be restrained and controlled. Nor can one be excused from the exercise of control merely because it is found to be difficult. It is also difficult to control the movements of the sensitive appetite opposed to chastity or temperance, yet all realize the seriousness and reality of the obligation to control them. Control of emotions and passions is basic to any spirituality. Their subjection to reason is absolutely necessary if a man is to fulfill the commandments.

Neither are defects or differences, whether physical, social, educational, economic, or even moral, valid reasons for a denial of charity. While these differences may, in some instances be present, nevertheless charity does not regard its object as being separate and different, but as identical and united. This union and identity with our neighbor come from his relation to God. He is to be loved by us because he is loved by God, created by God, redeemed by Christ, and called to eternal beatitude.

Charity, practiced as Christ wanted it practiced, will solve the problem of race relations. Other remedies, whether in the field of social welfare, establishing or improving educational, health, and recreational facilities; or in the field of justice and legality, granting and protecting rights and establishing equality before the law, will only be temporary alleviations and incomplete stopgaps. Only Christian charity which recognizes the Negro as a fellow creature of God, who is working and striving, like ourselves, toward his ultimate goal, which sees him as beloved by God, and redeemed by the sacrifice of Christ, and sees Christ in the individual Negro, even when it is difficult to do so, only this divine charity can permanently extinguish the fires of prejudice, injustice, and hatred. Nor will this charity wait until justice has finished its task, or until social services have expended themselves and completed their tasks. Even within social disabilities and injustices, and while there are still economic, social, and educational differences, charity operates and performs acts of supernatural love. Indeed it is these preliminary acts of charity which will spur on the completion of the job of social services and justice. Waldo Beach, using the scriptural *agape* for what we commonly designate as charity, expressed the duties of the Christian in regard to the performance of acts of charity to effect a Christian solution to the race problem, even within the framework of prejudice and injustice which are still existent.

> The Christian response is not trust in racial integration, or any other human arrangement as final, but a radical obedience to the God and Father of our Lord Jesus Christ who gives and requires the love of the neighbor in and for himself. Walking the difficult borderline between segregation and integration, the response of obedience is a double one: (a) an ethic of alleviation within segregation and (b) the radical ethic of reconstruction which cuts through the lines that segregation draws. It is important that both of these be maintained. Even within a fallen and interim order of segregation, there is room for Christian action, for expressions of *agape*, for the unconventional tasks of tenderness which are to be done out of love, without waiting for the removal of segregation. Also, there is a Christian obligation to seek the greatest possible equality *within* the segregation that stubbornly prevails. One who would defy all segregation, and never compromise with it, has lost sight of the Christian insight that human beings are the ultimate units in question whose needs must be served, despite and within a bad order. At the same time there is the revolutionary redemptive task of the overthrow of the system of segregation and the support of policies of integration.[7]

The precept of charity demands in the practical order the bestowal of what theologians call signs of charity (*signa dilectionis*). These are usually distinguished as common (*signa communia*) and special (*signa specialia*). By common signs are meant all those courtesies, urbanities, or benefits which, by reason of general charity, must be shown to all. They include the exchange of greetings, nonexclusion from common prayers or alms, response to questions, and sale of

---

[7] Waldo Beach, *loc. cit.*, pp. 223–224.

displayed merchandise. The extraordinary or special signs include those things which are symbolic of a great intimacy and familiarity. They are not due to anyone by reason of custom or person, but are reserved to those who are intimate friends, and include such things as the exchange of personal letters, special prayers, invitations and visits to the home, and dining together. Though the designation and determination of a common sign depend to a large extent on custom and locality, nevertheless, the following rule of thumb for their discernment, given by Prummer, is useful and valid:

> As often as a prudent and equitable man would immediately conclude from the denial of a sign or benefit that there is enmity present, such a sign is common and must also be shown even to an enemy.[8]

Common signs, since they are demanded by the law of charity, must be extended to Negroes. It cannot be objected that, since common signs are determined to a great extent by custom and locality, custom has established that these are not common signs when applied to the Negro, but special signs to which the Negro has no right, nor is there any obligation to extend them. Certain acts have, regardless of intention, an objective meaning, so that many forms of discrimination cannot be interpreted otherwise than as signs of contempt.

It can be stated, as a principle, that Catholics are obliged by the law of charity to show the common signs of friendship to Negroes, and that this is per se a serious and grave obligation. In practice, what does it mean? It means that those forms of politeness, courtesy, and urbanity which are shown to all white people, must also be shown to all Negroes. Father Gerald Kelly, speaking of this obligation, states that if you address a white man as "sir," you should say it to a Negro; if you tip your hat to a white person, you should do it to a Negro; if you say "Good Morning" to your white neighbors, you should also say it to a Negro neighbor. And he states as his belief that the obligation to extend common signs includes such things as public buying and selling and public services:

> I think we may safely add that in the concrete situation existing in our country, the exclusion of the Negro from the common signs is harmful to the common good and a sign of contempt. This principle, of course,

---

[8] Prummer, I, No. 575.

works both ways, it applies equally to the Negro in his dealing with white people. But the abuse is largely on the white side, and it is mainly with white Catholics that we must insist on the principle. If this principle were rigorously observed in the daily lives of individuals, it would considerably diminish, if it did not entirely remove, the large-scale social problem.[9]

St. Alphonsus and other theologians, treating of common signs, include the sale of displayed merchandise as a requirement of charity. It is difficult to see why hotels, restaurants, and theaters should not be considered as "displaying merchandise" for sale. The fact that their product is "consumed" on the premises (food in the restaurant; room accommodations in the hotel; entertainment in the theater) does not seem to alter the fact that they are "displaying merchandise for sale," just as a grocery or department store. The refusal of stores to sell to Negroes or of restaurants and soda fountains to serve them or of hotels to rent a room, solely because of race, appears to be a denial of one of the common signs of friendship. This would also include the obligation of hospitals and theaters to make their services available. We shall speak later of the obligation of stores and other businesses to make their services available without discrimination because of the relationship these bear to the common good.

Vermeersch, speaking of the gravity of the sin of denying common signs, states that it will be mortally sinful if it proceeds from grave hatred, or if it seriously offends the other person or is a cause of scandal. But if there is no interpretation of hatred, it is not a grave sin. This interpretation of hatred will vary according to time and place so that the examples of even outstanding authors must be considered according to the time and circumstances in which they wrote. Particular cases should be subjected to a prudent examination according to customs and circumstances of present-day life before grave obligations are imposed. Vermeersch also gives this principle:

Today in many places, a man who would omit the mere signs of friendship, but at the same time refrained from injury and detraction, and did not refuse to fulfill the strict obligations of charity which arose

---

[9] Gerald Kelly, S.J., "Notes on Current Moral Theology," *Theological Studies*, VIII (1947), 114. Cf. also, Gerald Kelly, "How to Think and Act about the Race Problem," *Review for Religious*, X (1951), 316–324. This enlightening and informative article is reprinted in Gerald Kelly, *Guidance for Religious* (Westminster: Newman Press, 1957), pp. 303–316.

from necessity, would seem, for the most part to be excused from grave guilt.[10]

Unfortunately, in practice there would appear to be many who do not fulfill all other requirements, including refraining from detraction and contumely, and merely omit common signs. The denial of a common sign is evil not as a mere denial of politeness, but precisely because it is a positive sign of hatred which extends and intensifies hatred in the neighbor, and frequently is a cause of scandal. According to Suarez, the denial of even common signs is deemed sinful because:

> . . . morally such exception is a sign of hatred, and it stirs the other to hatred. Hence it begets scandal and division of soul and is harmful for it makes an exception of the neighbor as more unworthy than any others.[11]

Prominent among signs against practical charity is scandal. It is commonly defined as any action, word, or omission which is the occasion of spiritual harm to our neighbor. The action need not be sinful in itself, it suffices that it appear to be evil. Speaking of the nature of scandal, Father Francis Connell, C.Ss.R., writes:

> We say that even an action "which has the appearance of evil" may be active scandal, as in the case of a Catholic who has a dispensation to eat meat on Friday and does so in the presence of others who do not know of this dispensation and may be led to follow his example. Hence scandal in the theological sense is not mere surprise or shock at the action of others, nor is it uncharitable talk, although in common speech the word scandal is often used in these senses. The main feature of scandal, as the term is used in Catholic theology, is that it furnishes a bad example to someone, furnishing him with an occasion of sin.[12]

The spiritual harm occasioned need not be of the same species. It can be, and often is, of an entirely different species. Actions of Catholics scandalize non-Catholics who perceiving their conduct are repelled from the Church, or are confirmed in their indifferentism, judging one Church as good as another. Father Victor J. Donovan

---

[10] Vermeersch, I, No. 80.

[11] F. Suarez, De Praeceptis Charitatis, Disp. V, Sec. V, ad 7, Opera Omnia, 27 v. (Paris: L. Vives, 1858).

[12] Francis J. Connell, C.Ss.R., Outlines of Moral Theology (Milwaukee: The Bruce Publishing Co., 1953), p. 96.

reports a conversation that he had with a Rabbi who told him that several members of the synagogue had actually gone a long way on the road to joining the Catholic Church when the shock of anti-Semitism as practiced by Catholics with whom they had been placed in contact because of their interest in the Church, drove them back to the synagogue where they became more zealous and confirmed in Judaism than they had been before becoming interested in Catholicism. The prejudices of these Catholics manifested in anti-Semitism was a scandal to those men — it kept them out of the Church and extinguished any interest they may have had in it. Surely this is the greatest of all scandals!

Discrimination and segregation, as practiced by Catholics, are succeeding in doing the same thing to the Negro. Considered under this aspect, discrimination and segregation constitute a scandal because they make it almost impossible to convert Negro non-Catholics, and render it difficult for Negro Catholics to practice their religion. Thoughtless and heedless Catholics often overlook the spiritual harm their actions and their conformity to custom are inflicting on the Negro and the difficulties they are creating for the Church in the spread of the Gospel.

Over twenty years ago, Father John Gillard, S.S.J., indicated that the conversion of the Negro is not an easy task even when viewed solely from the aspect of the prejudice of the Negro against the Church which he had absorbed from the misrepresentations and libels of anti-Catholicism through the years. The popular notion that the Negro is just waiting to be swept into the arms of the Church is not true. Father Gillard also indicated that the conversion of Negroes was no easier to accomplish than the conversion of any other people, and there is also the added difficulty of the repulsion of the Negro from the Church caused by practices of Catholics. Non-Catholic Negroes, seeing the treatment Negro Catholics receive from their co-religionists, are not encouraged or inclined to leave the relative security of the Negro Protestant church and make themselves partakers of similar treatment.[13]

The difficulty experienced by the Negro Catholic in the practice of

---

[13] John Gillard, S.S.J., "Catholicism and the Negro," Interracial Review, XII (June, 1939), 89–91.

his religion is evidenced by what is commonly called "leakage." The loss of Negro Catholics through abandonment of the practice of their religion can be seen in the vast amount of reclamation which must be done by priests working among the Negroes in the South. In some sections, at one time the majority of the Negroes were Catholic, but today there is only a handful who still profess allegiance to the Church. Father Gillard reports that in one section of Louisiana, 65,000 Negro Catholics fell away from the Church in the few years immediately following the Civil War.

Various factors, of course, contributed to the situation. Shortage of priests, relative fewness of Catholics, their lack of influence, poverty, etc., all played a part. But the segregation and discrimination practiced by Catholics have not been the least of these causes. Besides the scandal which has repelled non-Catholics and made it more difficult for the Catholic Negro to practice his religion, the segregated facilities, often consisting of a few pews reserved for Negroes, were manifestly inadequate. These deficient facilities, added to the lack of instruction and pastoral care caused by the shortage or indifference of priests, can account for a good share of this "leakage."

This aspect of scandal as a hindrance to conversions and taxing the faith of Catholic Negroes has been considered by Monsignor Gilligan.[14] Condemning segregation and the exclusion of Negroes from church, he states it is certainly wrong, and lists some of the evil effects flowing from it: preaching is rendered useless because it is contradicted by practice; the Church cannot condemn others while doing the same things; a source of ridicule is given the enemies of the Church, and scandal is given to well-meaning whites who are alienated from the Church. Father Coogan, S.J., also stresses the scandal which segregation in Catholic churches and schools involves:

We oppose segregation in our Catholic churches and schools, because it is unjust, impious, and scandalous — a bar to the conversion of non-Catholic Negroes, and a cause of perversion of the Catholic.[15]

The deterrent to conversions afforded by practices of white Catholics was recognized by the Fides Documentation Service in Rome,

---

[14] Francis J. Gilligan, *Morality of the Color Line*, pp. 208–211.
[15] John E. Coogan, S.J., "Christian Untouchables?" *Review for Religious*, V (1946), 107–113.

an agency of the Sacred Congregation for the Propagation of the Faith. In the report of March, 1950, the Service states:

> The major obstacle to the conversion of the American Negro is the attitude of white Catholics themselves. As the Negroes have become more educated, they have grown aware of the extreme discrepancy which exists between such an attitude and the real spirit of the Catholic Church. They read of the great pronouncements of the Holy Father, the Head of Christendom, and contrast his words of friendship and affection with the unfriendly attitude of the white people next door. They are particularly sensitive when they find Catholics practicing such discrimination in the Church itself.[16]

The scandal given to well-meaning white non-Catholics is only too often overlooked or not sufficiently appraised. Today, there are thousands upon thousands of good people, with high ideals and desires, who are searching for moral and spiritual leadership. But when they perceive Catholics acting in contradiction to what they profess to believe, they are unable to see in the Church the source of truth and spiritual and moral leadership.

Social Charity: We have seen that justice, considered as the rendering of our neighbor's right on an individual basis, must be informed and sustained by charity if it is to avoid minimalism and mechanism. So too, social justice considered as the obligation to promote the common good must have a counterpart in social charity. Social charity is a distinctly Christian virtue taking its source from the great law of love of God. Being true charity, it is supernatural in motive, ends, and means. Pagan philosophy by the light of reason alone, was able to attain to the idea of a collective justice due the city. Christianity, however, endowed with the entire revelation of the New Testament, cannot conceive of a social order which is purely rational and divorced from charity. The Christian is obliged to defend a social order which is inspired by justice, but if this order is based only on justice and lacks charity, it is soulless and would constitute an abstract and impersonal, rigid and mechanical social order. The ideal order for the Christian is one that was taught and preached by Christ, which is modeled on the community of the Trinity and actualized in the Mystical Body of Christ.[17]

---

[16] *America*, XCIV (Feb. 4, 1956), 504.
[17] E. Rideau, "Charité Sociale," *Catholicisme*, II, 984–985.

The term "social charity" appeared for the first time in a papal document in *Quadragesimo Anno* of Pius XI. In speaking of the necessity of social institutions being permeated with social justice if they are to be preserved and their defects corrected, Pius mentions social charity which should be the soul of this order:

> Social charity, moreover, ought to be as the soul of this order, an order which public authority ought to be ever ready effectively to protect and defend.[18]

Social justice and social charity are the two pillars of the social system which advance and promote the common good. They are alike in that both seek to promote the common good, but they approach it in different ways. Social justice, as we have said, inclines individuals to give what is necessary or useful for the common good; social charity inclines individuals to a brotherly love of all in the society with a view of promoting the common good by extending mutual helps and cooperation.

Social charity is not satisfied with rendering merely the obligatory, or in paying exactly what is due. It gives in order to benefit the common good, even to the point of sacrifice. It does not calculate or measure its love or devotion, and like true charity it bears the mark of gratuity. Social charity concerns inner attitudes and acts insofar as they have some bearing on the common good. It inspires individuals to be willing to come to an understanding for the sake of the common good, and to do what is in agreement with a rightly ordered love of self in order to maintain and solidify social peace. The obligation of social charity is to effect an apportionment of material and cultural welfare even if it entails and necessitates some self-sacrifice, and demands a readiness to settle conflicts between different groups by peaceful means.

Social justice alone and separated from social charity is unable to procure the patience, toleration, and generosity which is required by its overall objective in correcting, rebuilding, and repairing social institutions. These repairs entail, in many instances, long years of endurance, understanding, and sacrifice. The attempt to accomplish them by justice alone may actually effect the opposite result. Limita-

---

[18] *Quadragesimo Anno*, Terence McLaughlin, op. cit., p. 250.

tion to a condemnation of social injustices may easily drive and divide society into warring classes. In this way, the search for justice may result in and produce a group or class struggle. The search for social justice must be complemented and completed by social charity. This is especially true because individuals are often entrapped in an unjust situation wherein custom, usage, and convention may induce them to conform to a social pattern which they recognize as wrong. This is particularly pertinent in the matter of race relations where many well-meaning individuals are forced by custom and social or economic pressure to conform to a pattern which they deplore. Speaking of this situation, Father Cronin says:

> Unless we take the pessimistic attitude that most men are evil, we should be willing to appeal to the better instincts even of those who are enmeshed in objective evil. Without such attitudes, it is difficult to see how we can achieve the cooperation and organization postulated by social justice.[19]

Social charity is extremely important in the solution of the race problem. We recognize that in many instances practices of segregation and discrimination entail violations of justice. This does not mean that we should abandon efforts to effect justice, but we realize all too well that any program of improvement calls for much understanding, patience, and goodwill from both sides. This is evidenced by the resistance, increase of tensions, deepening of prejudices, and actual worsening of discrimination in some areas, as well as the uneven pattern of conformity to court decisions in recent years.

> Carefully prepared and quiet programs of school integration succeeded. Ill-conceived and poorly prepared plans in the same area failed. It is easy to demand and denounce, while it is often most difficult to get a meeting of minds on complex evils rooted in long traditions. The former is the approach of justice alone, the latter involves justice tempered by charity. Lasting social reform usually needs the healing touch of social charity.[20]

Social justice needs social charity to bring the members of both races together in a spirit of service and cooperation. It will depress the individualistic strivings within man and create a balance between both races. Social charity will add understanding and goodwill for

---

[19] John F. Cronin, S.S., *Social Principles and Economic Life*, p. 77.
[20] *Ibid.*, p. 78.

the correction of social injustices produced in racial discrimination and segregation.

> Social charity embraces all men in a universal brotherhood. It takes up in its arms of love friend and foe: it is no respecter of persons. Still it has a special heart of pity for those in misery. Charity inspires mercy to have a compassionate heart and to be bountiful to others. With its almsdeeds social charity builds a bridge across the gap that separates rich and poor. It helps level down social inequalities between classes in conflict over material possessions. Recalling to all men the profound truth that in the Creator's sight all are equal, it invests the outcasts of society with dignity and nobility, it levels men down to an equal plane of democracy and yet does not degrade them in doing so.[21]

Cardinal Aloisius J. Muench, in his article "Social Charity" has pointed out the role of social charity in racial conflicts. Indicating the rise of racism as a consequence of the denial of the natural and supernatural brotherhood of men, he continues:

> Social charity sets itself the task of restoring the high and sacred ideals of the brotherhood of man. For social charity proclaims the great dignity of man by emphasizing the fellowship that man has with God. . . . Charity is friendship of men for God, and for fellowmen on account of God. . . . Furthermore social charity inculcates the equality of men in this that all men share in the goodness of God. The divine life through charity is the common ground on which all men meet. . . . Such teaching leaves no room for race conflicts or class warfare.[22]

[21] Joseph R. Myers, *Social Distance according to St. Thomas Aquinas*, unpublished doctoral dissertation (Washington, D. C.: The Catholic University of America, 1955), p. 158.

[22] A. J. Cardinal Muench, "Social Charity," *Summa of St. Thomas Aquinas*, American Edition, v. III (New York: Benziger Bros., 1948), pp. 3326–3336.

CHAPTER 10

PRUDENCE IN RACE RELATIONS

Prudence is the virtue which gives a man the know-how to enable him to lead a moral and virtuous life. His mere desire to be virtuous does not suffice. He must know how to actualize that desire in a concrete situation. If he wishes to bestow alms, it is not almsgiving if he were to indiscriminately distribute money on the street to every passerby. He must know to whom to give, how much, when and where, if there is to be real almsgiving. Prudence gives him this information. It judges the acts and their means in reference to the end and then selects those which will attain that end with facility and success.

Frequently, however, modern man understands by prudence a practice or action marked by caution, or one which is certain to produce profit and gain for him.

In the matter of race relations, many, while they admit that violations of charity and justice are often involved, advise that we must approach the problem with prudence. Confronted with court decisions and suggested legislation, they plead that implementation of these decisions or enactment of the statutes must be accomplished with prudence. However, it is necessary to ascertain just what they mean by prudence.

All too often they mean that nothing is to be done. Prudence is used here as a euphemism for the notion that nothing should be said, nothing should be discussed, nothing should be done which would disturb the status quo. By prudence, they mean that a hands-off attitude must be adopted by the civil and religious authorities and that the situation should be left to itself to evolve its own cure and

98

remedy. Obviously, this is an abusive use of the notion of prudence, which does injustice to the nobility of that virtue. There is a place for prudence in the solution of the racial problem, but this must be true prudence and not pseudo-prudence so often substituted. Every change of a social pattern, especially where there is an emotional background, requires prudence. This must be exercised no matter how evil the social pattern may be. Prudence, in choosing the proper and effective means, has to include patience with those who are stubborn and perverse. It must include avoidance of actions, words, and attitudes which would only increase prejudice, without helping advance justice. But prudence does not mean silence about the moral principles at stake, or a policy of waiting for several generations for the situation to straighten itself out. Prudence cannot be used to justify attacks against obviously just court orders or resistance, open or clandestine, against a bishop or pastor who is attempting to end racial discrimination in his diocese or parish.

Perhaps one of the clearest and most extensive official statements of the role of prudence in racial relations was given by the bishops of South Africa in July, 1957. After condemning the principle of segregation as intrinsically evil, they warned that perfect equality of the various races in South Africa could not be established merely by passage of a law. Recognizing the existence of educational and cultural differences between the various sections of the people, they stated that "all social change must be gradual if it is not to be disastrous." The statement continues saying that a change is essential if national disaster is to be averted. The bishops felt that if the energy and effort being expended in the extension and defense of segregation could be properly directed and channeled, it would be sufficient to effect this change. They believe that formulation of a just policy, granting all citizens, regardless of race, enjoyment of full civil rights is a basic requirement and a goal which statesmanship must achieve despite fears, prejudices, pressures, or resistance. Addressing themselves directly to the Catholic population, the bishops continued in words which apply to our situation as well as theirs.

> The practice of segregation, though officially not recognized in our churches, characterizes, nevertheless, many of our church societies, our schools, seminaries, convents, hospitals, and the social life of our

people. In the light of Christ's teaching this cannot be tolerated forever. The time has come to pursue more vigorously the change of heart and practice that the law of Christ demands. We are hypocrites if we condemn apartheid in South African society and condone it in our own institutions. This does not mean that we can easily disregard all differences of mentality, condition, language, and social custom. The Church does not enforce human associations which, because of these differences, can produce no good. She understands that the spiritual welfare of her children cannot be fostered in a social atmosphere wholly alien and uncongenial. But the Christian duty remains of seeking to unite rather than separate, to dissolve differences rather than perpetuate them. *A different color can be no reason for separation when culture, custom, social condition, and, above all, a common faith and common love of Christ impel toward unity.* (Ital. added.)[1]

Their emphasis is the urgency of responsibility of the whites in South Africa to try to effect a change in the situation and to give full-hearted cooperation to such efforts. The same obligations apply in the United States. In practice, it can be said that whites are obliged to refrain from internal approval of evil social patterns. Active or external disapproval, however, is not obligatory in all instances. However, if a man is endowed with sufficient knowledge to give effective instruction or rebuttal, or if he has sufficient influence, he is obliged to use that knowledge or influence to help weaken the walls of an evil social structure. He is obliged also to use this influence or knowledge in instances where economic or political pressure is being used against Negroes, e.g., in the denial of bank credit or public services, or where it will be useful to bring about cessation of an unjust boycott of Negroes. Lacking this ability or influence, he may be obliged to express his disapproval of the defective social system by utilizing opportunities or occasions to state his opposition to discrimination. This obligation of expressing disapproval may, in certain instances, be a serious one, especially when silence would lead others to adopt stronger or bolder positions, or lead them to the performance of acts which are seriously unjust or uncharitable. More often, however, the obligation of expressing disapproval will not bind under pain of serious sin, or there may be no obligation in instances where he knows that he cannot possibly influence the situation. The obligation of doing something to better the situation is expressed by Father Gerald Kelly:

---

[1] Statement of the Bishops of South Africa on Segregation, *The Shield-Collegian,* XXXVII (March, 1958), 14–16.

In private discussions on this so-called Negro problem, many of my Jesuit colleagues have impressed upon me the fact that, even though a moral theologian may be forced at times to admit the existence of an excusing cause for not immediately stopping some practice of segregation, he must also point out the duty of doing what can be done to remedy the situation. Failure to protest against the evil or to try to change it looks very much like approval of it.[2]

The Supreme Court order directing that school desegregation be implemented with "all deliberate speed" is nothing but a juridical expression of what a theologian would understand as a call for prudence. It entails a demand that something be done, that efforts be made, plans and definite programs be mapped out to provide for fulfillment of the court's order. It also demands deliberateness and consideration which include prudential evaluation of the means best suited to obtain the end. This too is the role of prudence. Something must be done to improve the situation, and this cannot be precipitous and rash. It must be carefully considered, studied, and planned.

It can be readily agreed that more than a century of prejudice, inferior educational, social, and cultural opportunities, has made its mark on many Negroes. It has produced educational and cultural lags in many instances, which are used as reasons for keeping Negro children out of white schools and restricting them to "their own" schools. Here is the key to the perpetuity of segregation! It constitutes a vicious circle. Segregation produces educational and cultural differences between the races, and then these differences are used as the basis for the necessity of segregation.

Since these differences do exist, prudence demands that they be considered. But instead of assuming a "do-nothing" attitude, it demands that a corrective be applied. Hence, if a Negro child is burdened with an appreciable educational handicap, it would be wrong both to him and the other children to place him in a school where his deficiency would retard the others and create an unsurmountable obstacle for his own adjustment and learning. But if this deficiency does not exist in the individual, or if it has been remedied, then it is wrong to exclude him merely because of race. Many who have examined the educational situation believe that since this educa-

---

[2] Gerald Kelly, S.J., "Notes on Current Moral Theology," *Theological Studies*, VIII (1947), 113–114.

tional lag is minimal at the preschool age, school integration should be started at the first-grade level. Others, on the other hand, maintain it should be started in upper grades and gradually extended down to lower classes. The virtue of prudence will also play a large part in determining for educators which is the better of the two methods. But prudence is not operative where there is no planning, no deliberation or consideration or study, but merely impulsive or rash action which eventually does more harm than good; and neither is it operative where nothing is being done.

Father Yves Congar believes that the exercise of prudence in race problems will preclude thoughtless, rash, and brash measures, but that the solution must also take its leadership from charity and be accompanied by justice:

> Prudence will avoid desperate remedies or spectacular measures that will do more harm than good. Charity will supply the driving force and the illumination throughout, always provided that it goes hand in hand with an effective attempt at justice. Justice prescribes recognition of the rights of others, more particularly those rights flowing from the very nature and constitution of man.[3]

And Bishop Sheil, speaking of false prudence, denounces it as a sham and an excuse for compromising moral principles:

> Too often in the past religious leaders, under the plea of prudence, have failed to appreciate or to teach fearlessly what the Brotherhood of Man means in terms of simple justice for the poor, the underprivileged and the oppressed. Too much respect for the local banker, industrialist, realty operator, or politician has caused them to be silent when the teachings of Christ should have been literally shouted from the housetops. . . . There is a time for the exercise of the virtue of prudence. There is also a time for courageous thinking and action; but there is never a time for compromising with fundamental moral principles.[4]

The appeal to pseudo-prudence is often coupled with the platitude, "You can't legislate morality." Here, as in the case of prudence, it is important to determine what is meant by this. There is a sense in which this is true. If morality is understood as the conformity of actions to a norm or rule of morality, then while man possesses free

---

[3] Yves M.-J. Congar, op. cit., p. 44.
[4] Most Rev. Bernard J. Sheil, "Restrictive Covenants vs. Brotherhood," *Catholic Mind*, XLIV (1946), 713–717.

will, no law can force him to be moral or to conform if he does not personally will to do so. The existence of sins in violations of the Ten Commandments is obvious proof that, understood in this meaning, even the divine law "cannot legislate morality." But, more frequently, it is intended as a reason why no attempt should be made to alleviate injustices by means of legislation, or by the repeal of discriminatory statutes or laws. In these instances, it means that even though there are injustices and violations of the moral law, nothing should be done in the way of enacting laws to prevent these injustices because there is something irresistible and inevitable in patterns of segregation. These patterns are supposed to be so permanent and rigid that there has never been, nor can there ever be, any change by any conscious or deliberate effort, and it is thus rash and imprudent to try to change them by law. "You can't legislate morality. . . ."

Understood in this sense, it would mean that laws against murder, robbery, theft, etc., should not be enacted or punished because despite the laws and punishment, murder and robbery occur. Our legal system would be rendered useless and void if men refused to obey the laws, and the axiom "You can't legislate morality" were accepted. This is moral relativism whereby solely the will of the majority and their obedience determine what laws should be enacted. If they refuse to obey certain ones, these should not be enacted, or should be repealed. The repeal of the law is equivalent to establishment of the licitness of the act, at least civilly.

The axiom originates relatively late in American history. It owes its beginnings to William Graham Sumner (1840–1910), a sociologist and a disciple of Herbert Spencer. In 1907, he published a study and analysis of customs, under the title *Folkways*. In this book, which enjoyed wide circulation, he maintained, in regard to the origin and stability of customs, that laws could not establish "mores," nor could "stateways change folkways." This principle, typical of the *laissez-faire* attitude current at that period, applied to Southern race relations, found support in the writings of Franklin Henry Giddings (1855–1931), and in the racial interpretations of the psychologist, William McDougall (1871–1939), in his *Introduction to Social Psychology* published in 1908. These writings are typical of the social thinking of the period and it is easy to recognize their influence on thinking

on the race question, as well as the coincidence of their appearance
with the rise of Jim Crow.

It must be realized, of course, that it is not the obligation of the
state to enact legislation requiring acts of all the virtues, but only
of those which are necessary to promote the common good. Further,
the mere enactment of a law is no guarantee that it will be obeyed or
succeed in fulfilling its purpose. In other words, the axiom can be
considered true in the sense that "morality cannot be legislated"
effectively without a considerable degree of support and concurrence
from those for whom the laws are made. St. Thomas indicates the
scope of human laws, their relation to the common good, and the
fact that the community cannot enact laws prohibiting all sins and
vices:

> Human laws do not prohibit all vices from which virtuous men abstain,
> but only the more serious vices which it is possible for the larger part
> of the community to abstain from, and particularly those vices which
> inflict harm on others and because of which, human society could not
> continue unless they were forbidden. For these reasons, human law
> forbids murder and theft.[5]

However, the purpose of legal prohibitions of racial discrimination
is not the performance of virtuous acts by the citizens, but the defense
of the rights of the Negro community and the prevention of harm
being inflicted on them. Of course, prudence should guide any decision
as to the methods and means of protecting these rights and prevent
harm both to the individual and to the common good.

Father William Kenealy, S.J., because some states insist on imposi-
tion of segregation by law, has proposed the use of federal judicial,
executive, and legislative powers to combat the evils of segregation.
His advocacy of the use of legal methods, however, is not based merely
on the coercive power of law, nor does he seek legal enforcement for
the sake of virtuous acts by individual citizens, but for the promotion
of the common good. Describing his position, Father Kenealy states:

> My proposition is not based upon the naïve thesis that government,
> state or federal, should attempt to enforce all morality. I essay no
> lyric leap from morality to legality. Morals and laws are related and

---

[5] *Summa Theol.*, I–II, q. 96, a. 2, corp. "However, human law does not command every act of virtue, but only those which are ordainable to the common
good." I–II, q. 96, a. 3, corp.

interdependent. But they are not identical. Their respective fields are not coterminous. The field of law is not private morality but public morality only: that is, justice and liberty as they affect the common good and public welfare of society. But equal liberty under law, equal protection of law, and equal voting rights by law, regardless of race or color, are obviously matters of social justice, and, therefore, of public morality. Moreover, and of critical importance to my argument, they are social rights which have been expressly incorporated into our federal Constitution and thereby solemnly guaranteed to all Americans as fundamental federal rights.[6]

Law has more than a coercive effect. Father Kenealy indicates that it has an educational effect on public morals, either for good or bad, e.g., the proliferation of segregation laws as a result of *Plessy v. Ferguson,* and also the development of the law of property, from "raw power to social duties." Another effect of law is the cooperation and encouragement it affords to those who desire to act properly, but who are unable to do so without these legal supports.

Another aspect to be considered in regard to the prudence of legal regulations of behavior in race relations is the degree of success which such means have had. There can be little doubt that legal remedies have had, in many cases, a high degree of success. This success, of course, has not been complete, and in some instances, legal measures have been completely unsuccessful and ineffective. Prudence will guide a decision as to the chance of success. Greenberg, in a chapter on the ability of law to change race relation behavior patterns, carefully distinguishes the varying reactions to legal remedies which have attempted to alter race relations:

> . . . the thesis of this book is that law often changes race relations, that sometimes it has been indispensable to changing them, and that it has in fact changed them, even spectacularly. Indeed, it might be said that in many places law has been the greatest single factor inducing racial change. But law alone, like other social forces, and like laws affecting other institutions, may not be able to alter these relations beyond a certain point, and in some situations it cannot make much difference.[7]

Prudence realizes that enactment of legislation or repeal of Jim Crow laws is not the whole answer, just as a solution based only on

---

[6] William J. Kenealy, S.J., "Desegregation: Challenge to Conservatives," *Social Order,* XII (June, 1962), 250.

[7] J. Greenberg, *op. cit.,* pp. 2–3.

justice is not the whole story. But as justice should not be disregarded and forgotten, so also legal remedies cannot be spurned and rejected. There is a world of difference in the situation where racial injustice is protected by law or even demanded by statute, and the situation where those laws have been removed and its protection of injustice precluded. Where many of the racial practices violate justice, these laws encourage the situation by affording protection. None of those who say, "You can't legislate morality," in reference to the racial situation would say it about murder or robbery. They would not want to see laws punishing such crimes removed from the statute books since the very absence of such laws would be an encouragement to those inclined to commit these crimes.

Legislation, while not the whole answer, is certainly needed to help effect individual right thinking about the problem. Even in instances where court decisions and civil rights legislation are ahead of private sentiment and feeling, these laws and decisions help establish a moral atmosphere and produce a moral tone which is most apt to be conducive to personal change. Personal reform is more difficult in a situation where custom and law support a defective social structure. Only this change of interior attitude on the part of individuals can effect a true and lasting solution. Morality and conscience exist only in individuals, and obligations can be fulfilled by persons only. The Christian solution calls for a correction of attitudes, the recognition of the sinfulness and evil of the situation. It calls for interior and exterior support of juridical decisions and legislation which is aimed at stopping and curtailing this evil. But above all, in his actions and in his thoughts, the Christian will behold the Negro in the light of Christian charity, fulfilling all those obligations required by the law of Christ that "you have love one for another."

CHAPTER 11

THE RIGHT TO LIFE

The 1961 United States Commission on Civil Rights indicated that lawless actions of public officials and instances of police brutality, victimizing racial minorities and the poor, still represent a serious problem. They further declared that it was not always possible to determine whether a particular instance was motivated by racial prejudice or occurred because of the helpless condition of the victim:

Members of minority races, of course, are prevented by discrimination in general from being anything but poor. So, while almost every case of unlawful official violence or discrimination studied by the Commission involved Negro victims, it was not always clear whether the victim suffered because of his race or because of his lowly economic status. Indeed, racially patterned police misconduct and that directed against persons because they are poor and powerless are often indistinguishable.[1]

Although it cannot be said that all such instances are the result of racial prejudice, some of this lawless action must be attributed to that motive. This is indicated by police violence and brutality exercised for the purpose of enforcing racial segregation or the maintenance of a subordinate status for the Negro group. The Commission emphasized that where police violence was most vicious and brutal, the complaints have usually charged that the officers involved gave racial motives for their conduct.

The report also indicated instances of "private" racial violence, abetted by police inactivity and connivance. Some of this "private"

---

[1] *1961 Commission on Civil Rights Report*, Book 5, "Justice" (Washington, D. C.: U. S. Government Printing Office, 1961), pp. 2–3.

107

violence, which takes the form of mob attacks, has occurred in the South on such occasions as the appearance of Freedom Riders or Sit-In demonstrations, school or bus integration, and arrests or accusations of Negroes for crimes. Instances have occurred in the North on the occasion of a Negro family moving into an all-white neighborhood, use of swimming facilities by Negroes, and the like.

Essentially, both police violence enforcing segregation and this "private" violence are the results of racial discrimination. The brutalities frequently have for their specific purpose either the frightening of the Negro community to "keep them in their place," by making an example of what happens to "uppity" Negroes or the prevention, by violent and lawless means, of desegregation or the exercise of civil rights, e.g., voting.

When we speak of violations of the right to life, the most immediate and obvious form that comes to mind is lynching. No doubt, the stark horror of its dramatic explosive violence is responsible for its long-lasting impression. In the South, previous to the Reconstruction era, lynching was directed chiefly against whites, but during Reconstruction, the pattern changed. Lynching then became an instrument, not merely for punishing the individual, but also for the control and discipline of the Negro.

Between 1882 and 1959, there was a total of 4735 recorded lynchings in the United States; of these almost three quarters involved Negro victims. Of the 3441 lynchings of Negroes, over 97 percent occurred in the nine Southern and eight border states. In other words, in this seventeen-state area, 3332 Negroes were lynched. During the 1890's, there were approximately 200 lynchings each year. Fortunately, there has been a decrease from this high, and in 1951 there was only one lynching. In 1957, 1958, and 1959 there was also one reported each year. The last recorded lynching occurred in 1959. Happily the decrease has been regular and steady, and lynchings have become so rare that the Tuskegee Institute had discontinued issuance of its annual report.

Studies have indicated that besides the homicide or mutilation effected by the mob, other evil effects accompany mob violence. Relations between the Negro and white community deteriorate as mutual antagonism, fear, and distrust arise. Further, lynching brutalizes the feelings and emotions even beyond the locality in which they occur, and has a psychological impact which is vastly disproportionate to its relative frequency.

It is difficult for a white person to realize the atmosphere which lynchings and riots create for the Negro community — an atmosphere of fear, doubt, and uncertainty of which they are extremely conscious. The Negro is punished through any member of his race victimized by mob violence. In lynching, it makes no difference whether the victim is guilty. He is to serve as an example to others. After interracial troubles, especially in small communities and rural areas, the entire Negro community is frightened. Dollard asserts that every Southern Negro knows he is under a kind of death sentence which may or may not fall, and that this fear tends to intimidate him. This contention is supported by the report of the Committee on Civil Rights of 1947 which studied the atmosphere of fear generated in the Negro community by mob violence:

> Lynching is the ultimate threat by which his inferior status is driven home to the Negro. As a terrorist device, it reinforces all other disabilities placed upon him. The threat of lynching always hangs over the head of the southern Negro, the knowledge that a misinterpreted word or action can lead to his death is a dreadful burden.[2]

Though lynchings are infrequent today, their actual occurrence in the past and the deleterious side effects indicate that the matter is not of purely speculative interest. Scarcely anyone will question the moral responsibility of participants in lynchings which result in death or mutilation. There can be no doubt that participation in such crimes is a serious violation of the fifth commandment. Also guilty are those who cooperate by encouraging, approving, or urging such acts, as well as those who by their inactivity make such crimes possible, e.g., police and prison officials who neglect to take proper precautions to prevent lynching. Their passive or negative assistance makes them participants in the sinful acts. Thirty-five years ago, Monsignor Gilligan called participation in lynching, murder, and succinctly summarized forms of participation and their moral responsibility:

> [Lynching] constitutes that injustice which is more commonly designated as homicide or murder. All who actively cooperate in the lynching

---

[2] *To Secure these Rights*, pp. 24–25.

are in some degree guilty of the same sin. Among that group of co-operators must be included not only the man who fires the shot or who holds the rope, but all who deliberately assist the action in any way; those who by their presence encourage others to action, the sheriff who without great inconvenience could protect the Negro prisoner, and especially the agitators who arouse the crowd. Truly in many communities men participate in lynchings without any conscious-ness of sin and are not regarded as murderers. Yet they directly and unjustly destroy human life, so no other statement is possible.[3]

He also recommended a great emphasis and constant repetition of religious teaching on the true nature of lynching, and urged the enact-ment of state antilynching laws as antidotes. Likewise, he stated that the legislator who would refuse to support or to vote for such laws could sin grievously.

While lynching is a phenomenon which has been more prevalent in the South, the race riot has been more common in the North. A race riot differs from a lynching since in the lynching the mob acts against an individual who is unable to defend himself and is completely at their mercy. In a race riot, violence is directed against a few individuals or small groups who can and do fight back even though they may be outnumbered. In a race riot, the Negroes fight as fiercely as the whites. Many instances of so-called race riots are not properly such. They are really mass lynchings, following the pattern of a lynching with the mob using violence against several individuals who are incapable of retaliation or striking back.

The history of the race riot goes back to the Civil War era. At that time, there were several riots in the North where the free Negroes were regarded as competitors for jobs sought by newly arrived immi-grants. It is of interest that Irish workers showed more hostility to the Negro than other immigrant groups, although in some instances Ger-man immigrants participated to a lesser degree. In July, 1862, Irish and German workers began an attack on Negroes in Cincinnati, beat-ing them and burning their homes. These riots, lasting from July 15 to July 20, were caused by competition between Negro and white river-boat hands. The whites feared the loss of jobs and their replacement by Negroes at the end of slavery. In the following month, in Brooklyn, Negro employees of a tobacco factory were attacked by whites; in

---

[3] Francis J. Gilligan, *The Morality of the Color Line,* pp. 67–68.

Chicago, the hiring of Negroes in packing plants caused a protest from the white workers; and in Buffalo, there were anti-Negro riots by Irish dock hands because of the hiring of Negro stevedores. Even the famous New York City Draft Riots of July, 1863, which were provoked by the provision for exemption from the draft by payment of $300 allowed by the Draft Law, were also protests against Negroes because of association of the Draft Law with the cause of Emancipation. When the rioting began, it was directed equally against the military forces and the Negroes. But by the second day, mob anger concentrated more and more on the Negro. Mobs hanged, beat, and injured Negroes; Negro homes were sacked. Even the Colored Orphans' Home in the city was attacked. The riots brought about a mass exodus from the city and when the riots ended, 3000 Negroes were homeless and several hundred had sought refuge in the suburbs. The clergy of New York City demanded an end of the riots. On July 17, 4000 people gathered before the residence of Archbishop Hughes and heard him caution against further riot participation. Sermons were preached against all such participation in the Catholic churches on Sunday, July 19. The general opinion of historians is that the chief rioters were Irish and this seems to receive support from the fact that of those killed 52 were Irish and 7 were Germans.[4]

A race riot is a two-way battle. Casualties are produced on both sides. In the famous Chicago riot of 1919, 23 Negroes and 15 whites were killed, 342 Negroes and 178 whites were injured. As we have indicated, race riots in the past occurred mostly in the North but there has been a decrease in recent years. Apparently the worst period occurred immediately following World War I. In 1919 there were race riots in twenty-six cities. There are indications, however, that they may become more frequent in the South, as the Southern Negro becomes more determined to obtain his rights and decides to resist obstacles to their procurement, and particularly if the "passive resistance" movement fails.

In considering the morality of this problem, similarity of a riot to a battle may give rise to an inclination to judge it in terms of warfare. However, I believe it would be an error to do so. No racial group,

---

[4] Williston H. Lofton, "Northern Labor and the Negro during the Civil War," *Journal of Negro History*, XXXIV (July, 1949), 251–273.

no matter how large, enjoys the nature of a perfect society. Only the state possesses the moral power to wage a just war to repel aggression. No minority group, or, for that matter, no majority group within the state can arrogate to itself the privileges and obligations of the state in reference to the procurement of the common good. It would appear that the morality should be considered precisely under the aspect of permissible self-defense against an unjust aggressor. Self-defense, of course, can extend to the slaying of an aggressor, if this is required to prevent injustice. This right can be exercised to defend life and other goods of great import, e.g., bodily integrity, chastity, or property.

The right to self-defense against a mob can be used to prevent loss of these goods by innocent victims of aggression. It would make no difference whether the aggressors were whites or Negroes, their victims retain the right to use such defense as is necessary. This principle, however, by no means applies to marauding bands of either race who roam about seeking victims on whom to take revenge. The right of self-defense is not the right of retaliation. It operates only for the repression and frustration of an actual aggression. Raiding parties are morally reprehensible no matter which race instigates them and no matter how unjust the provocative incidents. Their victims are usually incapable of any defense and these actions are nothing more than lynchings.

Public officials have a serious obligation to maintain order and to prevent situations where the right of self-defense will have to be operative. As in the case of all crimes, it is, of course, impossible to foresee and to prevent every instance of unlawful force. Nevertheless, greater vigilance and precaution would help reduce the occasions. Officials, who, when they see the beginning of the assembling of angry mobs, do nothing to dispel them or to indicate that they will oppose violence and maintain peace, sin seriously. Further, law officials who neglect the obligation to prosecute and secure the punishment of participants in riots and lynchings, are giving encouragement to the repetition of those acts and are injuring the common good by the resultant cultivation of a spirit of disregard and contempt for law and right order. Too often, they attempt to excuse their inaction and connivance by a claim of impossibility of judicial proof, even though in some instances, newspaper photographs and newsreel movies clearly identify participants.

A fairly recent example of inactivity can be seen in the lynching of Mack Parker, whose murder, incidentally, represents the last known lynching in the United States. Parker had been accused of rape and placed in jail in Mississippi and was awaiting trial. On April 24, 1959, a group of white men took him from the jail, shot him, and threw his body in the Pearl River. The FBI offered its help to the governor of Mississippi, was successful in identifying many of the lynching group, and even obtained admissions from some of them. However, the prosecutor refused to present the FBI report to the grand jury, saying that it represented only hearsay evidence. Further indication of the atmosphere in court can be seen in the statement of the presiding judge to the jury. According to the 1961 Commission on Civil Rights Report, the judge is quoted as telling the jury that they were soldiers fighting to save freedom and a way of life. He is further quoted:

> We should have the backbone to stand against any tyranny, even including the board of sociology, sitting in Washington, garbed in judicial robes, and dishing out the legal precedents of Gunnar Myrdal.[5]

The report makes the following remarks regarding the Parker case:

> Although the Department of Justice brought the case to the attention of a Federal grand jury in January, 1960, the jury found no violation of Federal law and returned no indictment. The Federal grand jury had the benefit of the FBI report. The Department of Justice has not closed the case. . . . There is evidence that the lynching took place with the cooperation of a jail official who had the duty to protect Parker.[6]

Despite the fact that antilynching laws exist in over twenty states, almost half of which are Southern, they have been the basis for very few prosecutions and even fewer convictions. Some of these laws prohibit mob violence in general; others pertain solely to seizure of a prisoner by a mob. Sanctions include automatic suspension of the sheriff from office, various penalties on the county, fines and imprisonment for participation in lynchings, and, in some cases, capital

---

[5] Quoted by *1961 Commission on Civil Rights Report*, Book 5, "Justice," p. 42.
[6] *Ibid.*

punishment. However, no convicted lyncher has ever received the death penalty under these laws.[7]

Analogous to the problems involved in race riots and lynchings is the question of the morality of Freedom Rides and the Sit-Ins. The liceity of these methods is questioned by some who claim that not only do these actions violate private property rights through trespass, but they also increase racial antagonism and provoke riotings and disturbances of the public peace.

The Freedom-Ride movement began in May, 1961, when a group of six whites and seven Negroes boarded a Washington to New Orleans bus. According to *Time*, they intended to demonstrate "by provoking trouble, that Southern interstate travel is still segregated in fact, although integrated by law."[8] En route, the group experienced no serious incidents until the bus reached Alabama. In Anniston and Birmingham, they were attacked by mobs and beaten. After these incidents, the group decided to discontinue the bus journey and went on to New Orleans by plane. College students who had participated in Sit-In lunch-counter demonstrations rallied to the support of the Freedom Rides. They were guided in their conduct on these rides by the directive enunciated by Martin Luther King, Jr., who had modeled his tactics on Gandhian principles of nonviolence. Dr. King has described the principle of nonviolent resistance as meaning not only the avoidance of external, physical violence, but "also of (avoidance) of internal violence of spirit. This type of resistor not only refuses to shoot his opponent, but he also refuses to hate him. At the center of non-violence stands the principle of love."[9]

Utilizing this method, Dr. King had effected a victory in 1956 in desegregating buses in Montgomery. The nonviolent resistance preached and practiced by King and his followers was also used by these later Freedom Riders. Adhering to these nonviolent principles, Negro students rode interstate buses into various muncipalities in the South, using bus station facilities, such as waiting rooms, rest rooms, lunch counters, and restaurants which, either by local law or

---

[7] J. Greenberg, op. cit., pp. 394–396, for summary of various state laws prohibiting lynching and rioting.

[8] Time (June 2, 1961), 14–19.

[9] Martin Luther King, Jr., *Stride Toward Freedom: The Montgomery Story* (New York: Harper & Bros., 1958), pp. 103–104.

custom, had been reserved for the whites only. During the period from May 24, 1961, to July 6, 1961, in Jackson, Mississippi, a total of 172 Freedom Riders were arrested when they insisted on using segregated facilities. However, this figure does not represent merely those who were arrested for using segregated interstate facilities since the report includes four arrests of Negroes who sat on a bench reserved for whites in a public park in Jackson and refused to vacate.

Objections have been made to the Freedom Riders on the basis that they were outsiders from other states who intended to stir up trouble and cause rioting and public disturbances. Let us examine briefly these objections and test their validity:

a) *They are outsiders:* This is true. A great number of the participants are from other states. In fact, even those who may happen to be natives of a particular state usually begin their participation in another state. However, this is necessitated by the nature of the Freedom Ride. The intention is to use facilities which should be available to interstate travelers on a nonsegregated basis, but which have been segregated by local laws in contradiction to rulings of the Interstate Commerce Commission and the decision of the Supreme Court. When local officials attempt to enforce laws demanding segregation in these facilities, the Freedom Riders refuse to comply and submit to arrest without resistance. Their arrest and imprisonment are their protest against the unjust local segregation statutes, as well as often being the means of obtaining judicial relief through a testing of these laws in the Courts.

To qualify as interstate commerce, the trip must cross state lines. The very nature of the situation thus requires that they be outsiders in order to be considered passengers in interstate commerce. The federal regulations, established by the Interstate Commerce Commission and upheld by the Supreme Court, do not apply to intrastate facilities.

b) *They intend to cause trouble:* Obviously, this is the more serious charge. Intent to incite or stir up mob violence and riots would make the morality of any action questionable since public peace and order is a good of such importance and it cannot be lightly disregarded. But the actions of the Freedom Riders seem to deny any intent to disturb the peace or injure the common good. The nonviolence and their nonresistance to the violence inflicted on them in various cities corroborate their averred intention of a nonviolent protest against local segregation laws. The purpose is to force desegregation of interstate travel facilities or else be arrested and imprisoned for violating these statutes. Their peaceful submission to arrest and imprisonment is intended as a reproach to the conscience of the community. Perhaps this intention to reach indirectly the heart of the segregationist is best explained in the words of one of the Freedom Riders who had been arrested at Jackson:

> A Freedom Ride through the South, testing segregated terminals and the laws that enforce them is a personal witness against unjust institutions and laws, and at the same time an effective political action against them. . . . Even though the Freedom Ride acts directly upon laws and institutions, its power is chiefly that of Christian witness; its effect is to reproach the conscience of the segregationist. If the ride leads to arrest and a prison term, it is fitting that we accept it.[10]

Frequently jail sentence for these violations is used as a basis for a test case to have the local laws declared unconstitutional, although some of the Freedom Riders are opposed to posting of bond as well as appeal to higher courts since they consider these actions lessen the impact acceptance of jail sentences has on the conscience of their neighbors:

> I know that some other Freedom Riders will not agree with me, but it seems to me that the alternative of posting bond and appealing to higher Courts blunts our appeal to God's justice and human conscience and instead invokes Federal power. What is most important, it seems to me, is the acceptance of a prison term as a testimony of our belief in personal suffering as the way by which the world can be changed. While our countrymen look to power, publicity and plenty of cash to cure the world's ills, should not we Catholics seek a way of reaffirming the lesson of the Crucifixion? I think people do not really believe any more that personal suffering can change the world.[11]

I believe that Freedom Rides are morally justifiable, especially where civic disorders are not intended and where passive resistance is manifested by the Riders. The instances of violence which have occurred, or which may, in the future, occur, should not be considered as being

---

[10] Terry Sullivan, "What Is It Like To Be A Freedom Rider?" *Interracial Review*, 35 (June, 1962), 145.
[11] *Ibid.*, p. 145.

occasioned by the action of the Riders. The real cause is the action of those white citizens, who are themselves often outsiders, in disregarding law and order and in demanding the bestowal of rights on themselves only. This occasioning of disorders can be justified by the long-range good which will eventually accrue to the Negro community as they secure individual liberty and freedom of movement with the removal of discriminatory statutes.

The question of the morality of the Sit-In demonstrations is somewhat different from that of the Freedom Rides since the demonstrations do not involve interstate facilities, but rather privately owned and operated businesses. For the most part, Sit-In demonstrations involve lunch counters in department and variety stores. Negroes are welcomed and their patronage is sought in all but one department of these stores — the lunch counter of the store is the exception. There, either a segregated section is provided or a side of the counter, lacking seating facilities, is available to them. Participants in the Sit-In demonstrations occupy seats at the white section in one of these stores and request service. Upon either being refused outright or else being ignored, they continue to occupy the place, preventing others from securing a seat at the counter. White participants are accompanied by a Negro and ask that both be served. Eventually, the store either closes down the lunch counter or restricts it to "Employees Only," although in practice all white customers are freely admitted.

It has been maintained that the Sit-In demonstrators by these actions were restraining trade, violating the freedom of the store owner to select his customers, preventing him from making sales, and trespassing on private property. However, these objections cannot, I believe, be maintained in view of the facts.

I do not believe that a storekeeper has the right to select his customers on such arbitrary criteria as race or religion. Obviously, if a prospective customer is a poor credit risk; if he intends the items purchased for criminal purposes; if his demands for service, delivery, repairs, or guarantees are unreasonable a store owner would be justified in refusing to sell to him. We have instances in which stores are specifically enjoined from selling to certain people, e.g., liquor stores and bars cannot sell to minors; druggists cannot dispense certain drugs or medications without a doctor's prescription; gunsmiths are prohibited from selling various types of guns and ammunition. These restrictions are reasonable in that they intend the prevention of injury either to the purchaser or to society. But to say that business firms which provide necessary and useful services or products to the public have the right to decide arbitrarily to whom they will or will not sell, seems to be against public policy. No one will grant that the telephone company or the electric company, even though privately owned, is free to select its customers, or that a bus company or airline is free to determine whom it will transport. Nor can it be claimed that these companies are not free to select their customers merely because they are quasi-monopolies. Even if there were, in the same area, two or three telephone companies or electric companies from whom a man could purchase services, nevertheless, if the first company had the right to refuse arbitrarily to provide him with services, so too would the other companies. Companies and stores, even though privately owned and operated, have a semipublic character. Their owners cannot use and operate them solely for selfish aims, since their relation to the public-at-large has removed them from the realm of the strictly private in many aspects — they are not private in the sense in which we say that a man's home is private.

This notion of the public character of lunch counters and restaurants formed the basis of a separate but concurring opinion written by Justice Douglas in Garner v. Louisiana, which involved the arrest of Sit-In demonstrators at a lunch counter in Baton Rouge. They had been charged with and found guilty, by a lower court, of "disturbing the peace." The Supreme Court held that the arrests and convictions violated the constitutional rights of the Sit-In demonstrators. But, in arriving at the majority decision, the Court refused to consider the broader constitutional questions which were raised, i.e., the denial of freedom of expression and the very fact of racial discrimination. Justice Douglas, however, agreed that the convictions should be reversed, but formulated his opinion on these constitutional issues and stated that he believed that these issues should have been considered by the Court and the convictions reversed on those grounds, rather than on the basis that the actions of the demonstrators did not constitute a violation of the peace. Justice Douglas stated:

Those who run a retail establishment under permit from a municipality operate in my view a public facility in which there can be no more discrimination based on race than is constitutionally permissible in the more customary types of public facility. . . . Some of the argument assumed that restaurants are "private property." They are, of course, "private" property for many purposes of the constitution. Yet so are street railways, power plants, warehouses, and other types of enterprises which have long been held to be affected with a public interest. Where constitutional rights are involved, the proprietary interests of individuals must give way.[12]

In regard to the prevention of sales which the Sit-In demonstrators occasion: strictly speaking, their presence at the lunch counter, without creating disturbance or commotion, is merely an occasion of the loss of other sales. Every time a customer engages the time of a clerk to show or exhibit an item, he is automatically preventing the clerk from making a sale to another customer. Every time a man sits at a lunch counter or occupies a table in a restaurant, he is preventing another customer from being served, and the length of time he remains will influence the number of customers he has kept waiting. This, however, is merely a necessary corollary of physical limitations. The Sit-In demonstrator who is being refused service is preventing someone else from being served, but his presence is merely an occasion of the prevention of other sales. The actual cause is the refusal of the owner to serve him. If the management would allow him to make his purchase, he would complete the sale, vacate his place, and make it available to others. However, since the owner refuses to serve him, this refusal is the actual cause of the loss of other sales. The customer has the right to make a purchase at that department the same as in any other department of the store, but the owner does not have the right to arbitrarily refuse to sell to him. The Sit-In demonstrator is demanding something to which he has a right, viz., to purchase merchandise and services offered to the general public; the owner is refusing to make available to him this service on an equal basis with other customers.

Father Kenealy, S.J., clearly states the morality of the Sit-In demon-

---

[12] *Garner v. Louisiana*, 82 S. Ct. 248; *Race Relations Law Reporter*, 6 (Winter, 1961), 952–953.

stration, indicating that it does not involve a violation of the rights
of private property:

> No moral rights of private property are transgressed. No man has a
> moral right to use his property, a creature of God, against the children
> of God. Racial discrimination, even in the use of purely private prop-
> erty, is immoral at least as transgressing the supreme law of charity.
> The sit-ins, however, are not concerned with purely private property,
> or with securing the observance of charity in private homes, private
> clubs, private activities. Their concern is with justice in public life,
> public businesses, and public accommodations. They are entitled to
> seek that end by peaceable, orderly, and by public means. Their dedi-
> cation to such a cause is not a violation or defiance of any just law —
> and only a just law can bind the human conscience. The public wel-
> fare and the peace of the nation will benefit from the inspiring self-
> sacrifice of the participants in the sit-ins. The law itself will be purified
> by their efforts. The cause of justice will be served.[13]

A further word must be said regarding the possible occasioning of
disorders and disturbances of public peace by both the Sit-Ins and
the Freedom Rides. Both these methods are not, we have shown,
actually causes of public disorders, especially where the principles of
nonviolence are the guiding rules. The actual cause is the prejudices
and perverse wills of those who resort to violence in order to prevent
the exercise of a basic right by minority groups. However, even an
occasion of danger to public peace requires a justifying reason. We
have mentioned the good motives and intentions in both these protests. Obviously, these are high and worthy motives, but the public
peace is of such importance that mere good intentions do not automatically justify a threat to it. Besides exalted intentions, a justification of a risk to public order also involves a practical aspect. In other
words actions which represent an occasion of possible danger to common good must achieve a degree of success in securing their goals,
otherwise they involve exposing the common good to possible injury
without sufficient reason.

However, both the Sit-Ins and the Freedom Rides have achieved
a high degree of success in obtaining their goals which is commensurate with the degree of danger which they have occasioned. In
regard to their immediate object, the Sit-Ins have effected the de-

---

[13] William J. Kenealy, S.J., "The Legality of the Sit-ins," *The New Negro*,
edited by Mathew H. Ahmann (Notre Dame: Fides Publishers, 1961), p. 86.

segregation of lunch counters in approximately one hundred Southern cities. The Freedom Riders through their sacrifices have brought about the actual desegregation of transportation facilities for interstate travel, and also to a large extent, have helped in desegregating intrastate facilities.

But more important than these have been the results which are not so tangible, but which are nonetheless real. Such effects have been the stirring of and appeal to the conscience of many white people who were impressed and moved by the nonresistance of these groups and their willingness to go to jail in defense of their beliefs and principles; the boost to the morale of the Negro community in the realization, perhaps for the first time, of what a unified and peaceful protest could accomplish to improve their condition, and the revitalization of a sense of human dignity which came to them as a concomitance of their success in breaking down some of the racial barriers; the dispelling of the myth that the Negroes were satisfied with their way of life; the necessity of meetings of white and Negro leaders for the negotiation of grievances; and an increase in the endeavors of political leaders on the national level to protect minority rights.

This boost in morale was expressed by Dr. King who described its effects in Montgomery after a boycott led eventually to desegregation of the buses:

> The increased self-respect of even the least sophisticated Negroes in Montgomery is evident in the way they dress and walk, in new standards of cleanliness and of general deportment. As one Negro janitor told a reporter from the North: "We got our heads up now, and we won't ever bow down again — no, sir — except before God!" There has been a decline in heavy drinking. Statistics on crime and divorce indicate that both are on the wane. . . . Saturday nights are less belligerent than they used to be. There is a contagious spirit of friendliness and warmth; even the children seem to display a new sense of belonging.[14]

The existence of results from both types of protest demonstrations makes it evident that the good effects actually produced are commensurate with the danger incurred and represent ample compensation for a toleration of that danger to civil order and peace. Naturally, there are some who do not believe that these are the best methods for

---

[14] Martin L. King, Jr., *Stride toward Freedom*, pp. 187–188.

obtaining rights and who sincerely desire the procurement of these rights. However, it seems that their objections are to the relative effectiveness of the means used rather than to the morality of those means. Edward Bennett Williams has stated that he prefers a policy of selective buying whereby Negroes refuse to purchase from merchants who retain discriminatory practices. Mr. Williams sees this means as equally effective as the Sit-In and as possessing the added advantage that danger of violence is avoided. However, it should be indicated that boycotts as an instrument of protest by the Negro community are not new. They were used fairly frequently in the past, particularly at the beginning of the enactment of Jim Crow laws. It should also be pointed out that they were, for the most part, unsuccessful because of the control over the political and economic situation wielded by the white community and the general approval of the nation of the then recent *Plessy-Ferguson* "separate but equal" doctrine. Georgia was the first state to permit segregation on streetcars when, in 1891, it enacted a law to this effect. By 1907, Louisiana, Mississippi, Tennessee, Florida, Virginia, and North Carolina required it on streetcars throughout the state. Boycotts of segregated street cars by Negro communities were unsuccessful, e.g., 1904, in New Orleans, Mobile, Houston, Jacksonville; and 1906, in Austin and Nashville.[15]

Others prefer utilization of the Sit-In as a challenge and a stimulus to the conscience of the community, hoping in this way to bestir the community to remedy the situation. However, it is interesting to note that Dr. Proudfoot, who participated in the Knoxville Sit-In, indicated three distinct phases which had to be entered upon there before success was ultimately obtained:

> Typically the lunch counter struggle went through three phases before a bargain was finally struck. Negotiation was the first phase. This failed in almost every instance, whereupon Negroes turned to the public protest — the sit-in — hoping to afflict the conscience of the community sufficiently to prompt action. But the sit-in, in and of itself, also usually brought no results. It was finally the economic boycott or threat of it which was effective in the key cities. This means that — much as we may prefer the contrary — the issue was not settled on the basis of morality, but on the basis of economics.[16]

---

[15] Edward Bennett Williams, *One Man's Freedom* (New York: Atheneum, 1962), pp. 304–305; cf. also August Meier, "Boycotts of Segregated Street Cars," *The Phylon*, XVIII (3rd Quarter, 1957), 297.

[16] Merrill Proudfoot, op. cit., p. 194.

This emphasis on the impelling power of an economic motive in accomplishing desegregation and its apparent greater effectiveness over moral considerations seems to be corroborated in the field of housing. According to a report in the *Washington Post*, on June 30, 1962, Mr. William Levitt, president of the Levitt Company, was requested by a minority stockholder (10 shares), at a stockholders' meeting, to have the company abandon its policy of selling only to white families at the Belair, Maryland, development in the suburbs of Washington. He said that he was aware of the moral and sociological factors involved, but made his request solely on economic considerations, i.e., the large potential Negro market in Washington. According to the report, Mr. Levitt replied: "You asked that we disassociate ourselves from the sociological and moral questions involved and consider this strictly on a business basis. I assure you we will do exactly that. We will integrate, or not integrate, solely on the basis of what is good economically."

However, it must be indicated that a program of selective buying or a boycott is no guarantee that violence will actually be avoided. The Negroes in Montgomery, under the leadership of Martin Luther King, in 1955, began a boycott of the public transportation system because of bus segregation and because of the abuses and discourtesies to which they were subjected by company employees. The leaders of this boycott were extremely successful in persuading the Negroes of Montgomery to refrain from riding the buses. The economic effect produced on the company can be appreciated when it is realized that the company admitted that 75 percent of its passengers were Negroes. An indication of the actual financial loss sustained can be garnered from the fact that the city of Montgomery lost more than $15,000 revenue as a result of the boycott. Since the city receives 2 percent of the revenues of the bus company, this would indicate that the company lost more than three quarters of a million dollars gross revenue during the boycott. But despite the fact that the boycott was carried out in accord with the principle of nonviolence, it did not succeed in precluding violence on the part of extremist white groups. During the boycott, there was harassment of the Negro community by city officials through a "get tough" policy involving arrests for minor or trumped-up traffic violations, threats of arrest of former bus riders for vagrancy and hitchhiking, and mass arrests, including Dr. King, for violations of an ancient antiboycott law. Extreme violence was manifested in the bombing of the homes of Dr. King and another Negro leader. Finally when the Supreme Court, in November, 1956, sustained the lower court decision that Alabama's laws requiring segregation on public transportation were unconstitutional, a reign of terror broke out in Montgomery, several Negro churches and homes were bombed, and there were shootings and beatings of Negro bus riders.

Thus selective buying or, in plain terms, a boycott, while it may be capable of producing results, cannot be said to be a method which will preclude danger of violence.

To sum up, I believe that the Sit-In, because of its more active character, may be required in situations where it is feasible in order to make an ostensible and powerful appeal to community conscience and to build up the morale and solidarity of the Negroes so that a pattern of selective buying may be successfully executed. Apparently this was the method utilized to achieve desegregation of lunch counters in Knoxville where the determination of the Negro community to refuse to buy was bolstered by the more ostensible and more positive action of the Sit-In.

While there may be disagreement as to whether the goal desired can be obtained best through the use of the Sit-In, or by a boycott, or by a combination of the two, I do not believe that a solution can be formulated on the presupposition that any of these methods are per se less likely to provoke general violence or public disorder. Father Kenealy's statement of his belief in the moral justification of the Sit-In represents an accurate evaluation of the morality of this method, and may, with even greater justification, be applied to the question of Freedom Rides:

Are the sit-ins morally justified? It seems to me that they are. Assuming as before that they are orderly and peaceful, they appear to be the only practical way to induce a moral and Christian practice into an important aspect of public life. The motive is exemplary: to arouse the conscience of the community in favor of justice and equality. The circumstances seem propitious: the failure of other means, the frustration of purely legal victories, the inspiration to the weak and frightened, and the signal success in many cities. The conduct itself is peaceful and orderly. The enormity of the moral evil to be overcome is apparent: the widespread denial of fundamental human dignity, freedom, and equality, the consequent moral evils both in the individual persons (persecuted and persecutors) and in the civil community.[17]

[17] William J. Kenealy, "The Legality of the Sit-ins," loc. cit., pp. 85–86.

CHAPTER 12

THE RIGHT TO WORK

Ability to secure the necessities of life is an important adjunct in the development of self — the goal of human personality. Not only the ability but also the method by which this is accomplished is of vital importance in determining the degree of perfection of personality development.

The present pattern of racial relations existing in this country has made it more difficult, and frequently very difficult, for the Negro to obtain employment and jobs suited to his needs and abilities. In fact, the U. S. Commission on Civil Rights in its 1961 report lays the blame for the heavy concentration of Negroes in less-skilled jobs and their consequent depressed economic status on multiplex discrimination against the Negro. This report included as factors: discrimination in academic, vocational, and apprenticeship training programs; discrimination by labor unions, especially the construction and machinist crafts; discrimination by State Employment agencies in their job referral policies; and discrimination by employers, including government contractors and the federal government itself.

It might appear that a discussion of slavery or involuntary servitude would be of historical interest only and lack any practical value a century after issuance of the Emancipation Proclamation and the enactment of the Thirteenth Amendment. There have been cases, however, brought before federal courts involving involuntary servitude as well as peonage. Implementing the Thirteenth Amendment, three sections of the U. S. Criminal Code prohibit involuntary servitude and peonage and provide penalties for infringements of these statutes.

Unexpectedly, the most recent decision based on violation of Section 1583 prohibiting "enticement into slavery" was handed down as recently as 1947. This was the case of United States v. Ingalls, heard on appeal in Federal Court for the Southern District of California.[1] Its sordid details make shocking reading, especially when it is realized that they occurred so recently.

According to the testimony, Dora Jones, a Negro, was kept in a condition of slavery for many years by Elizabeth Ingalls, receiving no pay or remuneration for her work; no days off, no vacation. When she wanted to leave, Mrs. Ingalls would remind her of an adulterous liaison which had lasted for three years between Dora and Mrs. Ingalls' first husband and of an abortion Dora had had thirty-eight years previously. Dora had been seventeen years old when she came to work and actually believed that, if she left, Mrs. Ingalls could and would have her put in jail. Mrs. Ingalls also told her that she was not very intelligent and would not be able to make her way in the world so that even if she did not go to jail, she would be put in an insane asylum, if she left. These threats of jail and the insane asylum kept Dora on the job until 1946.

Mrs. Ingalls was found guilty of violating Section 1583, but appealed the conviction on the grounds that the definition of "slavery" used in instructing the jury was incorrect. The District Federal Court denied her appeal for a new trial and approved the definition as used. The definition of slavery which had been given to the jury and later approved was:

> A slave is a person who is wholly subject to the will of another, one who has no freedom of action and whose person and services are wholly under the control of another, and who is in the state of enforced compulsory service to another.

Fortunately, instances of slavery are extremely rare and the Ingalls case is the only recently reported decision. But the facts in the case have been outlined here to indicate that instances of involuntary servitude are not impossible and, granted the proper combination of circumstances, e.g., ignorance, fear, personality, motivation, etc., can recur.

Comparatively more frequent, however, are cases involving the charge of peonage. This can be defined as the condition or status of compulsory service based on the indebtedness of the peon to the

---

[1] United States v. Ingalls, 73 F. Supp. 76, S.D. Cal., 1947.

master. The distinguishing element in peonage is always indebtedness, and this element of debt, actual or fictitious, constitutes the difference between involuntary servitude and peonage. Accusation and adduction of proof that a person is being held against his will and compelled to work in order to pay off a debt is sufficient for the prosecution of peonage.

The Justice Department in 1956 filed four peonage cases in federal courts, and two additional cases in 1957. These involved, according to a representative of the Justice Department, persons held against their will, such as Negro workers on plantations, usually under some spurious statement by the manager of the plantation, letting the worker know that if he leaves the job, he will get into trouble. The persons involved were, in practically all instances, members of minority groups, who because of lack of education, were frightened into remaining on the job against their will. The number of peonage cases has also decreased, even though they have not completely disappeared from the American scene. But it should be kept in mind that most likely many instances along these lines never come to public attention or reach the courts because of the poverty and ignorance of the victims.

One enlightening explanation of the factors involved in peonage was given at a hearing of a Senate Sub-committee on Labor and Labor-Management Relations in 1951. Practices which obtained in some Georgia sawmills involving unreported cases of peonage were described:

> Sawmill people — and I think they are the worst offenders I know of — get Negroes in debt to them purposely. They actually buy the debts from each other. If one Negro wants to go and work for someone else and it is satisfactory with the man for whom he is working at the moment, the man with whom he wants to work buys the debt from the other man. They hold it over this Negro's head. Great numbers of times, I think you would find if you checked — and I think I could lead you if you want to see it — a great number of times if this Negro does not want to work for this particular person, he is prosecuted. All he has to do is go back to work and the prosecution is dropped.[2]

---

[2] Hearing before the Special Sub-committee on Labor and Labor-Management Relations of the Senate on Labor Practices in Laurens County, Georgia, 82nd Congress, 1st Session, 79–88 (1951); quoted by Sydney Brodie, "The Federally Secured Right to be Free from Bondage," Georgetown Law Journal, 40 (June, 1952), 387.

Often these victims are Negroes or Mexican "wetbacks," who have been lured by promises of high pay and good working conditions to work on farm projects at great distances from their homes. When they arrive at the job, they are lodged in buildings unsuitable and unfit for human habitation; overcharged for travel and living expenses; and forced to work under intolerable conditions. Threats of violence or force itself is used against those who attempt to leave before they have worked off the debt incurred for travel and living expenses, or merely to keep them on the job until the season has ended. Obviously, not every such victimization is founded on racial prejudice, but the pattern of discrimination makes these minority groups easy prey either because of ignorance of rights or the realization that they cannot exercise those rights or will be punished for attempting to do so.

Another method of enforced labor, also becoming less common, is the use of law-enforcement agencies as labor recruiters to procure farm workers. Frequently this is done through a rigid enforcement of "vagrancy" laws by the police. The sheriff or police round up vagrants and offer them the choice of accepting employment or of serving a court sentence to labor in the chain gangs. Myrdal describes this form of oppression:

Negroes alone are subject to a special form of legal injustice which is, however, now becoming rather rare: when white employers are short of workers, they inform the sheriff, who will suddenly begin to enforce vague laws such as that against vagrancy. Formerly the employers could rent prisoners from the state; now they make a deal with the Negro defendant to pay his fine if he will work a certain number of days — fewer than the number he would have to spend in jail.[3]

One of the more notorious instances of obtaining Negro labor in this fashion was revealed in the *Dial* case. The Dials were white farmers living in Alabama, near the Mississippi border. They obtained Negro prisoners from Mississippi to work on their farms by paying the fines and having the prisoners released to them. It was shown at the trial that by beatings and threats they forced the Negro prisoners to work on their farms. At least one of the prisoners had been beaten to death. Two of the Dial brothers were found guilty and sentenced to 18 months in prison. However, evidence was not produced that the

---

[3] G. Myrdal, *op. cit.*, p. 551, also pp. 228–229.

police or prison officials had connived directly in the brutalities practiced by the Dials.[4]

There are indications that some state officials still try to enforce state laws which have been declared unconstitutional as violations of the Thirteenth Amendment and involving enforcement of servitude or peonage under color of law. In 1958, when the Justice Department was investigating a suspected case of slavery, a memo report of one of the attorneys to the acting head of the Civil Rights Division indicated this attempt:

> A Georgia statute made it a crime to contract to perform services with the intent to procure money or other things of value thereby and not to perform the services. It further created a presumption of intent based upon proof of the contract, the procuring, and the failure to perform. In *Taylor v. Georgia* (315 U.S. 25 [1942]) this statute was held to violate the 13th amendment. Nevertheless, local officials in Georgia still attempt to enforce this statute from time to time, by adding a charge of minor theft. The fact that the victim was charged with theft of a tool as well as with indebtedness indicates that the situation described in the Bureau's memorandum might be such an attempt. Further, the circumstances of the sheriff putting up bail in exchange for the prisoner's services indicates a possible violation of the involuntary servitude statutes in that he may not have given the victims any choice between jail and working or he may have compelled the victim to work until the amount of bail was paid off.[5]

Risks and financial dangers involved in planting or harvesting do not justify abuses of human liberty, nor have the courts tolerated such instances when brought before them. The morality involved in inflicting such subhuman living and working conditions, in violations of commutative justice through involuntary servitude and peonage, overcharging for travel and living expenses, and underpaying, is so immediately evident as to require no explanation.

Racial discrimination in hiring and on-the-job advancement is much more commonplace. Whereas forced servitude is something which most people come in contact with only through newspaper accounts, job discrimination, in one form or other, touches on areas of daily life of most of our working people. There are two forms of job

---

[4] *United States v. Dial*, Crim. No. 1348, N.D. Ala., May 14, 1954; cf. also *1961 U. S. Commission on Civil Rights Report*, Book 5, "Justice," p. 54.

[5] *1961 U. S. Commission on Civil Rights Report*, Book 5, "Justice," pp. 203–204.

discrimination which we shall discuss. The first involves the employer who refuses to hire nonwhites, or will employ them only in the lowliest and poorest paying jobs. The second is discrimination enforced by employees who either refuse to work with a Negro or use pressure to prevent job advancement for a racially unacceptable fellow employee, or to bring about his dismissal.

Discrimination in hiring is practiced not only in the South, but also in all sections, even Hawaii and Puerto Rico. The President's Committee on Civil Rights in their study of job discrimination in 1947 reported that a statistical count in Chicago revealed that 83 percent of all job orders placed with one of the largest commercial employment agencies included discriminatory specifications. They reported that many Northern businesses have an unwritten rule against advancing Jewish employees to executive positions; that railroad management, as well as the unions, discourage Negroes from being employed as conductors or engineers. They found that in areas which have a reputation of freedom from racial prejudice there were indications of discrimination in hiring practices, even though in other areas of social relationship there was relative freedom from prejudice. In Hawaii, large businesses will not hire clerical workers of Japanese ancestry when such a worker would be seen by the public. In Puerto Rico, for the most part only whites or very light colored are employed by banks, department stores, airlines, and sugar companies in clerical and executive positions. The result of discrimination in hiring has been to force these groups to accept poorer paying jobs as laborers and domestics.

Despite widespread discrimination in employment, very little of it is actually demanded by statute. Except for some recent legislation requiring segregated on-the-job facilities, such as washrooms, restaurants, or cafeterias, most employment discrimination is privately inflicted.

Discrimination in hiring makes it exceedingly difficult for the nonwhite to get a job. In those instances where he can secure employment, he is forced to accept the lowest paying and most menial jobs and is prevented from advancing to any higher position, especially one considered managerial or executive. Further, discrimination often results in his being paid less than white co-workers performing the same tasks.

What can be said of the morality of discrimination in hiring employees? At the outset, it is necessary to explain that in speaking of a *right to work*, it must not be understood as a title enabling one to demand from the state, society, or individuals that a job be made available to him. Calvez and Perrin caution regarding the proper understanding of the right to work:

> What we have just established is an inalienable and imprescriptible fundamental right of the human person. That is far from being a positive and concrete right established against society, or the state, for example. In the same way, the right to property is fundamental but does not of itself constitute a positive title to demand from society the grant of any particular piece of property. When they spoke of a right to work, therefore, the popes in no way subscribed to the naïve illusions of certain socialists in the 1848 Revolution.[6]

Every man has a right to work. This right derives from his nature and does not depend for its existence on the will of society. The right to work is founded on a threefold obligation: (a) The obligation to work in order to secure the means of preserving life. For most, work is the usual and ordinary means of procuring a livelihood. (b) The obligation to work to avoid idleness. This is founded on the fact that because of concupiscence which is the common lot of man as a result of the Fall, idleness exposes him to danger of sinning. Both the scriptural words, "For idleness hath taught much evil" (Eccl 33:29), as well as the commonplace "Idle hands are the devil's workshop" give evidence of a universal awareness of this danger. (c) The obligation to work in order to contribute to the common good.

Theologians distinguish between a *right to work* (*ius laborandi*) and a *right to a job* (*ius ad laborem*). The former is best described as the right to seek to obtain a job by just means, as well as the right to demand that no one unjustly impede the free exercise of that right. The latter (right to a job) is the right to demand that a job be offered or secured for one. No one has this right. Noldin notes that *legal justice* may oblige the public authority to provide jobs when the number of unemployed is so great that the common good is being impaired.[7]

---

[6] Jean-Yves Calvez and Jacques Perrin, *The Church and Social Justice: The Social Teaching of the Popes from Leo XIII to Pius XII*, translated by J. R. Kirwan (Chicago: Henry Regnery, 1961), p. 236.

[7] Noldin, II, pp. 68–69.

Although such factors as discrimination in vocational and training programs or in availability of union membership are, as have been indicated, responsible for many occupational and economic disabilities of racial minorities, nevertheless, the two more proximate causes are the refusal of employers to hire Negroes and the various pressures brought on the employer by customers or employees, either to keep Negroes out of jobs or restricted to lower jobs. We shall discuss the morality in general of these two proximate causes.

Refusal of Employers to Hire: Bearing in mind the explanation of the derivation of the right to work and its various distinctions, it can be stated that no one has a right in strict justice to demand that an employer hire him. A Negro applicant cannot claim that an employer, needing additional employees, who refuses to hire him because of prejudice or hatred, is violating strict or commutative justice. This does not mean that because strict justice is not involved such refusals do not violate other forms of justice. It is the writer's opinion that such refusals frequently violate social justice, in addition to the violation of charity when hatred is involved.

At first glance it may seem difficult to reconcile the statement that social justice is violated by discriminatory hiring practices with the right of private ownership. It has been objected that owners of businesses should be free to select or refuse to hire employees as they wish; that it is within their rights to establish any disqualifying conditions they desire. However, it should be remembered that these owners, especially when they employ many workers and provide useful or necessary services to the community, cannot be considered strictly as individuals. They perform a social function, and as employers act, although in a restricted way, as distributors of the goods of the community. There is an obligation for all property, even privately owned, to have a social goal and contribute to the advancement of the social order and common good. Pius XII gave a clear statement of the necessary connection of private property with the social order and its obligation to contribute to that order, and these words were repeated verbatim by Pope John in *Mater et Magistra*, reaffirming this obligation:

> The Church in defending the principle of private property seeks a
> high ethico-social end. She does not claim to support purely and

simply the present state of things as if that represented the divine will. Nor is it a matter of protecting, by establishing a principle, the rich and the plutocrat against the poor and those who have nothing. Far from it! From the beginning, she has always been a protector of the oppressed weak against the tyranny of the powerful. She has always supported the just claims of all workers' groups against every wrong. *The Church rather tries to bring it about that the institution of private property becomes what it ought to be, according to the plans of Divine Wisdom and the order of nature — an element of the social order, a necessary presupposition of human endeavors, a stimulus to work to gain the temporal and transcendant end of life* (Italics added.)[8]

And in quoting these words in *Mater et Magistra*, Pope John makes the obligation even more explicit when he adds: "Private ownership should safeguard the rights of the human person, and at the same time make its necessary contribution to the establishment of right order in society."[9]

Apparently some have claimed this teaching of the social function of private property represented socialism, but Calvez and Perrin, taking account of these objections, maintain that such a charge can only be made by those to whom any change of the *status quo* represents socialism, and that the aim of the Church is to see that all men have the means of acquiring "true security and a true personal responsibility."[10]

Employers have within their control the means of making a livelihood for large segments of the people in a community. In today's economic and industrial way of life, most men depend on employers for the opportunity to earn means of providing the necessities of life for themselves and their families. In such an economy, by far the greater percentage of men earn a livelihood by working for wages rather than by being self-employed. Today, most opportunities to earn a living rest in the hands of manufacturers, large merchants, and the directors of various industries who have a serious obligation as custodians and distributors of these opportunities. They cannot conduct themselves as if their actions were completely and solely private matters. They do not have the same right to select employees according to color that they have to select a tie. Discrimination in

---

[8] Pius XII, *Oggi, al compiersi*, radio message, September 1, 1944, *AAS* 36 (1944), 249–258.
[9] John XXIII, *Mater et Magistra*, N.C.W.C. translation, No. 111.
[10] J.-Y. Calvez and J. Perrin, op. cit., p. 214.

hiring has far-reaching social effects. Their actions often result in the deprivation of access to an opportunity to earn a living for many members of minority groups.

This does not mean that an employer is under obligation to hire an inept, inefficient, or incompetent worker. Requirements of skill, experience, or in certain instances, citizenship, may easily find justification according to circumstances. But where an applicant meets all reasonable requirements and qualifications, then the employer, I believe, has an obligation in social justice not to discriminate against him because of race or color, and this obligation, prescinding from charity, which may easily be involved, stems from the relationship to the social order borne by private property, particularly businesses and industries in our modern industrial economy.

Many years ago, Monsignor Gilligan summed up the employer's obligation when he wrote that it was a sin against charity and justice for an employer to refuse, without a valid reason, to hire a Negro. With the explicit qualification that this is an obligation in *social* justice, and that race or color does not represent a "valid reason," this statement is an accurate summary of the obligation of employers. Their refusal to hire qualified workers for no other reason than race will usually involve a sin against charity and social justice. This discrimination is contrary to the common good and it neglects the obligation of employers to contribute to the social uplifting and benefits accruing to society and the common good when opportunities to make a living are available.

Various Influences to Prevent Hiring of Negroes: The second more proximate cause of job discrimination, the morality of which we are treating here in a general way, is that of the pressures, usually economic, brought to bear on an employer to prevent him from hiring Negroes or giving them promotions and raises, or on Negro applicants to keep them from seeking jobs. Now, it should be immediately apparent that those motivated by antagonism, enmity, or hatred, who try to prevent someone from obtaining a job or a promotion, sin against charity. But the question requiring various distinctions is whether or not they also sin against justice. And, if so, what kind of justice? Are they bound to make restitution?

The nature and purpose of society and the social order show that everyone has a *strict right* that the acquisition of something due him in *commutative justice* not be rendered impossible by acts of others. Society should aid in acquiring those goods to which its members have a *strict right*. Peinador describes this right and the nature of its origin:

> Moreover, everyone has a strict right that the attainment of a thing which he may legitimately acquire not be rendered impossible by the voluntary action of another. That this right exists, and further that it is a strict right, is clear from the essential constitution of society which demands mutual help and cooperation between its members, and, at the same time, it can also be shown from the relationship existing between persons and external goods. If it follows from the nature of man that he can rightly have a relationship to a certain thing, then society, or the mutual association of men, must be an aid in his endeavors to make that relationship efficacious, and not impede his endeavors. Therefore, since every man has the right to the help of society, he has the right not to be impeded in his pursuit of a legitimate good so that his acquisition of it is impossible. . . . There is a sin of injustice, presuming theological culpa, when a man is impeded in any way from obtaining a good which is due him in commutative justice. As shown, the reason is because his strict right has been injured, namely the right he had to that object.[11]

But, as stated, no one has a *strict right* to a job. He has a right to work, but he cannot demand in strict justice that an employer hire him or that society supply him with a job. Hence it cannot be said that every voluntary action preventing his securing a job violates commutative justice. However, he does have a strict right that others do not use *unjust means* to prevent his acquisition of a good for which he may legitimately hope. The reason for the existence of this right is ultimately based on human nature and the purpose of society. If this right did not exist, human society would be purposeless and without a real objective. A sin is committed against justice when someone is prevented from obtaining a good to which he does not have a strict right, but to which he could lawfully strive, if the means used were *per se* causes of the loss and not accidental causes.

In these instances, such means are usually described as *unjust* because they involve a violation of justice, e.g., fraud or violence, efficaciously averting one who is hoping to obtain a good from attempting to secure it, or diverting the will of the donor so that he

---

[11] Peinador, II, v. II, No. 415–416.

does not bestow the good on the one on whom he had decided to confer it, or who had merely hoped to receive it. Violations of justice, such as calumny, detraction, force or violence, unjustly inflicted fear, and threats of harm, which efficaciously prevent the acquisition of licitly hoped-for goods are considered unjust means and, therefore, violate commutative justice. Applying this to the question at hand, it can be said that threats, fraud, calumny, and other such means used to prevent the hiring of a Negro violate commutative justice and demand restitution since they violate the strict right which he has that no one use unjust means against him to prevent his seeking a job, even though he does not have a strict right to the job itself. Further, these means are unjust interferences with his right whether applied directly against the employer to prevent his promoting or hiring a Negro or against the Negro to prevent his applying for a job, e.g., by threats of physical harm. As violations of strict justice, there is a concomitant obligation of restitution. Speaking of this restitution due in these instances, Lehmkuhl says that it is to be prorated according to the hope that there was of obtaining the good.[12]

Unjust means are considered to be applied against one effectively prevented from obtaining a good whether these means were applied immediately and directly (a) against the one who hoped to receive the good; (b) against the prospective donor; or (c) simultaneously against both. An example of the first would be when threats of violence are made against a Negro or his family if he applies for a job; an example of the second would be when an employer is threatened with physical or economic injury if he hires a Negro; an example of the third would be if calumny were used, telling a prospective employer that an applicant is a drunkard, or incompetent and dishonest. In this last example, there is an injustice against the applicant because of the lie which defames him and deprives him of his good name, and there is also an unjust circumvention of the free choice of the employer who is deceived by the calumny.

The obligation of restitution in such cases involving unjust means used either solely against the Negro applicant or simultaneously against both may be seen to flow from the nature of the injustices involved. But some may question the obligation of restitution to one

---

[12] Lehmkuhl, I, No. 1161.

who has been prevented from obtaining a good if the injustice was applied directly only against the donor, as would be the case where the employer is threatened if he hires a Negro. It is true that the injustice is directly inflicted on the employer, but there is an obligation to make restitution also to the one circumvented in his striving for a good since his hopes and chances were frustrated by the injustice inflicted primarily on the donor, but which is an effective or per se cause of his loss, though only redundantly. In fact there may be a twofold obligation of restitution: first to the donor when the unjust means resulted in an actual loss to him, and, second, to the one whose hopes were unjustly frustrated. Lehmkuhl describes this obligation:

> If, however, the injustice was directly inflicted on him from whom it was hoped the good would be obtained, there is an obligation of restitution present to the degree that the injustice has redounded to the one who hoped, or had hope, and has so redounded that the loss or non-attainment of the hoped-for good followed per se and not merely per accidens.[13]

Obviously, the first thing to be determined in each case, and which is, in practice, most difficult, will be whether the unjust means represent a per se cause of the loss of the anticipated good or were merely a per accidens cause. A rule of thumb to help determine whether they are to be considered a per se cause has been given by Lehmkuhl, which will be useful in determining whether a threat against an employer requires restitution to the applicant. This rule states that it should be first determined whether the benefactor, whose will has been fraudulently thwarted, is or should be opposed to the effect of that fraud which has redounded on the prospective beneficiary. If he is not and ought not be unwilling, then the injury suffered by the third party may more easily be considered a per accidens effect.

Drawing on these principles, the following represent the opinions of the writer regarding the morality of bringing pressure to prevent the promotion or hiring of Negroes:

1. If the employer is requested, urged, or counseled not to consider hiring a Negro, the one who gives this advice or makes the request does not violate strict justice because such action, considered objec-

---

[13] Ibid.

tively, does not violate commutative justice. Further, it is not an effective cause, but rather an accidental cause or an occasion of the loss of job opportunity. Even if the motive for such urging is hatred or vengeance, the action will not violate strict justice. Because of hatred, there will be a violation of charity, and in view of the importance and necessity of job availability in our economic order, there may be a sin against social justice.

Some theologians have maintained that to impede another from obtaining a good because of hatred, but without force or deceit, violates strict justice and requires restitution. They give the example of a man motivated by hatred, counseling the exclusion from a will of a certain person, and they hold that even though there was no deceit, fraud, or violence, nevertheless, because of evil intent, commutative justice is violated if the man is excluded from the will. They give a further example, which appears to be a parallel with the matter of influence being brought to prevent a Negro from getting a job, namely, if a bishop has decided to bestow a benefice, e.g., a parish, on a certain priest and someone persuades him, without force or deceit, but with the intention of injuring the priest, to give the benefice to someone else. They maintain that the evil intention renders the act a violation of strict justice. St. Alphonsus, speaking of this opinion, calls it probable; but he personally holds the opposite, maintaining that strict justice is not violated and there is no obligation of restitution, and he calls his opinion common and more probable.

2. If fraud or fear produced by threats or other unjust means are applied directly against the Negro to keep him from applying for a job, there is a violation of strict justice and an obligation, presuming theological *culpa*, to make restitution, particularly when the individuals who have suffered the loss can be identified. As stated above, the amount of restitution must be prorated according to the hope of securing the job. Obviously, a very difficult task, but, nonetheless, a real obligation to make restitution exists in this case.

3. If unjust means are applied simultaneously against the donor and the one who anticipates the good, because of hatred or other evil motive, there is a violation of strict justice and an obligation to restore, again prorated according to the expectation of success. If an employer is falsely informed that a Negro applicant is dishonest or

incompetent, in order to prevent his employment, this deceit or calumny represents a double injustice, and restitution may be required for both injuries.

4. The principle that unjust means preventing acquisition of a good which, though not due in strict justice, may be licitly sought or acquired violates commutative justice can be applied frequently in various other areas of race relations besides unemployment, viz., education, housing, public accommodations, etc., where the hope of securing such goods is frustrated by fraud, force, or other unjust means. For the most part, we have not made explicit application of this principle to every possible area. Because the right to seek employment is so fundamental and necessary in our modern economy, this principle is being explicitly applied to this matter, although it should not be construed as a minimization of the importance of charity in this area, as in all others.

Obviously it is not always a simple matter to determine in a specific instance whether pressure brought to bear was an efficacious cause of the loss. In instances where physical violence or force has been threatened or used, the causal relationship will be apparent. However, in other instances, it may be almost impossible to determine whether the influence was a real cause or merely an occasion of the loss. Speaking generally, it is the writer's opinion that the threat of a strike, made by a union or employees, to prevent the advancement or hiring of a Negro represents a truly efficacious cause, assuming, of course, that the employer would have seriously considered the Negro applicant and been willing to hire him in the event that he had the necessary qualifications. The same conclusion can, I believe, be made regarding the threat of a boycott by customers.

In both instances, fear is being *unjustly* inflicted on the owner by employees or customers. The fear may be of financial loss through work-stoppage or strikes; decrease of production because of the atmosphere of discontent; lessening of business prestige through loss of an appreciable number of customers whose purchases constitute an important part of his sales. The fear does not have to be of physical harm or violence to be considered unjust. The fear of these losses, which are obviously substantial, inflicted on an employer who desires to act rightly and in accord with obligations of social justice in employment practices must be considered unjust, particularly since those who inflict it have no right to demand that he refrain from fair hiring practices. Further, their action would, in this instance, appear to be a real cause of the loss to the prospective employee since he forgoes the possibility of being hired solely if, and when, such fear has been aroused. It would be a different situation if the employer is in accord with the aim of these demands. The threat of a strike or boycott, while it may be seriously made, would not, in this instance, be an efficacious cause of the harm done the applicant, nor would it actually produce fear since the employer has no desire to act otherwise. The threat has little, if any, influence on his decision and is merely a concomitant factor to his voluntary discrimination.

It cannot be maintained that the threat of a strike or boycott is not unjust since one has no obligation to remain on a particular job or to continue to patronize a certain store. It must be remembered that strikes and boycotts are powerful weapons, capable of inflicting serious losses and suffering not only on those immediately concerned, but also on innocent bystanders. A strike or boycott involves much more than the mere change of employment or transfer of patronage. A strike is a concerted action, and the right to strike cannot be spoken of or considered in the same terms as a strictly personal right, such as the right to marry.

Every strike or boycott cannot be considered just simply on the grounds that no one can be compelled to stay on the job or to buy at a certain store. Certain conditions must be verified before a strike can be considered just. These conditions may be summarized: (a) there must be no violation of a just contract; (b) no unjust means can be used in the conduct of the strike; (c) no unjust conditions must be involved, and its purpose must be just. In the case at hand, this last condition does not seem to be verified. Here the purpose of the strike is unjust because by establishing an unreasonable qualification for hiring, it seeks to frustrate the employer's right to select employees on a just and equitable basis, and it seeks to prevent utilization of privately owned property in accord with the relation it bears to the social order and its obligation to contribute to that order, which demands that employers, since they control, to a great extent, the distribution of the wealth of a community, have an obligation in social justice to make employment opportunities available on an equitable basis. The purpose of such a strike would, at least implicitly, be to prevent an act of social justice.

On the other hand, in instances where an individual customer or employee uses threats of withdrawal of patronage or resignation, these threats would not seem to be efficacious causes since it would be an unusual situation where the patronage or employment of one individual was so vital to the economic welfare of the company that it would suffer great loss and handicaps without it. However, though rare, it should be remembered that it could possibly occur.

It is more difficult to determine a violation of commutative justice where there is no concerted effort by customers or employees, but where many simply stop patronizing a store or many employees resign because of prejudicial attitudes. In these instances, it does not appear that they can be accused of violating strict justice even though, because of coalescence of losses, the employer may have to discontinue nondiscriminatory hiring. Such individuals would, of course, violate charity, and, with the possibility of closing down job opportunities to a large segment of the community, would also violate social justice.

In light of what has been said, Father Cronin's statement regarding the morality of job discrimination because of race, and the type of justice involved, appears as a good summary:

> The question as to which type of justice is involved is more obscure. Earlier it was stated that a worker does not normally have a claim in strict justice to be hired for any particular job. His right to a job obtains in regard to the economic system as a whole rather than any given employer. If such is the case, then an employer does not sin against strict justice in denying a job to a properly qualified worker because of race, religion, or national origin. But social justice requires that all concerned work as circumstances permit to change the institutions which bring about the evil of discrimination. Social justice applies here, in that rights are being denied under circumstances definitely contrary to the common good. When a group is being deprived of basic rights, the common good demands that steps be taken to remedy the evil. . . . At the same time, we should not overlook the serious personal obligation of employers and workers, at least in charity, to avoid discrimination in employment practices.[14]

---

[14] John F. Cronin, S.S., *Catholic Social Principles* (Milwaukee: The Bruce Publishing Co., 1955), p. 321; and John F. Cronin, *Social Principles and Economic Life* (Milwaukee: The Bruce Publishing Co., 1959), pp. 332–333.

Frequently, after a Negro has secured a job, the arm of discrimination reaches in and affects his status. In the first instance, after he has hurdled the handicap of firms which refuse to employ a Negro, he finds only the most menial and lowest-paying jobs are available. Length of service means little in relation to opportunities to advance to better paying and more skilled jobs. Speaking of Southern Negro steelworkers, James Rorty relates how they have been frozen in the worst paying jobs while white workers with less seniority were advanced over them to higher salary categories and better jobs. He reports the conversation of an investigator for the Committee on Civil Rights of the United Steel Workers' Union with a Negro steelworker:

"What are you doing?"
"I'm the blacksmith's helper."
"How long have you been employed?"
"Twenty years."
"Who's that white fellow over there?"
"He's the blacksmith."
"How long has he been employed?"
"He came here five years ago. I broke him in."[15]

In addition to job immobility, there is also the practice of paying a lower wage to a Negro worker than to a white worker performing the same work. Obviously this violates justice. If we assume that the white worker is not being overpaid but is receiving a just wage, a Negro, who performs the same service and has similar needs, has a right to the same wages. Monsignor Gilligan illustrated a further refinement of this injustice, where employers hire a Negro at a lower salary with the intention of eventually cutting the wages of the white workers. Besides the violation of justice in giving the Negro worker less than he has a right to, this also reduces the living standards of all workers, and in turn, reduces living standards of a large segment of the community. This practice is very instrumental in keeping racial antagonism alive.

So far we have spoken of the role of justice in relation to hiring practices. There can be no doubt that the bestowal of justice will go far to ease a situation productive of so many harmful effects. But the virtue of charity can also play an important role. The discontinu-

---

[15] James Rorty, "What Segregationists Really Fear," *Ave Maria*, 88 (July 26, 1958), 5–7.

ance of job discrimination can be an act of charity as well as an
exercise of justice. The good example shown can be an incentive and
an encouragement to others to change their attitudes. It will also help
alleviate friction between racial groups and remove causes of mutual
distrust and discord. Job promotions and advancements, with concomitant financial and social advantages, will help ease the economic
pinch of many families and will eventually promote their well-being.
In a case of equally qualified white and Negro job applicants, the
order of charity will indicate that he is to be helped first who is in
greater need. Under present circumstances, job prospects for the
Negro are poorer and thus, as a rule, his need for that job is greater.
The Negro applicant is not preferred over the white because of his
race. If he were, it would merely be prejudice in reverse. Rather, with
all things else being equal the Negro's need of a job is usually greater.
The law of charity will move us to help first those whose needs are
greater.

Indeed, in charity the claim of the American Negro to a share of
job opportunities in American industry and business is greater than
that of the immigrant regardless of racial or national origin.

Since the enactment of various FEPC laws and regulations, as well
as the insistence by the federal government on nondiscrimination in
plants producing goods under government contract as a condition for
procurement of government business, management has shown itself
more and more ready to abandon discriminatory practices. Others
maintain they would cease discrimination completely, but they fear
the dissatisfaction of white workers and the possibility of strikes,
walk-outs, or slow-downs if they hire Negro workers.

As we have seen, workers who threaten work stoppages or strikes
if Negroes are hired or advanced to higher jobs violate strict justice.
The right to work includes the right that no one shall do anything to
prevent the obtaining of a job. These white workers, by threats, are
effectively precluding job opportunities. Such violations can entail
an obligation of restitution when they violate commutative justice.

Fortunately, the reaction of the majority of white workers to the
appearance of a Negro co-worker is not so violent. Studies of these
situations have indicated that when strikes and violence have broken
out over the hiring or advancing of Negro workers, these have been

instigated through the activities of a small group of workers, and once this clique has been isolated, the majority of the workers tend to adjust peacefully. Apparently this was the situation in the Philadelphia Rapid Transit strike of 1943. The issue which disturbed most of the strikers was fear that the seniority rights of the newly upgraded Negroes would injure their own seniority rights. The grand jury report indicated that there was only a "comparatively small number who really seriously opposed the employment of Negroes in platform positions." However, a small nucleus of race agitators was able to camouflage their prejudice as protection of seniority rights and in this way enlisted support for the strike among the rank and file workers. Viewed in this light, these agitators can be seen as playing a role similar to that of those who stir up and instigate mobs to violence.

More frequently, the reaction of workers who dislike having a Negro co-worker is silent resentment. If attempts to prevent hiring or advancing a Negro have been unfruitful, many workers will adopt the attitude of ignoring the presence of the racially undesirable. All social and friendly contact with him will be refused. Even associations required by the nature of the job will be kept to a minimum and discontinued as quickly as possible. They will speak to him only if business requires it. They will exclude him from social gatherings organized in the plant or office for the workers, either neglecting to invite him or ignoring him if he should attend. Some will go beyond this conspiracy of silence and seek opportunities to use insulting expressions and derogatory remarks in his hearing. In short, they try to make his working with them as difficult as possible.

There can be no doubt that charity must be considered in instances of this kind. Christians reacting in this way to the presence of a Negro co-worker violate the law of charity. Their actions are sinful, and gravely sinful where the offense given is serious. Charity demands that we show to all, even enemies, the common signs of friendship. These signs are described as courtesies and social amenities ordinarily given to others and whose denial must be considered as indicative of hatred or contempt. Refusal to greet or to return the greeting of a Negro co-worker is to deny him that which he has a right to in charity. To exclude him from office socials for no other reason than the fact that he is a Negro also violates charity. To limit all contact to the minimum demanded by the exigencies of business and at the same time to exclude him from any social contact is to deny the common signs of friendship and is a cause for offense.

Over and beyond the common signs, charity should urge the Christian to further acts. He will not be satisfied with the minimum required to avoid sinning against charity, but will seek ways and opportunities of showing friendship and making life a little easier for his Negro fellow worker. These are acts of supererogation, and they have a twofold effect. They are acts of charity to the Negro worker, easing the tensions caused by resentment and helping him in a difficult situation. They are acts of charity to other white workers, giving good example and encouraging them to show charity when they have been afraid to deviate from common practices. Christians who go beyond the minimum can act as leaven and do much to raise the moral tone of the attitudes of their fellow workers. Even bestowal of the minimum demanded by charity goes far in dispelling prejudice and fear. Experience has shown that in plants where Negro workers have been hired, frequently those who objected find that their fears were baseless. However, a Negro worker cannot be released from the tensions produced by fear and hostility if his co-workers refuse to have anything to do with him — if they refuse to extend the common signs of friendship. Fulfillment of the law of charity is required not only for the spiritual welfare and progress of the white workers, but also for the relaxation of tensions and fears introduced by prejudice and ignorance.

A counterpart of discrimination in hiring is discrimination by unions and its effect on the availability of jobs, as well as the question of the moral obligation of unions to admit qualified nonwhite members. Several states have enacted laws prohibiting racial discrimination in enrolling union members, e.g., New York, California, Nebraska. However, there is no federal statute imposing such an obligation.

Over 18 million American workers hold jobs covered by collective bargaining agreements. This means that about 25 percent of the jobs in the nation are influenced in some way by union policies. Policies exercising this influence may be either internal or external policies. By internal policies are meant union regulations controlling such factors as membership requirements, job referral practices, and participation in apprentice training. The external policies are those expressed by the strength and power of the union and its influence in negotiating conditions and terms of employment with management, regulating such vital items as wages and hours, promotions, job transfers, seniority rights, and the like.

According to the 1961 U. S. Commission on Civil Rights, craft unions and industrial unions manifest racial discrimination differently. Discrimination in the craft union is exercised chiefly in internal policies. Since in these trades, the union hiring hall is the usual instrument for the recruitment of needed craftsmen by contractors, the refusal of union membership can easily mean disbarment of a Negro from a job. On the other hand, industrial unions usually are quite willing to admit Negroes to membership, and since these unions do not control the hiring or the training programs in the way craft unions do, membership refusal would not automatically mean inability to secure a job or training. However, when discrimination occurs in the industrial unions, it is usually in the external policies, particularly the process of collective bargaining. There have been instances of unions being parties to agreements or practices which prevent Negro union members from enjoying equal opportunity, as when a union agrees to the inclusion in a work contract of "separate lines of promotion" for Negro and white workers in which the Negro line of promotion does not permit advancement to skilled jobs, whereas the white line provides for availability of all skilled jobs.

The 1947 Report of President Truman's Committee on Civil Rights pointed out that 6 percent of the complaints received by the FEPC were against union discrimination, and that private industry, when admonished by the FEPC, corrected abuses more readily than the unions. Fourteen years later, the 1961 Commission on Civil Rights still listed union discrimination among factors responsible for the depressed economic situation of the Negroes and admitted the inability of existing governmental machinery to cope with this discrimination, with the possible exception of the President's Committee on Equal Employment Opportunities which has a degree of control over union discrimination when work on government contracts is involved. Among recommendations of the Commission was a proposal that the Labor-Management and Disclosure Act of 1959 be amended to include a provision that no labor organization shall refuse membership, segregate, or expel any person because of race, religion, or nationality.

Most union discrimination has been on the level of the local organization rather than the national or international parent organization. Even when the CIO and AFL were separate, the national bodies constantly condemned discrimination. However, those ideals and practices did not completely filter down to the local level. In the past few years the situation has improved somewhat, especially in the industrial unions. Some have learned through experience that discrimination against Negro workers worked against white members. For example, to escape union influence in the North, industries would frequently move South where the union movement was not so strong or influential, and where there was a supply of cheap labor, with the Negro worker on the bottom. Unions soon came to realize that to guarantee the success of the union movement through the country, Southern labor had to be organized. But when strikes broke out, the companies brought in Negro strikebreakers whom the unions had previously refused to admit to membership. Eventually many unions realized that they could not continue to discriminate if they wanted to succeed.

The Oil, Chemical and Atomic Workers International Union, AFL-CIO, insisted that Negro oil workers in Gulf Coast refineries be unionized because, since both white and Negro worked in the same plant, both should be in the union. It had discovered that a low wage paid to anyone in the plant hurts everyone in the plant. The oil workers were among the first Southern unions to hold integrated meetings. Their record for action in obtaining justice for Negro workers is outstanding. In instances where Negroes were being paid lower wages than white workers doing the same job, the OCAW obtained a federal court order to end the dual wage system. They also forced a discontinuance of the "master-servant" practices prevalent in the plants at that time whereby Negro refinery workers on their days off had to mow lawns and do painting at the homes of white supervisors in order to protect their jobs.[16]

Despite improvements on the local level, many still refuse membership to Negro workers. In Washington, in 1960, AFL-CIO President

[16] *Ibid.*

George Meany spoke of the existence of racial discrimination in the building trade unions:

> Labor cannot in good conscience urge Congress to act against racial discrimination when some of our own affiliated groups themselves are guilty of practicing discrimination . . . here in the District of Columbia . . . there are local unions whose membership and whose apprentice rolls are closed to Negro applicants. Such practices violate every basic tradition of the free trade union movement.[17]

Do unions have a moral right to reject applicants on racial or religious grounds, or must they accept all qualified applicants? We wish to draw attention to the specification *qualified*, for there is no question of a necessity to admit the unqualified. It would be an anomaly for a salesman to seek membership in a mechanics' union. But by *qualified applicants*, we do not mean to include racial origin. The color of a man's skin has nothing to do with his ability as a mechanic. And further, we are prescinding from the question of the right of the union to prevent a surfeit of workers in a certain trade and the danger of depressing wage scales.

Now, some defend the right of a union to reject an applicant on racial or religious grounds, maintaining that the union is a private association with the right to admit only those who have qualities pleasing or agreeable to the majority of its members. However, it is the opinion of the writer that this is not true. The union is not a private association or a private club. Compared to the state, of course, the union is a private society while the state is a public society.

Though in one respect unions can be considered private societies, nevertheless, in another respect they are, at least, semipublic institutions, just as an inn or a hotel is a privately owned public establishment. Railroads and bus lines, despite the fact that in this country they are usually privately owned, are called common carriers, indicating that they must transport all who apply for use of their services. As public institutions, unions must act to serve the good of those qualified to become members. Under present socioeconomic conditions, the rights of workers usually can be effectively protected only

---

[17] Address by George Meany, president, AFL-CIO, 6th National Legislative Conference of the Building and Construction Trades Department, AFL-CIO, Washington, D. C., March 14, 1960, quoted, *1961 Civil Rights Report*, Book 3, "Employment," p. 131.

through a union. Just wages, protection of seniority rights, settlement of grievances, bestowal of pensions and retirement benefits, hospitalization and medical-care insurance — are only some of the benefits which unions have worked diligently to obtain for labor, and which they still protect, to say nothing of the alleviations of rank injustices and unhealthy or dangerous working conditions which they have procured.

Union-shop agreements permit the hiring of nonunion men with the understanding that they will join the union within a specified period, usually thirty days. These agreements have helped to strengthen the ability of the union to protect the rights of the workers. On the other hand, some union leaders believe that the closed shop agreement, whereby union membership is a prerequisite for employment, is necessary for greater security. Obviously, under both arrangements, the ability of a worker to obtain or continue to hold a job is contingent to some degree on union membership. Under these circumstances, refusal to admit to union membership a worker, qualified in all respects except the arbitrary qualification of race, is tantamount to the placing of an obstacle to his exercise of his right to work. This involves a violation of the strict right which he has that unjust means not be used to prevent his securing a good to which he may licitly aspire even though he does not have a strict right to it.

It is the writer's opinion that refusal of union membership can be called unjust since, where the motive is race prejudice, an injustice is involved, namely that contained in contumely which, as we have seen, is a denial of the respect and honor due to a person and is a violation of strict justice. Denial of respect and honor is present because the refusal manifests their opinion that he, because he is a Negro, is not fit or worthy to associate with the union members. Further, I believe that such refusals are unjust because they perpetuate a tragic social disorder, and the intention or desire to enforce such a perpetuation is opposed to social justice. Obviously, if an employer's property must be oriented to advance the social order, it is at least equally necessary that such an association as a union has an obligation to the social order and the common good. The union is more intimately and immediately involved in obligations of social justice than an individual. Discrimination in extending union membership should, it would appear, be considered as unjust means used to prevent a

Negro from securing a good, viz., a job or promotion, to which he has no strict right, but to which he could lawfully aspire, safeguarded by the strict right that no one use unjust means to frustrate his endeavors.

The Labor-Management Relations Act contains a provision intended to protect minority groups. It states that an employer who has entered a union-shop contract cannot justify the firing of an employee who has not become a union member "if he has reasonable grounds for believing that such membership was not available to the employee on the terms and conditions generally applicable to other members." It is, however, unfortunate that the relief provided is available only if, and when, it can be proved that dismissal was based on the fact of membership or nonmembership. It does not provide relief if dismissal was based on race. Thus, if an employer refuses to hire a Negro *because of nonmembership in a union* which has refused to grant membership to him, the employer violates the law and the employee is entitled to compensation for his losses. But if the employer refuses to hire him *because of race*, there is no violation of the statute although there may be a violation of a local FEPC law if one exists in that area. On one occasion the General Counsel for the National Labor Relations Board ruled that a union did not violate the Labor-Management Relations Act when it secured the discharge of a Negro employee on *racial grounds*. Thus while there is some provision for relief for losses incurred because the union will not admit to membership, it is clear that presentation of proof of motivation, showing that loss was sustained *because of nonmembership in the union and not because of racial prejudice*, will involve a long and costly court fight which, in practice, would be impossible for an individual employee fighting against a union and a large corporation, both of which have ample funds and a formidable battery of legal experts.

Further, in instances of open-shop agreements where only some employees are union members, it is the opinion of the writer that the refusal of the union to admit qualified applicants also violates strict justice. Even though in this instance, a worker is able to retain his job without being a member of the union, nevertheless, his right to protect and utilize opportunities of advancement, and his right to a just wage and proper working conditions are all being jeopardized.

It seems to this writer that the union, even in this instance, has an ex officio obligation to admit to membership all the qualified workers in the unit who apply and it cannot justify its refusal on the basis of race. The reason for this conclusion is based on the obligation of the union to provide fair representation not only for union members, but for all workers in the unit it represents.

The Labor-Management Relations Act grants a union statutory power to represent all the workers of a certain craft within a given unit. One of the powers of the NLRB is the certification of a union as collective bargaining representative. The process of obtaining this certification is for the union to file a petition stating it represents certain employees. The NLRB will then designate a bargaining unit; that is, it will determine which employees are to be included in the group to be represented by this union, and it then conducts an election among the members of that unit. If a majority of them desire to be represented by the union, the Board will certify the union as representative for all the members of the unit, and the employer must bargain only with that union. In this way, the union receives the power and authority to make contracts with employers regulating hours, wages, and working conditions. Since the union receives this power from the law, it has an obligation to give fair representation to all the workers within the unit, whether or not they are union members. The principle of the obligation of fair representation was given legal expression in Steele v. Louisville and N. RR. when it was determined that Negroes working within a certain unit, even though they had been refused union membership, were entitled to be represented by the union, and that the union had an obligation of providing fair representation.[18]

In 1957, the U. S. Supreme Court declared that this obligation included making day-to-day adjustments in various work rules, settling problems not covered by agreement, and protecting the rights granted in the work contract for nonunion workers.[19] However, to date the Court has not declared that this obligation of fair representation includes admittance to union membership on a nondiscriminatory

---

[18] Steele v. Louisville and N. RR., 323 U. S. 192 (1944); also Syres v. Oil Workers International Union, Local No. 23, 350 U. S. 892 (1955).
[19] Conley v. Gibson, 355 U. S. 41 (1957).

basis. In addition, the NLRB has, for the most part, shied away from making specific requirements for union membership, and, in fact, has declared that exclusion from membership or segregated union membership would not *per se* violate the obligation of fair representation.

Despite the refusal of the NLRB to declare that fair representation includes availability of union membership on nondiscriminatory basis, and the Court of Appeals' support of the right of a union to set up discriminatory qualifications for membership, it does not seem that a union can provide fair representation to a worker whom it has turned down as a member. Remembering that the law gives the union the right to make work contracts binding all the workers, including the excluded nonmembers, and that these contracts affect wages, hours, working conditions, opportunities for advancement, as well as rights of seniority and the settlement of grievances, I cannot understand how the union can be said to be fairly representing when it has excluded certain workers from any voice or participation in union policies or decisions. For these reasons, I believe that the union has an obligation *ex officio* to make membership available to all workers within the unit it represents without discrimination, and that the refusal to to do this violates commutative justice.

Father Gerald Kelly, speaking of the fact that discrimination in hiring by an employer violates social justice even though the worker does not have a strict right to a job, has wisely added that this situation does not obtain in the case of labor unions refusing to admit Negroes to membership. He believes that when they discriminate on racial grounds, the violation of social justice is not so immediate, but rather there is a violation of commutative justice, and, as can be seen from above, the writer fully concurs with Father Kelly's contention.[20]

[20] Gerald Kelly, S.J., "Moral Aspects of Industrial Relations," *Theological Studies*, XII (1951), 59–65; reprinted *Catholic Mind*, 50 (1952), 33–39.

CHAPTER 13

THE RIGHT TO MARRY

No area of race relations is more highly charged emotionally than the matter of interracial marriage. Opposition to these marriages ranks first in the order of separations which whites are most insistent in preserving and retaining. Although resistance to school integration is often explained on the grounds of educational inability and inequalities, or health, more frequently there is a deep fear that educational integration will lead to interracial marriage. Recently this apprehension was expressed by some segregationists: "The key that opens the door of the schoolroom to niggers unlocks the door to the bedroom, too."[1] Racial purists insist on holding firm against any removal of social barriers which could lead to marriage and subsequent "mongrelization of the race." According to Virginius Dabney, all Southern resistance to school integration must be considered in terms of opposition to racial intermarriage in order to understand its vehemence:

> No argument against integrated schools carries greater weight with white Virginians and other white Southerners than the prospect that education of the races together in the elementary and secondary schools will lead to ultimate interracial amalgamation and make ours a nation of mulattoes.[2]

The deep emotionalism found in racial prejudices and especially in the opposition to interracial marriage often seeks an irrefutable argument against any alleviation of racial segregation in such clichés as, "Would you want your sister to marry a Negro?" This fear of racial intermarriage is not restricted to the American scene. Even in South Africa, under stricter and more odious segregation patterns of

---

[1] Wilma Dykeman and James Stokely, *Neither Black nor White* (New York: Rinehart and Co., 1957), p. 26.
[2] Virginius Dabney, "Peaceable, Honorable Stand," *Life*, September 22, 1958.

154

apartheid, this fear of intermarriage is predominant and is an important factor in racial relations. Trevor Huddleston has indicated the predominance of this fear of racial intermarriage.

> Miscegenation, that fearful spectre which hovers over all South African society, is certainly regarded as a sin more mortal than any in the handbook of moral theology. "Am I my brother's keeper?" is a question which must for ever take second place to "Would you like your sister to marry a black man?"[3]

Today the word "miscegenation" has acquired an aura of scientific respectability which completely overshadows and conceals its interesting, though dubious, origin. Rather than having a scientific origin, the word was coined in a political struggle to obtain votes. It appeared for the first time as a neologism in a small pamphlet entitled: *Miscegenation: The Theory of the Blending of the Races, Applied to the American White Man and Negro*, published anonymously in New York in 1864. Ostensibly, it purported to be written by an abolitionist who advocated not only emancipation, but also marriages between the newly freed slaves and white women. In reality, it was authored by two journalists on the staff of the anti-Abolitionist paper, *The New York World*, David Goodman Croly, the managing editor, and George Wakeman, a reporter.

In this pamphlet, two new words are used and explained which were coined for use in this work. These were *miscegenation* (Latin: *miscere*, "to mix" and *genus*, "race"), and *melaleukation* (Greek: *melas*, "black" and *leukos*, "white"). Only the former neologism received popular acceptance and passed from the pamphlet into the English language and common usage.

By this pamphlet, the authors attempted to swing votes from Lincoln in the 1864 election by appealing to the fear of the voters, especially the Irish, of marriage between emancipated slaves and Irish women. With the memory of the New York City draft riots and the anti-Negro reactions still fresh in the minds of the people, this pamphlet proclaimed:

> Wherever there is a poor community of Irish in the North they naturally herd with the poor Negroes . . . connubial relations are formed

---
[3] Trevor Huddleston, *Naught for your Comfort* (Garden City: Doubleday & Co., 1956), p. 110.

between the black men and white Irish women . . . pleasant to both parties, and were it not for the unhappy prejudice which exists, such unions would be very much more frequent. The white Irishwoman loves the black man and in the old country . . . the Negro is sure of the handsomest among the poor white females. . . . The fusion, whenever it takes place, will be of infinite service to the Irish. They are a more brutal race and lower in civilization than the Negro . . . coarsegrained, revengeful, unintellectual . . . below the level of the most degraded Negro. Take an equal number of Negroes and Irish from among the lowest communities of the city of New York, and the former will be found far superior to the latter in cleanliness, education, moral feelings, beauty of form and feature, and natural sense.[4]

Then, in pseudo-support of Lincoln's reelection, the authors ask that the President declare that the "solution of the Negro problem will not have been reached in this country until public opinion sanctions a union of the two races . . . that in the millennial future, the most perfect and highest type of manhood will not be white or black but brown, or colored."

The pamphlet was an immediate success. Five months after its appearance, the miscegenation controversy had spread far beyond the New York City area and reached Boston, Philadelphia, Detroit, and St. Louis, and had become a major political issue. Politically, however, its success was somewhat limited. It failed to prevent Lincoln's re-election, although in New York City, where in 1860 he had polled 33,000 votes while his opponent received 62,000, in 1864 after the miscegenation controversy, Lincoln received only 36,000 votes compared to McClellan's 78,000. The flow of history has buried this pamphlet in obscurity, but its legacy of the word *miscegenation* to our dictionaries has endured.

Fear of interracial marriage is so widespread that there have been enacted specific statutes which prohibit it in states as widely separated geographically and socially as Mississippi and Nebraska, Alabama and Utah. Twenty-two states have laws forbidding interracial marriage. Some prohibit it between Negro and white; others extend the prohibition to marriage between a white person and a person of such races as Mongolian, Hindu, Korean, Malayan, Indian, or Mestizo. An

---

[4] Sidney Kaplan, "Miscegenation Issue in the Election of 1864," *Journal of Negro History*, 34 (July, 1949), 274–343; cf. also J. M. Bloch, *Miscegenation, Melaleukation, and Mr. Lincoln's Dog* (New York: Schaum Publishing Co., 1958).

interesting fact is revealed through a comparison of these laws. Nineteen states have laws which protect the "purity" of the white race by prohibiting interracial marriage if a white party is involved. Only three states prohibit interracial marriage if a white person is not involved — Louisiana prohibits marriage between Indians and Negroes; Maryland bans it between Negroes and Malayans; while Oklahoma prohibits marriage of one who is of African descent with one who is not of African descent. Apparently, in the other nineteen states, the purity of only the white race is of concern to the legislators and only marriage involving a white person with a member of another race is prohibited, but not marriage between members of various nonwhite races. Justification of these laws on the grounds that they insure "purity of the races" seems difficult in view of the fact that it is usually the "purity" of the white race which is being preserved.

Surprisingly, the Supreme Court has never ruled on the constitutionality of these state laws. Greenberg believes that this refusal to exercise jurisdiction in these intermarriage cases may be based on the fact that the Court did not believe that the practical advantages of airing this subject would work for the best interest of the public at the present time, especially while such strong antagonism and opposition are still being voiced to the school decisions.[5] Fortunately, the moral problems involved in the question of interracial marriage have been excellently handled in a dissertation submitted to the Catholic University of America by Rev. Joseph F. Doherty.[6]

Apparently the prohibition of interracial marriage has had a long history in American legal annals. In 1843, Francis Patrick Kenrick states that they have no force as impediments to the exercise of natural rights which rights extend to cases of interracial marriage:

> In some States, marriage between whites and Negroes is prohibited by law and considered invalid. However, they are valid by ecclesiastical law so long as the impediment of servile condition does not occur. If some wish to enter such a marriage, they cannot be forbidden the sacraments because of a legal prohibition or public opinion since they are exercising a natural right which the Church in no way prohibits.[7]

[5] J. Greenberg, op. cit., p. 345.
[6] Joseph F. Doherty, Moral Problems of Interracial Marriage (Washington, D. C.: The Catholic University of America Press, 1949).
[7] Francis P. Kenrick, Theologiae Moralis (Philadelphia: Eugene Cummiskey, 1843), III, p. 334.

It is interesting to note that in the 1861 edition of this work, there was added a caution to this paragraph which did not appear in the original edition: *Caeterum non decet sacerdotem suam operam iis conjungendis praestare.* Perhaps stricter enforcement of these laws with their heavy penalties of fines and imprisonment of officiating ministers had become more prevalent as a reaction to the increase of abolitionist propaganda between 1840 and 1860.

Monsignor Gilligan, speaking of the morality of interracial marriages, admits there is nothing intrinsically wrong with them, but that extrinsic factors make these marriages, for the most part, wrong. Father John LaFarge, who has written widely on interracial matters, says that they are inadvisable at the present time because of the opposition of public opinion and the existence of the various state laws, but that, nevertheless, these factors were not sufficient to render such marriages wrong or to impede them. Monsignor Gilligan expresses his objections:

> Even though the biological and social evils of miscegenation have not been proved and are probably incapable of proof, a marriage between a Negro and a white person in the United States at the present time, would place a considerable handicap on the moral life of the contracting parties. For that reason it would be wrong in an overwhelming number of cases for a member of either race to enter into an interracial marriage.[8]

Thus, writing over thirty years ago, he believes that prudence demands that the best means to guarantee a peaceful and compatible marriage be used, and, in addition, piety demands that the couple establish a home which will protect, safeguard, and guarantee the physical and moral well-being of the children. For these reasons, he believes, *in the light of circumstances of the 1920's* that it would be an extraordinary case where an interracial marriage does not carry a strong presumption of becoming an unhappy marriage and of eventually breaking up, and that such marriages expose the parties to grave temptations to violate their marital obligations. He draws a parallel between interracial marriage and a marriage between a European peasant and noble. Older theologians, treating of these peasant-noble marriages, held that because of quarrels and regrets on the part

---

[8] Francis Gilligan, *Morality of the Color Line*, p. 92.

of the couple, as well as the shame and dishonor inflicted on the relatives, such marriages were often illicit. Monsignor Gilligan concludes that if these peasant-noble marriages were frequently to be judged improper, then equally, most interracial marriages are wrong.

Father Doherty's study, however, disagrees with the conclusions of Monsignor Gilligan. He admits the role of prudence in considering the dangers in a given situation, and the necessity of weighing these dangers against the benefits sought in such a marriage, but he insists that there will also be natural and supernatural benefits produced by the marriage which must also be considered. Piety, of course, requires that provision be made for a home to safeguard the well-being of the children and promote their corporeal and spiritual education. But he maintains that the right of a man to marry the person of his prudent choice is more immediate and more urgent than obligations toward children who might be born in such a union.

It appears that the prudence of interracial marriage will have to be determined on an individual basis. Circumstances in each case will vary and this variation will determine, in a specific instance, whether entrance upon such a marriage is prudent for this particular couple. Personality characteristics of the couple; cultural, educational, and social background, common attitudes of their relatives and friends regarding interracial marriage; their economic situation; the place where they intend to establish a home; existent laws in the state which may subject them to harassment or civil disabilities — are some of the variables to be considered before an interracial marriage can be judged prudent or imprudent. These are factors arising solely because of the interracial character of the marriage and are in addition to the ordinary considerations which must be made before every prospective marriage. However, it does not seem that the social disadvantages which accrue to the children violate the virtue of piety. The writer would agree with Father Doherty's conclusion that the right of a person to marry according to his choice is more basic and fundamental, and that this right and its exercise take precedence over any such obligation to children who may be born of such a union. Hence these obligations to future children would not affect the judgment of an interracial marriage which otherwise could be judged prudent.

The impossibility of making generalizations regarding the chance of success of interracial marriage is underscored in Monsignor J. D. Conway's column where he indicated the difficulties imposed on such marriages by prejudice and the necessity of considering carefully these realities before entering upon such marriages. Later he published a letter from the partners of an interracial marriage who had been married for twelve years. They stated that they had not been rejected socially but had made numerous friends of each race and were on friendly terms with all their neighbors. Nor did their three children suffer the disadvantages so often feared. Monsignor Conway's comment on their letter represents an excellent summary of the various elements which must be considered in an interracial marriage:

> Never have I been so pleased to be refuted. But I did hedge my generalizations by stating that no type of marriage is doomed to failure. Your letter helps prove my prudence in leaving an avenue of escape. And you prove much more: that the success of the marriage depends on the partners, on their personalities and temperaments, their love and unselfishness, their willingness to make sacrifices and overlook the petty things of life, their faith and trust in God, their confidence in friends and neighbors.[9]

Regarding the justice of state laws prohibiting interracial marriage and which, with a single exception, declare such unions invalid *ab initio*, it can be said that as these apply to the baptized they are not just laws. They violate justice by imposing an obligation on the baptized in reference to the reception of a sacrament. Application of such laws to the baptized would be tantamount to the state's establishment of conditions for the reception of a sacrament and the constitution of a diriment impediment to the reception of the sacrament of Matrimony, which power the state does not possess. Father Doherty described these laws as unjust and summed up the basic and fundamental principles involved:

> As far as the baptized are concerned, these laws are not just laws. They offend against commutative justice because they impose an obligation on baptized persons who are not subjects of the State as to Matrimony. Only the Church founded by Christ and entrusted by Him with authority over *res sacrae* for the baptized can impose laws on baptized persons in matters pertaining to the sacraments. As a result, *per se* the laws forbidding miscegenetic marriages to baptized persons cannot be binding on these subjects. It makes no difference whether

[9] J. D. Conway, *What They Ask about Morals* (Notre Dame: Fides, 1960), pp. 332–335.

the baptized persons in this instance be Catholic or non-Catholic, for the State is incompetent in both cases. Marriage is a sacrament for all baptized parties if it is rightly entered upon.[10]

On the other hand, resolution of the problem of their application to the nonbaptized is not so manifest. Both civil lawyers as well as some canonists have seriously questioned the justice of these laws and their validity. Father Owen Cloran, S.J., in a recent canonical work on marriage, questions their validity as applied to the unbaptized:

> The justice of civil laws for unbaptized subjects, forbidding miscegenous marriages, as, for example, between whites and Negroes, or whites and Asiatics, or Aryans and Jews, under pain of nullity, can well be questioned. If such laws are shown to be invalid, even if restricted to the unbaptized, the validity of the marriage would prevail.[11]

Some Catholic writers, on the other hand, have maintained that these laws when applied to the marriages of nonbaptized were just. Father Goldsmith stated that he could see no reason which would prevent the state from establishing racial difference as a diriment impediment for marriages of the nonbaptized. These laws, he stated, did not oppose the natural law because they did not take away the right to marry, but merely placed certain restrictions on the exercise of that right.[12]

Others admitting the existence of a serious doubt as to the justice of these laws maintain that until the matter is definitely settled, the benefit of the doubt should be given to the state on the principle that in case of a doubtfully just law, the law is to be considered just until the contrary is proved.

It would appear, however, that instead of being unjust only in instances of marriage involving a baptized person, these laws are unjust and invalid in their application to all marriages, including those between nonbaptized persons. Even if we grant the right of the state to enact diriment impediments to marriage between infidels, nevertheless, it has a serious obligation to respect the basic right of

---

[10] Joseph F. Doherty, *op. cit.*, p. 101.

[11] Owen M. Cloran, S.J., *Preview and Practical Cases on Marriage* (Milwaukee: The Bruce Publishing Co., 1960), Vol. 1, "Preliminaries and Impediments," Canons 1012–1080, p. 13.

[12] J. William Goldsmith, *The Competence of Church and State over Marriage — Disputed Points* (Washington, D. C.: The Catholic University of America Press, 1944), p. 84.

individuals to marry, and hence, has an obligation not to restrict that right save for the promotion of the common good. Obviously, protection of the "purity" of the races cannot be offered as a good falling within the jurisdiction of the state, nor, as has been seen, has it been a consideration in the enactment of these laws. Hence, it does not appear that these laws can be justified on this basis. Prevention of public disturbances which may be caused by public resentment to such marriages seems to be the strongest argument that can be adduced to justify these laws. However, an examination of the origin of the laws indicates that there have been very few, if any, recorded instances of disturbances being the basis of such enactments. In an article on the history of miscegenous unions in the United States, Negro historian Carter G. Woodson indicates that opposition to these marriages sparked a riot in 1834 in Columbia, Pennsylvania, and another riot in 1849. Father Doherty indicates that as far as he can verify these are the only recorded instances of riots occasioned by interracial marriages, and that these occurred over a hundred years ago. It would appear the presumption or fear of the possibility of disturbances is a weak reason for suppression of such important human rights.

The right to marry is a basic human right and the right to marry a person of one's choice is a necessary corollary. Hence, laws which declare marriages invalid solely because of racial differences are unjust laws because they interfere with the exercise of this right. This right to marry a person of one's choice belongs to all, baptized or unbaptized, by reason of their nature. These laws are unjust not merely because they interfere with the right of the baptized to receive a sacrament, but because they impede a basic natural right.

To sum up, the writer would agree with Father Doherty's assertion that it is certain that laws forbidding interracial marriage are unjust even in their application to the unbaptized, and that the opinion maintaining that they are valid laws cannot be sustained; that there is no obligation in conscience per se to obey these laws; and that interracial marriages of the unbaptized are valid even though such a law may be in force where the marriages were contracted. Father Doherty's summary of his reasons for asserting that it is morally certain that these laws are unjust represents, I believe, the correct position.

1. There is no proportion between the good effects these laws are

supposed to produce and the deprivation of a fundamental human right.

2. Failure of these laws to obtain their objective, i.e., prevention of racial mixture; on the other hand, these laws have been encouragements of concubinage, sources of interracial conflicts, and instruments of deprivation of legal and property rights of widows and children which should have been theirs if the marriages were recognized as valid.

3. Other reasons offered to justify these laws are grossly inadequate, e.g., presumption that all interracial marriages are imprudent; protection of "purity of race"; the claim that these laws represent good public policy.

4. Racism which is the ultimate foundation of such laws is contrary to Catholic teaching.

It should not be thought that affirmation of the basic right to marry the person of one's choice as extending to interracial marriage is made without regard to or concern for the special problems and difficulties which such marriages entail in view of the racial attitudes presently prevalent in this country. Interracial marriages are subject to social, economic, and civil handicaps from which other marriages are exempt. Father Messner, speaking of the problems which beset interracial marriages, believes that they originate from the transfer of the partners to a different environment:

> It is this problem of the change of environment which is chiefly involved in the intermarriage of members of different races and as such it is a problem which equally concerns eugenics and ethics. Marriages resulting in the transplantation of one or both parties into an entirely different cultural environment may have favorable or unfavorable psychological effects. It is mainly by experience that the effects of such intermarriages can be judged, and the experience available up to the present day does not seem to permit the forming of a general principle, except that, on the whole, it is a matter of grave consideration for the parties before they contract such a "mixed marriage." The uprooting of one or both parties from their original environment involves the danger of failure to become "acclimatized," with the further danger that the parties may be unable to form that integral union of souls which is eminently desirable in marriage.[13]

However, I do not believe that this situation obtains in the matter of interracial marriages in the United States. The situation en-

---

[13] J. Messner, op. cit., p. 380.

visaged by Messner apparently seems descriptive of the peasant-noble marriage, and in which there is definitely a change of social milieu, mode of life, conduct, and responsibilities. On the other hand, interracial marriages in this country are usually between a couple economically, educationally, and more or less socially equal, even though their social standings will be within their racial groups. Indeed, it would be most unusual to find an interracial marriage in which there were vast differences of education, economic, and cultural position. In other words, an interracial "peasant-millionaire" marriage is most rare. As a result, the problems which interracial marriages have to face arise not so much from transplantation to different cultural environments, as from isolation from familial and social ties, nonacceptance in communities, and the overall racial discriminatory practices.

This newly experienced isolation from former social contacts can, in a certain sense, be considered as a change of environment for the racially mixed couple, but it is a change different from that depicted by Messner. He considers a common racial origin as supplying people with a twofold common environment. The first, a common spiritual environment which is the result of the use of one language as a means of expressing ideas and values held in common, and the second, an external environment, resulting from dwelling together in common territory.

But in the United States, the "change of environment" effected in interracial marriages comes from social pressures and rejections of the couple, which are the result of the action of free agents. Rarely are these couples fully and freely accepted by the opposite racial group, even within family lines. A son-in-law or daughter-in-law of a different race will almost always feel racial tensions and lack full acceptance by the spouse's family. The opposition, however, of the Negro and the white parents to the interracial marriage will vary in intensity and motivation. The Negro parents may doubt the intelligence of the white partner or his ability to realize the implications involved in such a marriage, or they may question his sincerity. But the interracial marriage does not mean the loss of status for the Negro parents that it would for the white parents, and they will usually accept the white partner when they become convinced of his sincerity. The white parents, however, because of the loss of status which this marriage means for them, will protest the marriage more violently and intensely.[14] Racially homogeneous groups of other married couples rarely give complete welcome to an interracial couple. Ordinary problems confronting married couples now have the added factor of a racial problem, and are increased because of it. In other words, ties and relationships which they had when they were single, within their own racial group, are not available to them as husband and wife. If these bonds of old acquaintances are not completely severed, they often can only be maintained on an individual basis. If one wants to see or visit old acquaintances or friends, it is necessary to leave the spouse home. All these things tend to magnify the problems which they face. Often, too, the children of such marriages are not accepted by grandparents on either side or by other relatives because of mixed race. Such rejections will embitter a parent not only toward the relatives, but frustration and inability to avenge the rejection of the children will move them to "take it out" on husband or wife.

Those contemplating an interracial marriage should be made aware of the peculiar situations and difficulties which they will have to face in addition to the usual problems of married life. Marriage counselors, advisors, and priests should not hesitate to expose candidly and realistically these future problems. In fact, they would be negligent if they underplayed or toned down such matters.

However, if after a prudent explanation and careful study of these problems, a couple believe and hope they are going to be able to overcome these difficulties and are willing to make preparations and take efficient steps to ameliorate the impact of social rejection and racial tension which most likely will arise, then no one can say that such a marriage is forbidden under pain of sin. Indeed, a Christian couple, whose marriage will necessarily be a sacrament, can rightly expect to receive those aids and graces from the sacrament which are proper to it and which will enable them to overcome the problems which arise from obligations imposed by the state of matrimony.

---

[14] Robert Senser, *Primer on Interracial Justice* (Baltimore: Helicon Press, 1962), pp. 102–103.

CHAPTER 14

THE RIGHT TO DECENT HOUSING

Segregated housing and discriminatory practices in making housing available to racial minorities form an iceberg in the sea of race relations. At first glance all that is seen is a racial group, restricted to certain sections in which, though much of the housing is substandard, there are some houses whose owners keep them up — the important thing is that "objectionable" people are kept out of white neighborhoods where they would cause deterioration of the neighborhood and a consequent depreciation of real-estate values. This, for the most part, is the usual superficial evaluation of housing segregation. But it exhibits only the surface. As with an iceberg, the greater and more dangerous part lies hidden and invisible, below the waterline.

Physical segregation into restricted areas of residence is a necessary condition for effective operation of many forms of racial discrimination and prejudice. School segregation, for example, is almost an inevitable consequence of housing segregation. Davis McEntire has summed up this important corelation:

A group segregated in residence is necessarily segregated in schools, recreation, and other facilities organized on an area basis. Discriminatory in itself, residential segregation permits and stimulates other forms of discrimination. When a minority group is physically isolated, differential treatment follows almost as a matter of course.[1]

Segregation seriously effects the amount of housing available to the Negro either for rental or purchase, as well as the price he has to pay

---

[1] Davis McEntire, *Residence and Race: Final and Comprehensive Report to the Commission on Race and Housing* (Berkeley: University of California Press, 1960), p. 89.

for it. One would expect that the law of the marketplace would have the primary influence on these items, and that where there was a demand, enterprising marketers would bend every effort to satisfy that demand, and the price would vary in accordance with the scarcity of the product and the size of the demand. The actual need of the Negro community for housing, however, plays only a secondary role in determining how much housing is to be made available. Factors such as the desirability of a section for white residency; the rigidity with which segregation to certain areas is enforced; and the resistance of whites to Negro entry are more important in the regulation of the amount of available housing. The fact that the population in a Negro section exceeds the amount of housing, so that there is serious over-crowding and a grave need for more housing, does not automatically make it available in adjacent areas. The selectivity range for a Negro home purchaser as to location, size, availability, age, or facilities is rigidly regulated by fluctuation in the amount of property available to him rather than by ability to pay.

Actually, the available supply is the product of a completely arti-ficial situation in which the law of supply and demand becomes opera-tive *after* the quantity which will be available has been determined. Then, if the supply exceeds the demand or is financially inaccessible, the price will drop. But if the demand and need are great, and there is financial ability to pay so that the demand exceeds the supply, a critical housing shortage is produced. But other housing is not auto-matically made available to satisfy this demand.

A further disability, indicated by McEntire, is that the available housing, for the most part, is of inferior quality for the price which the Negro family must pay for it. The Negro, as a rule, pays more than a white purchaser or renter does for similar housing:

> The housing for which minority homeseekers are permitted to com-pete is not only a small but on the whole a very inferior part of the total housing supply. Thus restricted, non-whites receive poorer housing than do whites, even when they pay the same rents or purchase prices. The differential is very wide in the South, but it exists throughout the country and through the whole range of rents. There are great numbers of non-white families who can afford only cheap housing; yet the dwell-ings they receive are poorer than need be on the basis of rent alone.[2]

---

[2] *Ibid.*, p. 92.

Robert C. Weaver, administrator of the Housing and Home Finance Agency in the Kennedy administration, has made the observation, based on his study of the 1940 census, that the Negro family gets less for its housing dollar than the white family and that even if the Negro family is able to pay an economic rent, it has less chance of securing decent housing for it.[3]

Further burdens of greater cost for the Negro are imposed in higher mortgage interest rates which are often charged. Frequently, since the only housing available is in an older section of town which is usually rundown, the financial institutions may refuse to make a mortgage loan. And in instances where they will do so, they allow mortgages only for smaller amounts and shorter periods at higher interest rates. This does not mean that all higher interest rates are instances of racial discrimination or represent excessive charges levied because of the Negro's need. Rather, the higher interest cost may be necessitated by the greater risk to the mortgagee when he accepts a mortgage on less desirable property.

Housing segregation, by producing large concentrates of racially distinct groups, causes distinctions to be more prominent and it enables whites to apply prejudicial axioms while they ignore individual abilities or characteristics. The very fact of segregation to a certain area is a bulwark to the notion that those who are segregated there deserve such separation and ought to be kept there.

But the most devastating effect of housing deficiencies is the disruption of family life. Inadequate housing, with a lack of facilities which would ensure cleanliness, privacy, and proper home life, take a great toll in precluding proper family relationships. To pay the higher rents and housing costs, the mother of the family may have to supplement the family income by accepting employment outside the home. She will have to leave school-age children alone and unsupervised, and will be compelled to bring babies and preschool children to day nurseries or entrust them to the daily care of a friend or relative. Another resource utilized for income supplementation is the renting of rooms. At times not only an individual is rented a room, but even a second family will move in to share the same housing in order to

---

[3] Robert C. Weaver, *The Negro Ghetto* (New York: Harcourt, Brace & Co., 1948), p. 261.

carry the high cost of purchase or rent. This solution too often results in overcrowded conditions, and in jealousy, fighting, immorality, and even the moral corruption of the children, especially when the parents are unable to be properly selective in the acceptance of an outsider. McEntire has stressed this harm done to family life by housing problems:

> Lack of space is probably the deficiency of minority-group housing most harmful in its impact on family living. Adequate space is generally recognized as an indispensable requisite of good housing whether the buildings be new or old, well or poorly equipped. A good family life is hardly possible unless there is space for carrying on and separating different activities, and for individual privacy. To maintain cleanliness and order is extremely difficult in cramped quarters used by too many people for too many purposes. The constant association of household members, unrelieved by opportunity for privacy, is apt to generate more tension than affection. There is evidence that crowding may be damaging to mental health and to the personality formation of children. Persons with concern for family life, when they are in the market for a house, try to pay particular attention to factors of design, facilities, and location which promote happy family relations. But most Negro or Puerto Rican families have little opportunity for these choices.[4]

Thus segregated housing produces effects which are far-reaching and extend beyond those immediately apparent. The psychological, spiritual, and moral, as well as the physical, damage is inflicted not only on the segregated minority group, but is also a threat and a problem for the entire community.

The development of segregated housing has a different history in the North than in the South. During slavery, in the South, a segregated Negro section did not exist. Slaves dwelt on the property of their owners. It is true they occupied small cabins, but nevertheless they lived close to the homes of the masters. In recent years, in the South, there has been a steady trend toward establishment of separate residential areas, even though racially mixed areas may be found in some of the older Southern cities. However, when new areas are developed or suburbs are divided into residential sections, the trend has been almost unanimously toward segregated areas. On the other hand, in the North, particularly in cities where the Negro population was small and to which they have since come as migrants, the Negroes

---

4 Davis McEntire, op. cit., pp. 93–94.

have always lived in segregated sections. Lack of cultural advancement, poverty, and the same tendency to congregate that was manifested by white immigrants were factors which led to this pattern.

In the North, Negroes usually lived in small groups, with a few Negro families living on the same street, and, according to their numbers, several of these small groupings might be found in various parts of a city. However, variations in this pattern can be seen in such cities as Minneapolis, where the Negro population was spread throughout the entire city, and this pattern has continued even though the Negro population increased. On the other hand, early in the history of Chicago and Detroit, there were clearly defined sections which became impacted as the Negro migration increased after the two World Wars.

To restrict Negroes to segregated areas and to prevent their "invasion" of all-white neighborhoods by buying or renting there, several techniques have been developed. First, an attempt was made to exclude them by direct racial zoning. Laws were enacted which prohibited occupancy of housing by nonwhites in certain areas. However, this excluding device was struck down by the courts and declared unconstitutional. The U. S. Supreme Court ruled racial zoning unconstitutional in its 1917 decision in *Buchanan v. Warley*. This case involved a zoning ordinance of Louisville, Kentucky, prohibiting residency by members of one race in areas predominantly occupied by members of another race. Despite the fact that the "separate but equal" doctrine of *Plessy v. Ferguson* was still the prevalent legal concept, the Court declared that such racial zoning denied the due process of law, and that the "separate but equal" concept did not apply to real property rights. Of further interest at this time is the comparatively early reply to the objection that such racial zoning was required to prevent riots and racial disturbances and preserve the public peace:

> It is urged that this proposed segregation will promote the public peace by preventing race conflicts. Desirable as this is, and important as is the preservation of the public peace, this aim cannot be accomplished by laws or ordinances which deny rights created or protected by the Federal Constitution.[5]

Since this decision, racial zoning has become a rarely used tool for

---

[5] 245 U. S. at 82 (1917).

housing restriction. However, it should not be thought that it has completely disappeared. In 1940, the North Carolina Supreme Court had to hear, for final disposition, a case involving such zoning. In 1949, the city of Birmingham enforced zoning on the grounds that it was necessary in order to prevent racial violence. The U. S. Circuit Court, however, ruled that the claim that Negro families moving into white neighborhoods produced racial violence was immaterial, and when the city authorities appealed this decision, the U. S. Supreme Court refused to consider the case. Greenberg reports that Palm Beach had a racial zoning ordinance, which was in force in 1959, at the time he made his study.[6]

The second form of racial housing exclusion, which is not as direct as zoning, but nevertheless effective as a means of enforcing segregation, is the "restrictive covenant." This restriction attached to the real property itself and was to last for a certain period of time, usually fifty years. It provided that if, at any time within that period, the property was sold or transferred in any way to a nonwhite, the nonwhite owner could be subject to legal action to divest him of his title and to revert the property to a white owner. In 1948, the U. S. Supreme Court decreed that restrictive covenants were *unenforceable at law.* The Court did not prevent or outlaw the making or entering into a restrictive covenant, but it decreed that if one was made, the state could not, through judicial enforcement, effect divestment of title to a white owner.[7]

Before the 1948 decision, restrictive covenants were widespread and covered the greater part of the most desirable residential properties. The extent of the property covered by such agreements can be seen in the 1948 report of the President's Committee on Civil Rights which estimated that 80 percent of the total amount of land in Chicago was covered by restrictive covenant.

Many devices and subterfuges have been evolved to evade the ruling of nonenforceability. For example, several real-estate brokers enter into agreement not to sell property to certain minority groups. Financial institutions agree not to lend to a Negro buying a house in a white

---

[6] *Holland v. Board of Pub. Instruction*, 258 F. 2d 730, 731 (5th Cir., 1958); cf. J. Greenberg, op. cit., pp. 275–279.

[7] *Shelley v. Kraemer*, 334 U. S. 1, 4 (1948).

neighborhood. Neighborhood improvement associations are formed by white owners who by united action are able to apply sanctions, financial and social, against members who are considering sale of their property to Negroes.

The third restrictive device is recourse to violence and force to keep out nonwhites or to terrorize and drive out those who insist on occupancy of their property. Unfortunately, there have been too many shameful instances of violence used to drive out Negro neighbors. The list of cities in which such violence has erupted since the end of World War II is long, and includes Southern, Northern, and Western cities. Bombings, stonings, and arson have occurred in such cities as Birmingham, Miami, Washington, Nashville, the Bronx, Houston, Dallas, Atlanta, and Los Angeles. In addition, there have been serious outbreaks in the Detroit area as well as in Cook County, Illinois.

The violence has run the gamut of variations and includes stonings, arson, assault, and bombings. The South African author, Alan Paton, was present at a housing riot and wrote a report of it. This riot occurred in 1953 at Trumbull Park in Chicago, when Donald Howard, a Negro mail carrier and a veteran of World War II, moved his family into one of the 462 apartments in a low-cost housing project operated by the Chicago Housing Authority. His was the first of ten Negro families that the Housing Authority had decided to admit after their restrictive policies had been under severe criticism. When the Howard family moved in, increasingly larger crowds gathered at the housing development in proportionately uglier moods. Rocks were thrown, windows smashed, buses and automobiles stoned, and fires set. For months the tension heightened and it was necessary at times to have as many as 1200 policemen on 24-hour duty at the housing project. Finally, after nine months of existence behind barricaded windows, living in constant fear, the Howard family, encouraged by the police, moved out. Paton, an experienced reporter of dialogue, relates a conversation with a teen-age member of the rioting mob:

> We crossed over and asked him how things were going.
> "We mean to get the jigs out, that's all."
> "Who's we?"
> "All of us," he said. "We've got no leader or president. We all feel the same. There'll be a race riot, sure enough. You wait a few weeks."
> "What do the Churches say?"

"I'm a Catholic," he said, "and a good one, I'd say. But the Church hasn't got a right to tell me who I should live next to. And the Church knows it, too, because it hasn't said anything about Trumbull Park."

"I read somewhere that it did," I said.

"That's Bishop Sheil," he said. "He's a liberal, and he talks too much."[8]

A moral and theological consideration of housing segregation will have to take into account what, for most people, is the most impelling and forceful argument for continuation of the *status quo*. This is the belief that when a Negro family buys and moves into an all-white neighborhood the section will soon become all-Negro; that property values will immediately decrease sharply; and that white owners will be forced to sell at considerable loss and move to another section which may, on considerations other than racial exclusiveness, be less desirable. The picture of the white family in a neighborhood which is "turning colored" being forced to sell at a loss of several thousand dollars and to purchase another house in a different section, at a considerably higher price, is the common one of white owners who have become victims of Negro "pushiness." The problem was expressed some time ago in a letter written to the *Michigan Catholic* in which the writer, a Catholic, expressed his dilemma:

I am sure that most Catholics don't feel that colored people are inferior to them, but it is an undisputed fact that, as they move into a neighborhood, property values go down. The investment that most of us have in our homes represents our whole fortune. Few people can afford to take a loss and then start over again. Their chief resentment against the Negro is the way his inroad affects their pocketbook.[9]

Even though this writer expressed his problem chiefly in economic terms, nevertheless, there is implicit in the general tone of his statement a moral dilemma and an awareness, even though at a low level, of the fact that more is at stake than economic considerations. Yet, these objections in the manner presented here are an accurate facsimile of those uttered time and time again.

It is true, under the situation as it exists today, that when an all-

---

[8] Alan Paton, "Negro in America Today," *Colliers* (October 29, 1954), 72–75, reprinted, *Readings in Sociology*, Gordon Zahn (ed.) (Westminster: Newman Press, 1958), pp. 236–239.

[9] Editorial, *The Michigan Catholic*, Aug. 8, 1953, reprinted in *Catholic Mind*, under title, "Interracial Justice and Home Values," 51 (1953), 730–731.

white neighborhood is opened to Negroes and they begin to move into homes there, after a certain percentage of the white residents have moved out and when, at the same time, other white families are not interested in buying or renting housing in that area, the remaining white residents will gradually be replaced. It is fairly certain that the entire neighborhood will change racially as the remaining white families move out and are not replaced by other white families. When this has been accomplished, the neighborhood becomes another part of the already existing segregated neighborhood, whether or not they happen to be contiguous. This means that where a housing development or a neighborhood has nonwhite residents, after a certain percentage of Negro residents has been reached, it is most likely that the entire development or neighborhood will be completely changed racially. Housing experts who have studied this phenomenon call the critical percentage the "tip point," which various authors have estimated to be anywhere from 10 percent to 60 percent. Unfortunately, the tip point is not the same for every section and situation, and the variation which may obtain in individual situations is surprisingly wide.

Thus there can be places in which 50 percent or even 60 percent of the residents may be Negro and yet the other residents will remain, and, in addition, new white residents will move in as housing becomes available so that the area remains a mixed or integrated neighborhood. Obviously, various factors of desirability and advantage for the white occupants, both old and new, enter into the consideration, and play a key part. It should not be thought that these situations obtain only because some old-time residents are determined and numerous enough to prevent the neighborhood from racially changing. Instances of this type are not only dependent on the old residents remaining, but on new white residents not hesitating to move into the area. In other words, the advantages of locating and living in that section must outweigh any disadvantage they perceive in the fact that the neighborhood is integrated. An instance of desirability of location taking precedence over any objections to an intermixed neighborhood can be seen in Georgetown in the District of Columbia. Several years ago, Georgetown had a relatively large Negro population, but the desirability and advantages of a Georgetown residence far exceeded any disadvantage which might have accrued from residence in an area which in other cities would have, for all practical purposes, been considered a Negro neighborhood. As a matter of fact, the desirability of George-town residence has had the effect of increasing real-estate values to the extent that today most of the Negro residents have moved to other sections of the city where rents and tax assessments would be economically feasible. The result has been that the section is now predominantly white with few Negro residents. Nevertheless, it is an example of the fact that residence of Negro families in an area is not necessarily a deterrent to new white residents.

From his study of housing developments and projects, Abrams believes that those are more successful in which the nonwhite representation ranges between 6 percent and 30 percent. He finds that when this range of percentages can be maintained, the minority group does not feel isolated and at the same time, the majority group does not feel overwhelmed by the others. In addition, the neighborhood immediate to the project accepts it more readily when these percentages have been maintained.[10]

The fact that no definite percentage can be labeled as crucial with any degree of certainty previous to the accomplished fact is unfortunate. In some instances, a single nonwhite family moving in is sufficient to convince the residents that the neighborhood is inevitably due to change, and panic selling begins immediately. Fear of neighborhood change was widespread in the Russell Woods section of Detroit and many of the residents were convinced of the inevitability of change after three Negro families had moved in. It should be added, however, that the Russell Woods section was bordered on three sides by highly impacted and overcrowded Negro areas whose residents gravely needed additional housing.

It is apparent, then, that neighborhood change does not depend primarily on the fact that nonwhite families have moved into it, but on the availability and willingness of other white buyers to come into the mixed neighborhood. If several nonwhite families come into a neighborhood, even though their neighbors refuse to panic-sell, nevertheless, over a period of time, and under the most normal circum-

---

[10] Charles Abrams, *Forbidden Neighbors: A Study of Prejudice in Housing* (New York: Harper & Bros., 1955), p. 311.

stances, the larger percentage of the homes will be offered for sale. If that neighborhood does not present attractions and advantages which appeal to white buyers, eventually the housing which they have rejected will be taken by Negroes who are limited in their choice, and the area becomes a nonwhite neighborhood. The change-over may take fifteen or twenty years, depending on circumstances, but if other white families refuse to move in, its change to a Negro neighborhood is inevitable.

There are several factors, in addition to prejudice, which tend to discourage white purchasers of homes in racially mixed neighborhoods. First, white families have available for their selection a wide variety of homes which are often superior to those in mixed neighborhoods. Some prospective buyers shy away from buying a house in a mixed neighborhood because they fear a decrease of value or the disapproval of friends. Finally, others are discouraged by brokers or the refusal of banks to extend credit or make mortgage loans on property in such neighborhoods.

The fear and belief that the appearance of a Negro family in a neighborhood will result in property-value depreciation, the deterioration of the neighborhood, its eventual change into a "colored section," and the reactions which actually tend to cause these results has been termed a "self-fulfilling prophecy." The prediction can be legitimately made only if certain conditions are verified: the minority group needs housing, and the white neighborhood contains housing not priced beyond the ability of most of the minority group, and has few attractions for white buyers. Such an area, under these circumstances, is a logical candidate for the relief of the minority's housing need, and for a change in its racial makeup. But if the area is at a distance from the settlement of the minority and the houses are high-priced relative to their ability and if the area offers attractions for white buyers, the presence of several Negro families, though displeasing to some white residents, will not cause them to believe that the area will change racially.

Nor should it be believed that there will be an inevitable depreciation of property values. Studies have been made of racially mixed areas and comparable white areas with particular emphasis on the change of property value. Luigi Laurenti has made such a study and published his findings in *Property Values and Race*. Real estate values in three cities, San Francisco, Oakland, and Philadelphia, from 1943 until 1955 were studied. Data on the selling prices of homes, usually one-family, owner-occupied residences in residential areas, during this period were gathered. The study analyzed the prices of 5417 houses in these three cities, in twenty neighborhoods, which had previously been all-white, but into which Negro families had moved. These mixed neighborhood home values were then compared with 4495 sale prices of homes in nineteen comparable neighborhoods which had remained all-white. The twenty mixed areas showed a variation of Negro population ranging from 2 percent in some instances to more than 70 percent in others. Stated briefly, this study indicated:

1. The values in 41 percent of the racially mixed areas were substantially unchanged in comparison with the all-white neighborhood, i.e., there was an increase or a decrease of value of less than 5 percent, which amount could not be considered representative of a substantial price alteration.

2. In 44 percent of the mixed areas, values showed increases ranging from 5 percent to 26 percent over corresponding homes in all-white neighborhoods.

3. In the remaining 15 percent of the houses in the mixed areas, the valuation decreased from 5 percent to 9 percent below corresponding houses in the all-white areas.[11]

The mythological element in the belief that real estate prices will automatically fall as soon as a colored family moves into a neighborhood is also indicated by Robert C. Weaver who stated that there is no univocal effect of Negro occupancy on real estate values — it may result in a decline or a substantial increase.[12] Obviously, if many owners simultaneously dump their property on the market and if the number of purchasers is limited, prices will definitely fall. But the indications from Laurenti's study are that if the supply of housing for sale remains normal, then in 85 percent of the areas property values should remain stable or increase over comparable housing in all-white areas. In the remaining 15 percent there will be a decrease below the

---

[11] Luigi Laurenti, *Property Values and Race, Studies in Seven Cities: Special Research Report to the Commission on Race and Housing* (Berkeley: University of California Press, 1960), pp. 50–53.

[12] Weaver, *The Negro Ghetto*, p. 292.

value of similar property in an all-white neighborhood. Incidentally, it should be noted that according to the Laurenti study, this decrease, on the average, is considerably less than the average increase, since the increases were found in 44 percent of the sales with a range from 5 to 26 percent, while the decrease was only in 15 percent of the sales, and in these, the decrease ranged from 5 to 9 percent.

Not every departure from a mixed area should be considered a result of prejudice, pride, or hysteria. Accusations of prejudice or unreasoning hysteria are not a true explanation of every situation. Needless to say, it is important to prevent panic reactions, and it is very true that because of fear and prejudice many areas have been changed racially by the thoughtless actions of residents who in panic and haste to sell have spurred others to do the same and thus have produced a surfeit of property and depreciated prices. On the other hand, in areas in which the conditions mentioned are verified, that is, where there is a shortage of housing for the minority, where the area is proximate to the impacted section, and where advantages to white buyers have decreased, it would seem that a change in the racial population of such an area is likely. There will be white owners who because of prejudice refuse to live near a Negro family. Economic, social, or moral and spiritual appeals have little, if any, effect of them. Inevitably they will be the first to offer their property for sale not only to protect their economic interests, but also to avoid living in a racially mixed area. Moreover, there are those who have no prejudice, and who firmly believe in the right of all to equal opportunities to live and work in areas of their choice. These may be determined not to panic; to maintain their residence and to act as good neighbors even though the neighborhood is changing. However, even for these, after the "tip point" has been passed, it becomes evident that the entire section has deteriorated or soon will deteriorate into a segregated one. At such a time, even though reluctant to do so, they will seriously consider moving. And this, not because there are Negroes living nearby, but because the neighborhood has become or soon will be a segregated one. As a segregated neighborhood, it labors under all the disadvantages characteristic of such areas — inferior and segregated schools; lack of better stores and shopping facilities; neglect of and decline in public services, e.g., street paving and cleaning, garbage and trash disposal, street lighting, and police protection. His may be the last white family in the area, but eventually, the needs of his family, especially if there are children of school age, will demand that he move. Such men cannot be accused of acting hysterically or irrationally. They are leaving the section for the same reason that the Negro family wants to leave it, namely because it is a segregated area and by that fact, an inferior one in which the protection and bringing up of a family is rendered most difficult. No one should point a finger of accusation at such a man whether he be white or Negro for his desire to leave a segregated neighborhood. Of course, the main difference is that it is relatively easy for the white family to protect itself and move. Unfortunately, the Negro family, which may have been one of the first to move into the area, now finds itself reenclosed by the completion of a vicious circle and again locked-in in a segregated neighborhood. The only alternative is to start all over again, with the risk of a repetition of the situation in another neighborhood.

The existence of the critical "tip point" has given rise to the conviction that maintenance of a racial balance in housing developments is not only useful, but necessary, lest white applicants be frightened off by a large racial minority group, and the development is left without a sufficient flow of applicants, or has only minority group applicants. Despite the realization of the need to retain racial balances in these developments, many of their sponsors are reluctant to apply racial quotas. A system has been worked out which has been called a "benevolent quota" system. Under this system, a percentage of the residential units are assigned to applicants of the minority group. When the quota established is filled, it means that individuals of that race making application will be turned down. Needless to say, the racial quota system presents several problems to advocates of interracial housing who are uneasy about using what appears to be discrimination in order to prevent racial imbalances. They are reminded of the quota system established by medical and law schools and colleges some years ago to keep out Jewish students, and they see too many resemblances in the racial quota. Abrams speaking of the quota system says:

> Normally this should be unnecessary. Where a minority is only 5 per cent of a city's population, the chances are that its proportion in the

project will be 5 to 20 per cent, depending on housing need and income ranges. If the percentage rises disproportionately it is because the site may be near a minority area, because poor public relations policy has discouraged white applicants, because income limits are so low that they abnormally favor non-white occupancy, or because minority pressure for housing is abnormally heavy. Where, despite authorities' efforts, project occupancy heads toward homogeneity — either majority or minority — an effort to keep the project in workable balance is desirable. There may be some who would call this a "quota" system. But it is far from that. A quota system is a device to exclude people, not include them; to effect segregation not to break it down. There would be no need to maintain a balance in any project if adequate housing were available for all, and there were no barriers. Until that has been attained the maintenance of workable communities during the development process is essential.[13]

In view of this, it is necessary to speak regarding the morality of a quota system. I am sure that the moralist feels the same reluctance that the open-occupancy advocate feels in establishing such "benevolent" discriminatory quotas. Despite this reluctance, however, I believe that in projects of the open-occupancy type, when it becomes apparent that the number of applicants of a racial group is producing a disproportion which will result in a racial imbalance, the setting up of a quota system by the owner or an association of owners is morally justified. Of course, in determining percentages, prudence must be exercised.

Obviously, those who are excluded when the quota has been reached will suffer some loss and inconvenience. The degree and amount will depend on several factors, chief of which will be the availability of other residential accommodations. In many instances, housing will be available to make their inconvenience less than it would be if there were a housing shortage. But, if, in some situations, housing available to the Negro is practically nonexistent, and the applicant is in grave need of housing, it would seem that the virtue of charity demands that the quota system be eliminated or at least not applied in this case. The grave need of a man and his family for housing can place a grave obligation of charity on one who has housing available and is aware of this need. The good which would eventually come through maintaining racial proportions in a development can compensate for many losses and inconveniences to individuals, but where the need of a

---

[13] C. Abrams, op. cit., pp. 311–312.

family for housing here and now is grave, it does not seem that it can be refused for the sake of retaining racial balances. Where there is an absolute lack of housing for many families, the state may be obliged to intervene in order to promote the common good. It may act to correct the situation either by construction of housing or by encouraging and assisting private enterprise to make sufficient housing available.

The ordinary citizen is usually not involved in the control or rental of developments, nor is he frequently involved in sales of real estate. But this does not mean that he is free from obligation in reference to housing and race relations. Indeed, he is either a homeowner or a tenant himself, he has neighbors and reacts to them in various ways, he has opportunities to influence and improve the moral tone of his neighborhood, and at times, he may be in the position of a home seller or lessor. Thus, the matter is not one which involves only the few, but can include every resident. This involvement means that the white resident may be called upon to make sacrifices if he wishes to lead a virtuous and moral life. Primarily, he must be ready to abandon his desire for and his insistence on residing in racially homogeneous neighborhoods.

It is immediately apparent that there can be no moral justification for participation in mob violence and rioting on the occasion of a Negro family moving into a neighborhood. The injury done to the common good and the disturbance of the public peace, as well as the physical injury and harm to persons and property, give ample evidence of the immorality not only of active participation in such violence, but also of the approval, condoning, or encouragement of those who participate in it. The appearance of a Negro family should neither be the occasion for such violence, nor should it produce a wave of panic selling and exodus from the neighborhood. The "self-ful-filling prophecy" has often come to actuality as panic gripped a neighborhood and produced the fear effect. McDermott and Clark have described a quite successful program used in a Philadelphia neighborhood to prevent this. A committee was formed to urge residents to stay put and not to sell from fear. It provided for the organization of a group, with membership open to all in the neighborhood, which would help stabilize the area by squelching rumors and cooperating with realty dealers in an attempt to maintain stability and to guard area housing standards. A welcoming committee was established to greet the newcomers and to assure them of the cooperation of the group, and in turn, to secure their cooperation. Obviously organization of and participation in such a program rather than panic or violence is the proper, virtuous, and truly Christian reaction. It is one which recognizes that housing discrimination is a *sine qua non* condition for the maintenance and continuation of racial prejudice and tension, and it attempts to contribute a share in the work of removing this bulwark of racial strife.[14]

Proper and suitable housing is a basic requirement for decent family upbringing. Disease and the consequent weakening of health, crime, and spiritual and moral dangers are frequent products of situations where there is unsuitable and inadequate family housing. However, it would be an error to estimate adequacy solely in terms of physical construction and facilities. A three-bedroom house, well built and equipped with heating, plumbing, etc., is not necessarily adequate even for a small sized family. For a determination of adequacy, location and neighborhood must also be considered. A family cannot spend its entire life within the four walls of the house. Availability of proper schools and stores is also important, and above all, the moral tone of the neighborhood must be included in any consideration. A house possessing adequate physical qualities, but located in an area in which crime and immorality are common certainly could never be considered adequate for the proper and moral upbringing of a family. Such areas with high incidence of saloons, low-class dance halls, and prostitution present a moral hazard especially to children. No matter how well equipped the house may be, if it is located in such an area the family living in it needs proper housing.

Many segregated sections in our cities, both Northern and Southern, have moral conditions which render any housing within the area improper and inadequate for family life. Unfortunately, the situation has been that when a man attempts to move his family out of such an environment and to transfer them to a neighborhood in which they

---

[14] John McDermott and Dennis Clark, "Helping the Panic Neighborhood: A Philadelphia Approach," *Interracial Review*, 28 (August, 1955), 131–135; reprinted, *Catholic Mind*, 54 (1956), 255–262.

will not be subjected to such moral dangers, he is prevented from doing so either by subterfuges replacing the unenforceable restrictive covenant or by the outright refusal of owners to consider sale of their property to a Negro family.

Speaking from a moral viewpoint, such a family is in need of housing, and where there is little or none available except the inadequate segregated section, then their need must be considered grave. True, a family in such a need cannot claim that an owner has an obligation in strict justice to sell or rent his property to them because of their need. But, because an owner has no such obligation in strict justice, he cannot thereby consider himself exempt from any moral obligations. The virtue of charity would oblige an owner having property for sale or for rent to help this family in their grave need by agreeing to sell or rent to them. Since their need is grave, it seems that this obligation of charity would bind the owner gravely, and his refusal to sell or rent to them would per se be a grave sin. However, in situations in which other adequate housing is readily available, we must conclude that their need would not be serious or grave. Their situation would be like that of a white family which ordinarily has a sizable selection of housing available so that while they may need more room, this need can easily be satisfied, and hence is not considered a serious need. The obligation in charity to help a neighbor who is in such need would, at most, be a light obligation.

Even in those instances where an obligation is considered to bind under pain of mortal sin, there can be circumstances in which the loss to the owner would be such that he would be excused from a grave obligation. In cases where physical harm or great financial loss is threatened if he sells to a Negro family, and there is real probability that those who have made the threats can and will execute them, this danger could excuse him from a grave obligation. Such an incident was reported by a member of the staff of the Philadelphia police commissioner. In 1955, a white woman who sold her home to a Negro family was threatened by her neighbors with physical violence. Apparently fulfillment of these threats was so likely that she was forced to live in virtual hiding for several months, and, in addition, required a police escort to accompany her to and from work daily. Life in such a state of apprehension and fear would be a serious hardship for almost anyone and hence sufficient to excuse from a grave obligation.

However, other forms of retaliation and harassment, which are not so drastic, may or may not be considered serious hardships, depending on circumstances such as personality makeup and vulnerability to adverse publicity or criticism. Such is the case of a white owner who, after he sold his home to a Negro family, was followed by representatives of the neighborhood civic association into his new neighborhood and his "betrayal" of the other neighborhood publicized to his new neighbors.

By the same token, those who use such means to prevent sale of property not only sin against charity by impeding an act of charity, but they also sin against justice because they use unjust means to prevent an owner from disposing of his property. Further, since they are using unjust means to prevent their neighbor from obtaining a necessity for the fulfillment of his obligations to his family and for the full development of personality, they also sin against the virtue of justice in violating this right of the Negro family.

It will be difficult for many white owners to retain a calm and dispassionate attitude when their neighbors begin to spread scare rumors. It will take moral stamina and courage for them to be prudent and to help lead their neighbors to a realistic acceptance of the fact that the price of a strictly homogeneous neighborhood is too high. Calm thinking is needed to help them realize the mathematical fact that there are not enough Negro families to be able to fill up all residential areas. The fact is, of course, that the Negro population is approximately 10 percent of the total, and if housing were available to them on the same basis that it is for most white families, namely on the basis of economic and social strata, the ideal would soon be accomplished where there would be a numerically proportionate distribution of the nonwhites among the general population on a social, educational, and economic parity. The same fallacy which impedes the Negro in his search for living quarters is faced by the Jews in reference to vacation facilities. Many summer resorts and hotels refuse to accept Jewish guests, reasoning that if they admit a few, it will only be a short time before their entire clientele will be Jewish. The same numerical fallacy is present here. If all the resorts were available without religious restrictions to applicants on the basis of social, economic, or even recreational abilities, there would not be enough Jewish vacationers to fill up all the resorts. The situation obtains because there are so few available in comparison with the number of vacationers seeking them. Naturally, the tendency to congregate stems from the fact that these are the only available places.

Advancements in other areas of race relations, e.g., employment, education, public accommodations, transportation, etc., have been made in recent years. But the problem of discrimination and segregation in housing has not made comparable advances toward solution. True, there has been a major increase in the amount of housing available to Negro families, but most of this is housing in previously all-white areas which have now been abandoned to Negro occupancy. The present problem is not immediately the amount or even the quality of housing available for Negro families, but the question whether they are going to be kept in separated areas or permitted to seek and purchase housing on the general market. The housing shortage, which for the Negro population was so very severe and critical immediately after the war, has been improved and corrected, but the problem of housing for them still exists and McEntire stresses its importance:

> Racial segregation in housing is sustained by widespread popular attitudes, the practices of the housing industry, and policies of governments. Probably no aspect of racial discrimination in the United States is more institutionalized and resistant to change. Correspondingly, the elimination of racial restrictions on residence would have consequences reaching far beyond the immediate facts of housing. Just as residential segregation serves to isolate the segregated groups from the activities of the general population, so integration in housing must stimulate participation in wider areas of community life. . . . It seems fair to say, therefore, that *the future character of majority-minority relations hinges to a great extent on the racial pattern of residence*.[15] (Italics added.)

Thus, because the housing problem is so important and may well be, as McEntire states, the key to the breakthrough in the solution of many racial problems, Christians and all men of goodwill will be anxious to bend earnest efforts to contribute to the advancement of solutions. They will use patience and prudence, courage and leader-

---

[15] D. McEntire, *op. cit.*, pp. 5–6.

ship, charity and justice, not only to improve their own attitudes and reactions, but also those of their neighbors. Apparently the solution is not easy, nor will it come easily, but the practice of these virtues within this field should go far to help effect a proper and a Christian solution.

CHAPTER 15

THE RIGHT TO EDUCATION

On May 17, 1954, the United States Supreme Court handed down one of the most far-reaching and controversial decisions it ever issued. This was the decision in the case of Brown v. Board of Education of Topeka.[1] An understanding of this decision and its implications is vital for a proper appreciation of the legal status of attempts to enforce segregation not only in education but in other fields.

The Court declared that the doctrine of "separate but equal" has no place in the field of public education and that "separate" educational facilities were inherently unequal. Recognizing that it was sounding the death knell of segregated schools, it took into account the difficulties, prejudices, and resistance which would immediately be aroused. To seek equitable means of implementation, the Court restored the cases to the docket so that the attorneys-general of the states which permitted school segregation, as well as the attorney-general of the United States, could make suggestions. A year later, on May 31, 1955, the Court issued its decree of implementation,[2] in which the phrase "with all deliberate speed" was used to describe the requisite compliance expected by the Court. This phrase "with all deliberate speed" is claimed by some to have its origin in Francis Thompson's Hound of Heaven — "But with unhurrying chase, And unperturbed pace, Deliberate speed, majestic instancy. . . ." Others

---

[1] 347 U. S. 483 (1954).
[2] 349 U. S. 294 (1955).

maintain that it is from English Chancery practice and that it does not have a literary or poetic origin.

The basis of the decision to discard the "separate but equal" rule, which had been in use for over a half-century, has become a subject of much controversy. In a discussion following the reading of Monsignor Francis Gilligan's paper on segregation in education to the Catholic Theological Society of America in 1958, it was remarked that the decision did not seem to stress the dignity of the human person. Monsignor Gilligan agreed and expressed the wish that the decision had explicitly expressed its metaphysical basis. However, he indicated that it stressed that there was a denial of rights and that this denial formed the basis of the decision. The nature of this right, however, whether it was a natural right or a civil right, he added, was not spelled out.[3]

The problem of explaining the Court's decision to depart from the "separate but equal" principle has been expressed by Father North:

> . . . six Courts prior to the Warren Court had found state laws segregating the races in public schools reasonable means of achieving a legitimate governmental end. Only the Warren Court said such laws are "not reasonably related to any proper governmental objective." What made these laws reasonable for all previous Courts but unreasonable to the Warren Court? Was it the "total view of education today"? Was it the sociological and psychological "predilection" of the Court? or was it "the felt necessities of the times, the prevalent moral and political theories," international and domestic, which induced the Warren Court to declare a hoary precedent unreasonable and discriminatory? That all these elements were somewhat intermingled with the Court's reasoning can hardly be denied. It is this intermingling of the disparate elements employed by the Court to spell out discrimination that has rendered the Brown decision subject to so much legal criticism.[4]

Apparently Father North believes that the rejection of the "separate but equal" rule was founded on the importance of education in American life as well as on the psychological trauma caused by

---

[3] Francis J. Gilligan, "Moral Aspects of Segregation in Education," *Proceedings of the 13th Annual Convention of the Catholic Theological Society of America* (1958), 51–64.

[4] Arthur A. North, S.J., "The Plessy Doctrine: Rise and Demise," *A Catholic Case against Segregation*, Joseph E. O'Neill (ed.) (New York: The Macmillan Co., 1961), pp. 22–23.

segregation. The idea of this sociopsychological explanation also finds favor with others:

> The Court was profoundly influenced by what it regarded as the neces-
> sity of keeping the law abreast with the changing conditions of Ameri-
> can life. It appeared to be more influenced by what it regarded as
> changing social fact than by the intent of those who adopted the
> amendment or by previous judicial precedent.[5]

Father John LaFarge has also expressed the opinion that the decision was not based on moral principles or the judgment of segregation as immoral because it offended the dignity of human personality.
To impress the general public a more powerful and moving argument
was required, an *ad hominem* reasoning was needed, and therefore,
the Court argued from a sociological premise.[6]

However, Blaustein and Ferguson, in their legal study of the school
decisions, assert that it is impossible to determine the exact role of
the psychological and sociological data. Frequently, about the only
thing that prosegregationists and the social scientists agree on regarding these decisions is that segregated public schools were outlawed
because of sociological and psychological considerations. However,
these two authors believe that the prosegregationists, as well as the
social scientists, overstate their case that these data were the sole
guides in formulating the final decision. It is their opinion that
although the Court weighed and cited these data in the decision, it
was actually declaring school segregation invalid and in effect, establishing a new law, but not without constitutional and legal precedent.

> The new constitutional standard was rooted in sound legal doctrine
> and based in large measure upon judicial pronouncements which long
> preceded the judgment in *Plessy v. Ferguson*. True, the Supreme Court
> gave new significance to those pronouncements as it disregarded the
> conventional test of the Plessy case. But it was also true that *Plessy
> v. Ferguson* had limited the meaning of many of these same cases
> when it made new law back in 1896.[7]

---

[5] Newton Edwards, *The Courts and the Public Schools: The Legal Basis of
School Organization and Administration*, rev. ed. (Chicago: University of Chicago
Press, 1955), p. 548.

[6] John LaFarge, S.J., "Decision on Segregation," *Catholic Mind*, 52 (1954),
577–587.

[7] Albert P. Blaustein and Clarence C. Ferguson, Jr., *Desegregation and the
Law: The Meaning and Effect of the School Segregation Cases* (New Brunswick:
Rutgers University Press, 1957), pp. 134–137.

These lawyer-authors maintain that the *Brown* decision was primarily founded on opinions previous to the "separate but equal" rule, and that these earlier cases all declared racial discrimination to be *per se* unconstitutional. They point out the statement of Chief Justice Warren that in the cases decided shortly after adoption of the Fourteenth Amendment, "the Court interpreted it as proscribing all state imposed discriminations against the Negro race." And in a footnote which is occasionally omitted in reprints of the decision, Warren cites four of these early cases utilizing this interpretation of the Fourteenth Amendment. Also included in the Warren decision is a quotation from the most famous of these cases, *Strauder v. West Virginia*, which was decided in 1880. This case involved the question as to whether exclusion by law of Negroes from jury service violated the constitutional rights of Strauder, a Negro, who had been convicted of murder in West Virginia courts. In a 7 to 2 decision the Supreme Court declared that this exclusion of Negroes by law from jury service did violate Strauder's constitutional rights, and in appealing to the protection afforded by the Fourteenth Amendment to the Negroes, the Court said:

> What is this but declaring that the law in the States shall be the same for the black as for the whites; that all persons, whether colored or white, shall stand equal before the laws of the States, and in regard to the colored race, for whose protection the amendment was primarily designed, that no discrimination shall be made against them by law because of their color? The words of the amendment, it is true, are prohibitory, but they contain a necessary implication of a positive immunity, or right, most valuable to the colored race, — the right to exemption from unfriendly legislation against them distinctively as colored, — exemption from legal discriminations, implying inferiority in civil society, lessening the security of their enjoyment of the rights which others enjoy, the discriminations which are steps towards reducing them to the condition of a subject race.[8]

The *Brown* decision approved the language of the previous cases and indicated that the *Plessy v. Ferguson* decision was an abandonment of precedent and an introduction of a completely novel distinction. *Plessy v. Ferguson* declared that the object of the Fourteenth Amendment was the absolute equality of both races before the law, but that this was to be a *political* equality and not a *social*

---
8 100 U. S. 303 (1880).

equality. From these facts, Blaustein and Ferguson deduce that the 1954 decision represents a return to precedents of interpretation of the Fourteenth and Fifteenth Amendments previous to the *Plessy* decision, and that the 1896 decision was a departure from the practice of the Court when it distinguished between social and political rights and classified transportation and education as pertaining to social rights not protected by the constitutional guarantee of equality.

The *Plessy* decision declared that a state could require racial segregation provided that in the judgment of a Court it was a "reasonable regulation," and sustained as constitutional the Louisiana statute requiring railroads to "provide equal but separate accommodations for the white and colored races." The decision in *Plessy v. Ferguson* was a departure from the previous decisions, a change from the *stare decisis* principle, and it gave a new meaning to the Fourteenth Amendment.

The first case involving school segregation was *Cummings v. Board of Education*, but it did not reach the Supreme Court until 1899, three years after the *Plessy* decision.[9] Negro parents in Richmond County, Georgia, sought an injunction to close the white schools until a school was provided for Negro children who would not be admitted to the white school, and for whom there was no public high school. The parents claimed that the failure of the Board of Education to provide a high school violated the "separate but equal" doctrine. It was not until the case had progressed to the oral argumentation that they first argued that segregated schools were unconstitutional. Technically, the contention was made at the improper time, and the Court expressly refused to consider that question because it had not been raised at the correct time. The final decision of the Court was that an improper remedy was sought in asking for an injunction since closing existing schools would not remedy the situation of lack of schools for the Negro children, and the relief sought was denied. Thus the Court, in the first segregated education case, explicitly refused to consider the constitutionality of segregated schools, and neglected to give standards for the measurement of equality. Yet this decision has been cited by some as the first decision upholding "separate but equal" schools. Blaustein and Ferguson insist

[9] 175 U. S. 528 (1899).

that in none of the cases involving segregated education, beginning with the *Cummings* case up to the later decisions regarding graduate schools, did the Court consider the question: *Is segregation in public education per se unconstitutional?* The Court faced this specific question for the first time in the *Brown* case. It decided to reexamine the "separate but equal" rule and to determine if segregation deprived Negroes of rights guaranteed by the equal protection clause of the Fourteenth Amendment. Its response was that segregated educational facilities were inherently unequal, and that segregation did deprive these children of equal protection of the law. When the Court had examined the evidence presented to it of the injury done those who were segregated, it may have concluded that this damage exceeded and outweighed the "way of life" argumentation offered by the lawyers for the defendants, and that this lack of proportionality was so great that the segregation legislation was unreasonable and, therefore, unconstitutional. But, on the other hand, they may have decided that any classification based solely on race is unreasonable and cannot be justified under any circumstances; therefore, the segregation legislation is unconstitutional. Blaustein and Ferguson contend that the language of Justice Warren could be adduced to support both these propositions.

In light of the implementation decree of 1955, they feel that the Court was not only declaring educational segregation unconstitutional, but was stating that all laws based on racial classifications are discriminatory, and discriminatory laws are *per se* unconstitutional. Support for this contention is indicated by the fact that while in the 1954 opinion, the Court consistently speaks of "segregation," in the 1955 decree of implementation, the word "segregation" does not appear. They state that the absence of the word in the implementation decree is not immediately apparent and many have assumed its presence. However, its absence cannot be considered an error or an accident since it was, without doubt, extremely difficult to write the decision without using the word "segregation." The word that is used and stressed in the implementation decree is "discrimination." This opinion begins by stating:

> These cases were decided on May 17, 1954. The opinions of that date declaring the fundamental principles that *racial discrimination* in public

education is unconstitutional are incorporated herein by reference. (Italics added.)

Actually, the previous decision had spoken of the question of the constitutionality of segregation and declared: "We have now announced that such segregation is a denial of the equal protection of the laws."

The word "discrimination" appears in the implementation decree five times and it describes the required quality of public schools as "nondiscriminatory." Important also is the statement regarding the invitation issued to the attorneys-general:

> We invited . . . the Attorneys-General of the states requiring or permitting racial discrimination in public education to present their views. . . .

Actually the wording of the invitation in the previous decision was:

> The Attorneys-General of the states requiring or permitting segregation in public education will also be permitted to appear. . . .

Obviously, the substitution of "discrimination" for "segregation" in these sections is deliberate. The Court must have been keenly aware of the difference in meaning between these two words. The authors, Blaustein and Ferguson, point out the significance of this substitution by indicating that the Court had been consistent in declaring laws and statutes invalid which it termed "discriminatory" even when, at the same time, it was upholding some segregation laws.

> When the Supreme Court holds that a statute is discriminatory, its conclusion embodies a finding that the legislative scheme was activated by bias and prejudice, and thus for that reason alone the statute violates the Constitution.[10]

It is their contention that the *Brown* decision declared all racial segregation to be in violation of the Fourteenth Amendment because it is discriminatory, and therefore, per se unconstitutional, and that segregated education is merely one form of discrimination. Support for this contention, they believe, can be seen in cases in which the *Brown* principle was applied to segregation issues outside the field of education.

The use of the Brown decision can be seen in *Holmes v. City of*

---

[10] Blaustein and Ferguson, op. cit., p. 153.

Atlanta, involving segregated municipal golf facilities. A lower court hearing the case stated that the *Brown* decision outlawed the "separate but equal" principle only in the area of education:

> . . . "separate but equal" doctrine as recognized by our courts is not in conflict with the Fourteenth Amendment — is unaffected by the ruling in *Brown v. Board of Education* . . . as in that case the doctrine of "separate but equal" was rejected only as it applied to public education.[11]

In view of this, the lower court decreed that while the city was obliged to make golf facilities available to Negroes if it provided them for whites, it could, if it so desired, provide segregated facilities. But this decision as well as an affirmation of the Court of Appeals were vacated by the Supreme Court which ruled that Negroes could not be excluded from using a municipal golf course on the basis of race. The Court reversed these decrees and ordered relief to the petitioners in conformity with the decision in *Mayor and City Council of Baltimore City v. Dawson*, which in turn had been decided on the basis of the *Brown* decision even though it concerned segregated municipal beaches.

Further corroboration of the claim that the *Brown* decision declared all compulsory racial segregation to be discriminatory and, therefore, unconstitutional, and further that it based its decision on basic human rights can be seen by the interpretation and use of this decision in foreign courts. Such an instance is the decision of the Southern Rhodesia High Court on October 13, 1961, in a case involving racial segregation in a municipal swimming pool. The plaintiff, an Asian, was refused admittance to the all-European pool and brought suit claiming that the enforcement of segregation by the city was illegal. The decision indicated that although there were no inequalities in the "tangible facilities" since each race had a pool assigned to it, there were, however, "intangible discriminations" because the segregation, which was instigated by the prejudices of whites, produced feelings of humiliation and resentment among the Asians. The presiding justice stated that although this distinction had not received much consideration in the South African courts, it had in the courts of the United States.

---

[11] U. S. District Court, Northern Dist., Georgia, 124 F. Supp. 290 (1954).

He cited the *Brown* case as having been decided on this distinction between "tangible" and "intangible" factors, and also used *Holmes v. City of Atlanta* and *Mayor and City Council of Baltimore City v. Dawson* as examples of the application of the *Brown* principle to areas outside education. He pointed out that although these opinions did not have binding force on him, they did have persuasive force as "indicating the modern trends in this field of jurisprudence."

Further, that he considered the *Brown* decision as involving natural rights rather than strictly civil rights can be seen in this South African judge's statement:

> Dividing people up according to race, if based on race prejudice, may amount to an infringement of what Melius de Villiers calls "primordial rights," while dividing them up according to the commencing letter of their name cannot possibly amount to such an infringement. The American cases quoted strongly support my view.

These "primordial rights," which nomenclature is attributed to Melius de Villiers, are based according to de Villiers on what he calls man's *dignitas*. In this quotation cited by the Court from de Villiers, it is apparent that he is describing what moral theologians term the right of a man to esteem, honor, respect, and reputation:

> By a person's reputation is here meant that character for moral or social worth to which he is entitled amongst his fellow-men; by dignity that valued and serene condition in his social or individual life which is violated when he is, either publicly or privately, subjected by another to offensive and degrading treatment, or when he is exposed to ill-will, ridicule, disesteem or contempt. The rights here referred to are absolute or primordial rights; they are not created by, nor dependent for their being upon any contract; every person is bound to respect them; and they are capable of being enforced by external compulsion. Every person has an inborn right to the tranquil enjoyment of his peace of mind, secure against aggression upon his person, against the impairment of that character for moral and social worth to which he may rightly lay claim and of that respect and esteem of his fellowmen of which he is deserving, and against degrading *and humiliating* treatment. . . . (Italics added by presiding Justice.)[12]

If these conclusions are correct, they would solve the problem of the basis of the Court's decision, and would indicate that it was not

---

[12] *Sumanrai Nagarji Mehta, Applicant and City of Salisbury, Respondent,* Southern Rhodesia High Court, October 13, 1961, Judgment No. 64/61; *Race Relations Law Reporter*, Vol. 6 (Winter, 1961), 1123–1131.

founded solely on sociological or psychological data. Though not explicit, it appears that the Court did establish its decision on solid metaphysical grounds, namely, that segregation on the basis of racial distinction violates the rights of the individual, or that compulsory racial segregation is always discriminatory. And further, the right to immunity from the disadvantages of segregation, while stated in terms of constitutional rights, is, nevertheless, a natural and personal right protected and guarded by the Constitution.

The function of the Supreme Court is determined by the Constitution, and because its appellate and juridical review jurisdiction for the most part involves cases arising under the Constitution, its decisions will necessarily be expressed in constitutional terms. Consequently, even natural rights, which are protected, and not created by the Constitution, will be vindicated under the title of constitutional protection.

The Court, in fact, has explicitly admitted the existence of rights, protected by the Constitution, and not originating from it. In *United States v. Cruikshank*, speaking of the right of free assembly, the Court stated that this was a right preexisting the Constitution and that it is and has always been "one of the attributes of citizenship under a free government. . . . It was not, therefore, a right granted to the people by the Constitution. The government of the United States when established found it in existence, with the obligation on the part of the States to afford it protection."[13] At another time, it stated that the denial of rights, *created or protected*, by the Constitution could not be used as means to secure even important and desirable ends, such as the avoidance of racial conflict.

But the Court decisions do not usually distinguish rights as "natural" contrasted to "civil." It is sufficient for its purposes to adjudicate the existence of a right and its violation by some statute. It could fulfill its role if it designated all rights protected by law as civil, regardless of their origin. The *Plessy* decision attempted a distinction between social and political equality, but it did not speak of "natural" and "civil" rights.

It should be indicated that in the *Civil Rights Cases* of 1883 when the Court struck down the Federal Civil Rights Act which prohibited

---

[13] 92 U. S. 542 (1876).

discrimination in public accommodations and provided penalties against individuals who discriminated, the Court construed the Fourteenth Amendment as binding only on the states, and not applying to actions of individuals. Speaking of slavery, it indicated that there were many a freeman at that time who enjoyed all the essential rights of life, liberty, and property, the same as the white citizen, but who, at the same time, did not consider it a violation of personal status if he did not enjoy all the privileges of the white citizen, or if he was the object of discrimination in public accommodations, such as inns, public transportation, or places of amusement. How realistic this statement was and how representative of the actual situation may be doubted in view of contemporary accounts written by freemen. Frederick Douglass, probably the most famous of the ex-slaves, describes his situation as being jobless, friendless, poverty-stricken, and without any place to secure help. "No colored man," he said, "is really free in a slaveholding state. He wears the badge of bondage while nominally free and is often subjected to hardships to which the slave is a stranger."

The Court decision continues, stating:

> Mere discriminations on account of race or color were not regarded as badges of slavery. If, since that time, the enjoyment of equal rights in all these respects has become established by constitutional enactment, it is not by force of the 13th amendment (which merely abolishes slavery), but by force of the 14th and 15th amendments.

Note that the Court did not answer the question: Is immunity from racial segregation in public accommodations a right guaranteed to all citizens by the Fourteenth Amendment. The Court would not face that problem or attempt to answer it. It reached its decision for adjudication of the case before it by restricting the binding force of the Fourteenth Amendment to state actions.

> We have discussed the question presented by the law on the assumption that a right to enjoy equal accommodation and privileges in all inns, public conveyances, and places of public amusement, is one of the essential rights of the citizen which no State can abridge or interfere with. Whether it is such a right, or not, is a different question, which in the view we have taken of the validity of the law on the ground already stated, it is not necessary to examine.[14]

---

[14] 109 U. S. 3 (1883).

It appears that the Court considered that such rights, if they did exist, were only granted through enactment of the Fourteenth Amendment, and did not preexist it. However, actually it did not affirm or deny their existence under that Amendment or attempt to solve the case before it on the basis of the reality of the existence of these rights.

In view of the consistent designation of segregated schooling as "discrimination" and the avoidance of the word "segregation" in the implementation decree of 1955, as well as the application of that decision to areas other than education by the courts, it would appear correct to infer that the Court declared all racial segregation is discriminatory and, therefore, unconstitutional, and that the rights involved can properly be called natural rights based on the dignity of man.

As is well known, the decisions did not meet universal approval. The reaction was violent especially where segregation had been rigidly enforced. Legal devices were constructed to frustrate the mandate of the Court and to hold off desegregation. Basically, these attempts to avoid desegregation of schools fall into four classifications:

1. State interposition and nullification. This was based on the doctrine of states' rights widely held previously to the Civil War. It maintained that the state had the obligation to interpose its sovereignty between the federal government and the people when there had been an invasion of powers constitutionally reserved to the state.

2. Statutes disbarring plaintiffs from court actions to end segregation.

3. Alteration of the basis of segregation from race to such classifications as scholastic and psychological aptitudes, or free choice, and the various pupil placement plans.

4. Removal of the school system from state control and placing it in private control.

Possibility of variations within each of these groups is very great. It would be beyond our purpose to attempt a detailed examination either of the forms, possible legality, or effectiveness of such devices. Many have been tested in the courts where many were struck down and the others retained; others are in preparation for judicial consideration or actually in process. Eventually, it is likely that the majority of these will be tested. It will be time-consuming and expensive, but, in many instances, these burdens for the plaintiffs are intended in enacting the statute. It would appear, in view of the general pattern of decisions, that the courts will eliminate all schemes formulated with race as the criterion. Further indication of the probable disposition of these cases can be seen in the fact that legal precedents are being established which will influence future adjudications. An example of this was when the U. S. District Court for the Eastern District of New York handled a case involving de facto segregation, i.e., situations in which because of certain conditions, such as proximity of a school to a Negro neighborhood, a school would have an almost 100 percent Negro enrollment. The Court declared that even de facto segregation is a violation of constitutional rights. It indicated that by law, education is compulsory and that "the educational system that is thus compulsory and publicly afforded must deal with the inadequacy arising from adventitious segregation."[15]

It should be recalled that de facto school segregation is ultimately attributable to housing discrimination. If the school district represents a fair territorial division (and is not the result of gerrymandering) the reason why school attendance will be entirely Negro is because that school is located in an area populated almost entirely by Negroes. Where this situation does obtain, the problem of a de facto segregated school can be efficiently resolved only if the housing discrimination is ended. Until such time, it would seem that each instance of de facto school segregation must be judged separately and according to its peculiar circumstances. There are various factors which must be considered before a judgment can be made as to the suitability of terminating such a school situation while the housing problem remains unchanged, e.g., a pupil transferal plan which may make it necessary for children to travel daily long distances from their homes, often through hazardous traffic, and at considerable expense. The better solution would, of course, be to end the segregated housing so that various neighborhoods, and their educational and recreational facilities, would reflect a more realistic population representation.

The morality of advocating, supporting, or voting for legislation to "avoid" fulfillment of the Court order will depend on the inten-

---

[15] *Branche v. Board of Education of Hempstead, Southern School News*, May, 1962, p. 11.

tion of the individual. Where actions are motivated by a desire to retain or encourage segregation for racial reasons, he would act immorally. Even though such "avoiding" devices were to pass the test of review and be sustained as legal, it would not morally justify his action. Intention and desire to perpetuate a situation productive of such harm cannot be rectified by the fact that he had discovered a legal loophole. This immorality is, of course, immediately apparent if, holding a position of responsibility and authority, he adopts a do-nothing attitude or its equivalent. Monsignor Gilligan, speaking of the morality involved, stated:

> The members of the executive and legislative branches of state governments are guilty of an objective sin of injustice; positively, if they encourage segregation, negatively, if they remain inactive. Their primary obligations are the protection of *natural rights* and the promotion of the common good. Guilty also of injustice are the vociferous moulders of public opinion who influence citizens to perpetuating the institution in schools. Then the conscience of white parents may also be burdened if they try to arouse public opinion by inflammatory statements.[16]

A chief consideration will always have to be the necessity of education in our civilization and the effects of segregated education on training and education. These effects should not be considered as limited to educational deficiencies, but extend to psychological injury produced by the generating or reinforcing of feelings of inferiority. This psychological harm was one of the considerations of the Court in the Brown case when it declared that the segregation of Negro schoolchildren from others of similar age and qualifications caused feelings of inferiority as to their status in the community which could effect irreparable injury to their hearts and minds.

On the other hand, measures which propose a solution of various problems involved in complying with the mandate cannot be condemned. The Court itself, it should be remembered, took cognizance of the fact that the problem was complex both by reason of its scope as well as by variations in local situations. For this reason, it remanded the cases for a year before the decree of implementation. Even then, it ordered the admission to schools on a nondiscriminatory basis "with all deliberate speed." Situations may exist in certain locales,

---

[16] Francis J. Gilligan, "Moral Aspects of Segregation in Education," *loc. cit.*, p. 59.

which present serious difficulties, when a delay in implementation would be legitimate. There could be situations with problems of availability of administrative or teaching personnel; lack of school buildings or accommodations of proper size or condition; problems of pupil transportation; and even financial problems stemming from the endeavor to execute plans of compliance. These situations could easily require and justify a deferral and extension of time before complete compliance. In these instances, it is possible that segregated schooling must be tolerated until the problems have been faced and solutions worked out. But it is neither the intent of the Court nor in accord with ethical or moral principles that this latitude in implementation be used as a subterfuge to disregard or frustrate the law or as a means to continue segregation.

It has been over eight years since the *Brown* decision, yet some states, under the name "token" integration, have admitted only eight or twelve Negro students into white schools in the entire state; others have done absolutely nothing during these years except harass parents who seek to register their children in school or prevent them from seeking judicial relief — the record shows that they have not admitted a single Negro student to a white school in the entire state.

During the 1962–1963 school year, in seventeen Southern states and the District of Columbia, there was a total of 255,367 Negro students attending school with white students. This figure represents only 7.8 percent of the total Negro enrollment in that area. And almost 88,000 of these pupils are in the District of Columbia. Of the total desegregated pupils in this entire area, 95.2 percent of them are in the District of Columbia and the "border states," viz., Delaware, Kentucky, Maryland, Missouri, Oklahoma, and West Virginia. The remaining 4.8 percent are in eight Southern states. Alabama, Mississippi, and South Carolina have no integrated pupils at the elementary and high school levels. This 4.8 percent in the eight Southern states represents *12,217 Negro students attending school with white students while the total Negro pupil enrollment in the eight state area is 1,985,523.* This figures out to little more than half of 1 percent of the Negro students in an eight-state area who are attending nonsegregated schools.[17] It may be seriously doubted that

---

[17] *Southern School News*, December, 1962, p. 1.

such statistics represent a sincere effort to solve problems and implement the mandate. The "all deliberate speed" admonition loses all meaning in view of such performances. It would appear that many persons with administrative and legislative responsibility in these areas sin at least materially either positively in their efforts to perpetuate segregation or negatively in their do-nothing attitude.

There is a variety of explanations for the efforts to prevent school desegregation. Some are expressions of fear: fear of racial intermarriage receiving first consideration. This fear is probably the most frequently used explanation of opposition to school desegregation by those who see the opening of schools to Negroes as the first step of an inevitable progression to interracial marriage. This fear is more real and imminent to Southern whites because of a different attitude toward the school in the South. Schools are regarded, for the most part, in the North as public institutions established for the purpose of supplying an education. They are regarded impersonally. Establishment of friendships at the school is an optional factor of attendance, distinct from any real school purpose. On the other hand, in the South, the school is almost as social as it is educational. The social body is practically coterminous with the student body. This co-extension is possible because of a homogeneous school population, for the most part white, Protestant, and Anglo-Saxon. Sororities and fraternities do not play the important role that they do in the Northern schools because the whole Southern school is a white, Protestant, Anglo-Saxon fellowship.[18]

Many objections to desegregation are, of course, thinly disguised manifestations of bias or prejudice. Among these are claims that Negro children are dirty and uncared for, and that they are infected with venereal diseases, hence must be kept in their own schools lest they contaminate or infect white children.

Regardless of the possibility of a higher incidence of Negro pupils being dirty or unkempt (incidentally, the writer has never seen this claim supported by verifiable statistics or studies), it should be immediately apparent that maintenance of segregated schools will neither remedy the situation nor prevent its repetition. If a Negro

---

[18] Walker Percy, "The Southern Moderate," Commonweal, 67 (Dec. 13, 1957), 279–282.

pupil arrives at school unkempt or dirty, the proper solution is for the authorities to impress on the parents or guardians the fact of their obligations, and, where this is of no avail, apply judicial and punitive measures for child neglect. Remedies, however, should be applied whether the child is white or colored; it is no solution to permit the situation to continue so long as it is in segregated schools where such disagreeable facts can remain hidden from the sensitivity of the white community. No consideration is given to the dislike or fear of conscientious Negro parents that their children must be subjected to such conditions in segregated schools. Demands for segregated educational facilities in such circumstances apparently mean that it is all right for Negro children to come to school dirty provided they come to a segregated school.

The same applies to cases of disease. Medical care, supervision, and guidance of such pupils should be provided whether they are white or Negro. Health hazards, from whatever source, must be controlled, and where isolation is demanded in a certain medical situation, it should be enforced strictly. But isolation must be of sick persons only, not of an entire race. If certain classes or national groups appear to have a high incidence of an infectious disease, e.g., tuberculosis, it would be ridiculous to isolate every member of that group, sick or well. The so-called social diseases most often are contracted through some form of sexual contact. Fears of contamination from germs carried through the air or lurking on pencils or books are not well founded. Again, proper precautions should be taken in instances of communicable disease to guarantee that it does not become a health hazard to the community, or to individuals, but the strictures should be placed only on persons constituting the menace.

All these objections should be faced on an individual basis and proper corrective measures applied, whether they are the coercive sanctions for negligent parents, medical care, even compulsory when the common good makes it imperative, or punitive and restrictive measures for pupil delinquency, etc. But they must be applied on an individual basis not a racial one. If a white child is offensive to moral or hygienic standards, or is a health threat to others, he or his parents, as the case demands, should be forced to correct the situation just the same as the Negro child or his parents.

A more realistic objection is the fact that there is an educational lag between Negro children, seeking transfers from segregated schools, and white children. Sometimes this lag amounts to as much as several years of education. This means that when a sixth-grade Negro pupil transfers from the segregated school, he is likely to find that his new classmates are considerably ahead of him academically, and that his scholastic equals are more likely to be found in the fifth or even the fourth grade. If he is retained in the upper class, he either fails because he cannot keep up with the other students, or the teacher has to downgrade the teaching program. The obvious result of this latter solution is that the others are held back, suffer a loss of time which could have been used to advance their education, and further, finding the retarded pace boring, they lose interest in classwork and often misbehave and become disciplinary problems. This solution is not fair to the pupils who are losing so many educational opportunities.

The problem is a vexing one, particularly when the number of new arrivals is large. Most likely this was foreseen as part of the situation by the Court in using the phrase "with deliberate speed." In some areas there are thousands of students in segregated schools whose education has been deficient and who are victims of this lag. Explanations of the cause of this educational lag are varied. At times, deficiencies attendant on segregated education are explained as the product of the massive inequalities of Negro schools, with their substandard physical plants and equipment; underpaid and overworked teachers; lack of sufficiently trained teachers; curricula deficiencies; truncated scholastic years, etc. Many of these defects are caused by discriminations in allotment of school funds. In 1940, in the Southern states, for each prorated $1.00 spent on education of Negro children, $2.58 was spent on each white child. By 1952, the situation had improved, but even then the ratio was $1.47 for each white child compared to $1.00 for each Negro child.[19]

Psychological factors have also been offered as an explanation. Feelings of inferiority and frustration have been indicated as important factors in discouraging scholastic endeavors. Aggression and hostility

---

[19] Truman M. Pierce, et al., White and Negro Schools in the South: An Analysis of Biracial Education (Englewood Cliffs: Prentice-Hall, Inc., 1955), p. 164.

toward whites which the Negro must transfer to members of his own race frequently result in rebellion against the teacher and school authorities. In addition, lack of jobs, except as laborers, truck drivers, or domestics, for Negroes with only a high school education, acts as a deterrent to study and ambition for those high school students who realize that they will not be able to overcome the problems, chiefly financial, of securing a college education. The principal of a Negro high school pointed out this lack of job opportunities for high school graduates:

> As far as economic opportunity is concerned, if our students don't go on to college, they might as well not have gone to high school; they end up as janitors, maids and porters.[20]

But even a college degree is only a partial key to job opportunities for the Negro. His education will open the door to a career with the federal government, in social work, or in teaching, but if his aims have been directed to finance, or his interests have been in the field of industry or business, a college degree will be of little value.

This lack of job opportunity is causing many Negro college graduates to leave the South and go North, or to the West, particularly California. Southern states are spending more money each year on Negro education in a belated effort to try to make them "equal," and in some instances the state is subsidizing Negro colleges. But after the expenditure of these sums, local hiring policies force the graduates from these colleges to leave the home state and seek jobs elsewhere. Those who should by reason of training and education form the backbone of the Negro community and become leaders are driven out, leaving the less educated Negro in the greater predominance, and thus reinforcing prejudicial attitudes of the whites.

Another explanation of educational lag is the claim that the Negro is intellectually inferior. This assertion of innate intellectual deficiency is not new. It has a history reaching back to pre-Civil War days. Charges of intellectual inferiority by reason of race were particularly widespread in the literature defending slavery. The charge is still being made today, both in popular written defenses of racial

---

[20] Statement of principal of a Negro high school in Winston-Salem, N. C., quoted by Gene Roberts, Jr., "Negro Education — For What?" *New York Times Magazine*, November 19, 1961, p. 26 ff.

segregation such as Stuart O. Landry's *The Cult of Equality*, and in technical studies such as Audrey M. Shuey's *The Testing of Negro Intelligence*. Dr. Shuey's conclusion of her study is:

> The remarkable consistency in test results, whether they pertain to school or preschool children, to high school or college students, to draftees of World War I or World War II, to the gifted or the mentally deficient, to the delinquent or criminal; the fact that the colored-white differences are present not only in the rural South and urban South, but in the border and northern areas; the fact that relatively small average differences are found between the IQ's of northern-born and southern-born Negro children in northern cities; the evidence that the tested differences appear to be greater for abstract than for practical or concrete problems; the evidence that the differences obtained are not due primarily to a lack of language skills, the colored averaging no better on non-verbal tests than on verbal tests; the fact that differences are reported in all studies in which the cultural environment of the whites appeared to be no more complex, rich, or stimulating than the environment of the Negroes; the fact that in many comparisons (including those in which the colored appeared to best advantage) the Negro subjects have been either more representative of their racial group or more highly selected than have the comparable white subjects; all point to the presence of some native differences between Negroes and whites as determined by intelligence tests.[21]

All admit that Negroes had a poorer showing in intelligence tests than whites as a group. In explanation it is pointed out that Northern Negroes do better than Southern Negroes; that in the army tests, the record of some Northern Negroes is better than that of some white Southerners; that there is an improvement corresponding to the number of years the Negro has lived in the North. This, some psychologists say, indicates that environmental factors account for the difference in group testings.[22]

Bertram Karon has written:

> One can conclude that whites and Negroes, and northern and southern Negroes, do differ in average intelligence as measured, that intelligence tests are affected by environment, that the environments involved do differ in respects known to be related to intelligence test scores. One cannot conclude that there is *no* difference due to hereditary factors between the groups, but only that there has been no *demonstrated*

[21] Audrey M. Shuey, *The Testing of Negro Intelligence* (Lynchburg: J. P. Bell Co., 1958), p. 318.

[22] Otto Klineberg, "Tests of Negro Intelligence," *Characteristics of the American Negro*, Otto Klineberg (ed.) (New York: Harper & Bros., 1944), pp. 23–96.

hereditary difference, whereas there has been demonstrated an environ-
mentally based difference of considerable magnitude.[23]

This is approximately the same conclusion drawn by Dr. Anne
Anastasi:

> On intelligence tests, the average performance of Negroes has generally
> been lower than that of whites. Although statistically significant, such
> group difference must be qualified in two important respects. First,
> they represent only a description of differences under existing cultural
> conditions, but provide no evidence for the racial or hereditary origin
> of such differences. . . . A second necessary qualification stems from
> the wide individual differences within groups and the consequent over-
> lapping of groups. As a result, group averages provide a very unreliable
> guide to the evaluation of individuals.[24]

On the other hand, some psychologists adopt a middle position and
do not consider the matter proved either way. Such is the report of
the British psychologist, Dr. P. E. Vernon, who in a discussion of the
problem of Negro intelligence states:

> . . . those psychologists and anthropologists who would attribute all
> test differences to differences in upbringing have quite a strong case.
> We can also agree that no one has yet proven the existence of any
> genuine racial or ethnic difference in intelligence A. But also we
> must recognize that no one has disproved them. It would, for example,
> be an entirely reasonable hypothesis that the Negro has much the
> same genes as the white underlying early perceptual and motor develop-
> ment, but that he tends to lack some of the genes which underlie the
> later maturation of advanced conceptual thought. This would fit in
> with a lot of the facts, though it cannot, as yet, be confirmed or
> contradicted.[25]

So the controversy goes. It is beyond our capabilities to judge
which viewpoint is correct scientifically. This is a matter for which
the theologian and the ethician, as well as the educator, must await
the research and conclusions of the psychologist and the anthropolo-
gist. However, the weight of authority alone inclines one to accept the
opinion that environmental factors are responsible for the test dif-

---

[23] Bertram P. Karon, *The Negro Personality: A Rigorous Investigation of the
Effects of Culture* (New York: Springer Publishing Co., 1958), pp. 52–53.
[24] Anne Anastasi, "Psychological Research and Educational Desegregation," *A
Catholic Case against Segregation*, p. 145.
[25] Philip E. Vernon, "Race and Intelligence," *Man, Race and Darwin: Papers
read at a Joint Conference of the Royal Anthropological Institute and the Institute
of Race Relations* (London: Oxford University Press, 1960), pp. 57–64.

ferences. By far the greater number of scientists are agreed that there is no innate mental difference in the Negro. When the state of Alabama allotted $3,000 to Dr. Wesley C. George of the School of Medicine of the University of North Carolina for an anthropological study to prove the existence of an innate intellectual inferiority of Negroes, which could be used to justify retention of segregated schools, the American Anthropological Association, at their convention in Philadelphia, on November 21, 1961, approved a resolution by a vote of 192 to 0, reaffirming its position that Negroes were not inferior to whites as a race. Their resolution read in part:

. . . The American Anthropological Association repudiates statements now appearing in the United States that Negroes are biologically and in innate mental ability inferior to whites, and reaffirms the fact that there is no scientifically established evidence to justify the exclusion of any race from the rights guaranteed by the Constitution of the United States.

But though proponents of segregated education claim innate inferiority as justification for their position, nevertheless, it is not a valid justification. Even if intellectual inferiority of the Negro as a race was scientifically proved, nevertheless, it would not be a warrant for segregation. All statistics employed are those of group testings, hence they do not indicate or consider individual abilities. Testings show that some individual Negroes tested did better than some of the whites. Psychologists call this an "overlap," that is, the percentage of Negro scores which equaled or exceeded the average white scores. Dr. Shuey, who maintains the existence of basic intellectual differences, reports that the "overlaps," when reported, "ranged between 0 and 69 per cent." Individuals capable of equaling or surpassing the median obtained by the white group certainly cannot be considered intellectually deficient. To force them to attend schools in which there is a preponderance of below-median students would be an injustice. If local school boards and educational authorities desire segregation of schools predicated on intelligence ratings, this would not necessarily be an unreasonable basis of distinction, although the effectiveness of such an arrangement might well be questioned. But intelligence requirements should be the same for all prospective students. It would be an anomaly to have a situation where the white median IQ is 105, and a Negro applicant with a rating of 103 is rejected, while a white applicant with 99 is accepted. If educational and curricula requirements justify the establishment of a minimum intelligence rating, justice and charity will demand that it be applied to both white and Negro children and not used as a means of racial discrimination.

To alleviate problems of the transitional period, the courts have approved various pupil placement arrangements. Under some of these plans, school authorities were permitted to use test criteria for Negro children applying for admission to previously all-white schools. The purpose was to enable authorities to select those who gave indications of succeeding in the new environment. These testings were required only of Negro children and not of white children. Such approval of pupil placement plans does not contradict what has been said about the inequity involved in establishing and enforcing certain requirements only for Negro students. In the first place, no judicial approval of such plans ever contemplates their permanency. They are temporary and intended to bridge the transitional period. Further, they are in accord with the Court mandate to end discrimination with "deliberate speed," since for approval of these plans, the courts must be convinced that local authorities are moving toward complete compliance, and that this plan is prudentially promoting and assisting such progress and is not a discriminatory subterfuge. Further, the burden falls on the local authorities to prove that such temporizings are needed and that they are in good faith in their assertions of intention to fully comply at the earliest date practicable. Indeed these requirements were stipulated in the Supreme Court's implementation decree.

Evidence of the thinking of the courts along this line and their strict enforcement of these requirements is seen in a U. S. District Court decision in Arkansas. Previously the Court had approved of a test criterion for Negro children applying to a certain school. Two Negro children applied for admission to the first grade. When both failed to acquire an "average or better" rating on these tests, they were refused admittance. In a case brought by their parents, the District Court indicated that when it approved the plan, it contemplated a situation in which there would be a substantial number of Negro applicants, but that this expectation did not materialize. The Court then decided that the use of selective testing was licit where the number of Negro applicants was substantial. In this way, a selection of the more apt would work to the best interests of the individual students, and, in the long run, to the school system and to the entire race. However, where Negro applicants were so few, the problem of selection was practically nonexistent and the officials must be careful lest the requirements become exclusionary devices which would perpetuate compulsory segregation, intentionally or unintentionally. The school board was consequently ordered to reconsider the two applications.[26]

In the years that have elapsed since the *Brown* decision, progress has been made. However, in some sections of the country, there are Negro children, born about the time of the decision, whose parents had hoped would be free of segregated education, but for whom, as they reach school age, only segregated schools are open. But the walls are weakening. Defenders of segregation are on the defensive. The legal bulwark upon which their system rested has been removed. In areas where local laws attempt to retain segregated education, their dubious constitutionality renders them vulnerable to federal court action and judicial review, leaving as the only alternative open defiance and violence.

Token integration, or even more, the complete lack of any desegregation in some areas indicates that it is not likely that numerically significant school integration in these areas will be obtained for some time. Hodding Carter, a Southern moderate, lists reasons why he believes that large-scale integration is not in the immediate offing:[27]

1. The continuation of housing segregation.

2. Gerrymandering of school districts by local authorities in an attempt to keep Negroes in certain school districts.

3. Pupil placement plans which have passed the constitutional test.

4. Economic and physical pressure brought to bear on Negro parents by employers and others not to enroll their children in white schools.

5. The preference of some Negro parents and pupils.

---

[26] *Earnestine Dove v. Lee Parham*, U. S. Dist. Court, Eastern Dist., Arkansas, Western Div., August 25, 1961, 196 F. Suppl. 944.

[27] Hodding Carter, "Desegregation Does Not Mean Integration," *New York Times Magazine*, February 11, 1962, p. 71.

6. Vested Negro interest in school segregation, e.g., administrative or teaching positions which would not be open or available to Negroes in a nonsegregated school.

7. Wide expansion of school-building programs and expenditures in certain areas for Negro schools.

The Courts have looked primarily to the individual states and the various local governments or agencies acting in their name, in determining obligations or violations of the desegregation order. They have been consistent in their interpretation of the Fourteenth Amendment as binding only the states or public authority, and as not applicable to actions of individual citizens, unless acting under "color of law." The Supreme Court in the *Civil Rights Cases* of 1883 declared that the Federal Civil Rights Act of 1875 was unconstitutional because it punished private citizens who discriminated on the basis of race. Private citizens who discriminate can be punished only by a state civil rights' statute, and not by an act of Congress, this decision declared. Unfortunately, only a few states have enacted such civil rights' statutes.

In addition to legal obligations, there are moral obligations which are not enforceable by law. This is particularly true of the obligation of charity, which obligation can and does apply in the matter of the right to education. It obliges (a) teachers, (b) pupils, and (c) parents.

Interracial charity, like interracial justice, is a virtue which should be part of a teacher's spiritual equipment. But, as with all virtues, it is not secured by mere desire. Acquiring virtue is the result of hard work, sincere and conscious efforts, as well as continuous practice. Every teacher is aware, from experience, of the alertness of a class to attitudes and prejudices of the teacher. Just as a class is aware in a short time of disciplinary strength or weakness or academic interest in a teacher, through what would appear to be an intuition, so too they are aware of likes or dislikes of the teacher. Lack of charity, resentment, impatience, and personal prejudice toward Negro pupils, though not overtly manifested, will not escape the attention of the students, and will tend to create and form prejudices and dislikes in them, or reinforce and strengthen them where they have already been acquired. Teachers have a moral obligation in charity to be diligent and careful lest prejudice be transmitted or strengthened through their actions and attitudes, and the only method of guaranteeing that they will not do this is the sincere and conscientious effort to develop that attitude within themselves. At the same time, charity, as well as justice, toward the Negro pupils demands this effort to overcome prejudice or dislike, lest the teacher's demands, expectations, disciplining, and teaching of the Negro children offend charity or justice.

In June, 1962, the public schools of the South marked the end of the first full year without violence since 1954. During previous years, mobs, boycotts, and bombings flared up each year as new schools were desegregated. These incidents included violence at the University of Alabama during the 1955–1956 school year when a Negro woman attended class for three days; riots in Clay and Sturgis, Kentucky, as well as in Clinton, Tennessee, which necessitated sending in the National Guard in 1956–1957; and the most noteworthy of all, in 1957–1958, at Little Rock, Arkansas, when the President sent federal troops to control the rioting. Participants in these various incidents included white students and their parents, as well as others who had no immediate connection or interest in the school, but who were opposed to desegregation. Participation in such violence by students or their parents is reprehensible and immoral, as is the participation of the other members of the mob, which occasionally included Northern prosegregationists.

Not all Southern students resented the Court order or attempted to frustrate it. The opinions and feelings of many Southern college students in this matter were much more moderate and advanced than those of their elders. Evidence of their attitude can be seen in the University of Mississippi's student paper which advocated and requested the admission of Negroes to the graduate school; other student papers supported this request. In the four years previous to 1957, an estimated 2000 Negroes were enrolled for the regular school year at publicly supported colleges which had previously been segregated.

However, when James Meredith, a native of Mississippi, after seventeen months of litigation, was enrolled in 1962 as an undergraduate at the University of Mississippi, the students did not reflect their earlier attitude. In July, 1962, the Court of Appeals for the

5th Circuit ordered that an injunction be issued constraining officials of the University of Mississippi to admit Meredith as a student. Meredith made four unsuccessful attempts to register. Twice the governor of Mississippi, Ross R. Barnett, personally rejected Meredith's application, and the lieutenant-governor, Paul Johnson, rejected the third attempt to enroll on September 26, 1962. Meredith's fourth attempt was unsuccessful when police refused to permit him to enter. Finally, on Sunday, September 30, accompanied by several hundred U. S. marshals, Meredith was brought on the campus. When it became known that he was on campus, rioting broke out. U. S. troops were dispatched, and within a few hours violence ended. However, two men had been killed, 166 U. S. marshals and 40 soldiers were wounded. Meredith was finally registered. The harm caused by the Mississippi riot was great. Besides the loss of life and the injuries, there was the destruction of property, as well as the loss of American prestige throughout the world and the cost of providing protection to Meredith in enrolling and remaining at the university. An estimate of this latter cost can be made from the realization that during the month when the situation was most critical, the U. S. Defense Department spent more than four million dollars and, at one time, deployed more than 30,000 troops to protect Meredith and maintain order.

Closely allied with the problems of education is the matter of discrimination in the use of library facilities. Several years ago, the courts had occasion to consider the role of the library in modern society and educational systems. It recognized that libraries are an integral part of public educational facilities, and an invaluable aid for advancing adult education.[28] Although it is generally recognized that libraries are necessary educational auxiliaries, it is not realized that many Negroes are either completely excluded from the use of municipal libraries, or else have restricted and limited facilities available. Librarians themselves are not, apparently, all aware of this discrimination. In 1960, in an article in the Library Journal, the librarian-author stated that most librarians did not know that Negro readers

---

[28] Kerr v. Enoch Pratt Free Library of Baltimore City, 149 F. 2d 212 (4th Cir. 1945; cert. denied, 326 U. S. 721) (1945).

in most Southern communities could not use white branches, and could not use the central library in which the larger book collections were kept.[29]

A 1954 survey of library services in Southern towns and cities revealed that in only sixty-two communities Negroes were allowed full use of the main library and its reference room, and twenty-four communities provided them with limited service at the main library. Eleven cities maintained unsegregated branch libraries. In South Carolina, Georgia, Alabama, Mississippi, and Louisiana there was no community providing full service for Negroes at the main library. The result of this discrimination has been that two thirds of the ten million Negroes living in these thirteen states have had no library service whatsoever, while most of the other three million Negroes, who had some access, were limited to Negro branches.

Few states have laws actually requiring library segregation. Most library boards are free of legal restrictions and can act to end segregation when public protests are made. In Memphis, a Sit-In demonstration, plus impending court action, brought about voluntary desegregation of the library in 1960. In Danville, Virginia, and Petersburg, Virginia, the city councils desegregated the libraries after Sit-Ins and impending court cases.

An indication of the extent of library discrimination obtaining today is seen in the results of a survey conducted in 1960 by the United States Commission on Civil Rights. A questionnaire was sent to 256 libraries in seventeen Southern states. However, the statistics gathered are incomplete since, for various reasons, only 109 libraries in eleven states replied. Nevertheless, the figures gathered can serve to indicate a general pattern. Where segregated branch libraries were operated, services were available in white branches on an average of 33.3 hours weekly, but in the Negro branches, only 15.2 hours of service were available. White branches had an average of over 28,000 circulating volumes and 959 reference books; while the Negro branches had an average of 4379 circulating volumes and 161 reference books. The conclusion drawn by the Commission was that where services were provided on a segregated basis for Negroes,

---

[20] Rice Estes, "Segregated Libraries," *Library Journal*, 85 (Dec. 15, 1960), 4418–4420.

the facilities were inferior to those provided white citizens, and that these discriminations violated federal law which made funds available to libraries, but required that they provide service for all.[30]

There is a negative obligation for students not to harass, insult, or ridicule Negro students who come to their school; there is a positive obligation of charity to show them the common signs of friendship, including the politeness and courtesy which would be shown to any fellow student, such as the returning of greetings, nonexclusion from general activities, etc., as well as an obligation to render the social amenities ordinarily required by etiquette. Greater charity will move a student to advance beyond what is obligatory and to practice forms of the virtue which are supererogatory, e.g., extraordinary signs of friendship, etc.

Parents have an important obligation to inculcate the proper attitudes and moral standards in their children. They should prevent their acquiring racial prejudices and dislikes by correct instruction and explanations, and, in particular, should be careful not to permit their own words or actions to become a scandal to their children. Besides the obligation of refraining from participation in violence, they must also refrain from nonviolent attempts to drive or keep a Negro child from school merely because of race. These acts include social or economic pressure brought to bear on Negro parents so that they will be deterred from registering their children in white schools. Threats of economic reprisal, loss of business or customers or employment, and even pressure in the form of ridicule or shame which are used in such situations to keep a Negro child out of school are violations of charity and justice. Whites who resort to such pressures are at least sinning materially.

---

[30] *1961 U. S. Commission on Civil Rights Report*, Book 2, "Education," p. 148.

CHAPTER 16

THE RIGHT TO WORSHIP

Nowhere is racial segregation more extensively and rigidly enforced than in South Africa. The official government policy of enforced segregation, apartheid, has been implemented to impose restraints on every facet of daily life. Separation is carried out to a degree surpassing the most stringent demands of American segregation. Apartheid restricts housing facilities and limits freedom of movement, prohibiting non-Europeans from entering certain areas; buildings must provide separate elevators; blood banks are required to keep blood donations from non-Europeans separate; airplanes must furnish separate sections, while dishes and headrests on seats occupied by colored must, at the end of each flight, be removed, tagged, and washed separately. Such prescriptions recall the requirements of the dietary and purification laws of the Pharisees.

Time, in an article on "Apartheid," spoke of the lack of charity manifested by the South African Dutch Reformed churches, most of which refuse to admit any native to their services. The article reported the story of a South African policeman who discovered a native in a white church on his knees. Being informed that the Kaffir was scrubbing the floor, the officer replied, "Alright, but God help you if I catch you praying."[1] The anomaly makes the reply laughable, but awareness that this does not necessarily describe a fictitious situation since it occurs in churches in this country, dulls any humor. The segregated church is not a phenomenon restricted to apartheid. Individual Protestant and Catholic churches in the United States have refused admittance to Negroes and at times have resorted to

[1] "This is Apartheid," *Time*, July 6, 1962, p. 19.

216

police authority to turn away Negroes who attempted to obtain admittance.

Previous to the Civil War, the various Protestant denominations faced a dilemma which eventually produced schisms which have continued to the present time. Among members of the Episcopal, Methodist, and Baptist denominations, the question of the morality of slavery was so vigorously controverted that schism was produced. The Southern Methodist Church and the Baptist Convention which still exist as separate entities were products of this controversy. Today the Southern Protestant churches are presented with an equally divisive question — the compatibility of Christianity with segregation. In a study of the reaction of Southern churches to this problem, John Wicklein has this to say:

> Today no major denomination in the South and few leading churchmen assert that segregation can be reconciled with their religion. And therein lies the dilemma: If Southern white churchmen follow their conviction and work for integration, they are damned at home; if they compromise their conviction and condone segregation, they are damned in the nation and the world. Many clergymen have made the difficult choice and placed themselves in the forefront of groups acting to end the "peculiar institution" of the twentieth-century America.[2]

The Wicklein study is chiefly concerned with the Protestant churches and considers their efforts to desegregate in Atlanta, Birmingham, and Montgomery, as well as the resistance or cooperation these met. (In the latter part of the survey, Catholic efforts in New Orleans are studied.) From his study, Mr. Wicklein believes that the Protestant clergy, especially the younger members who have attended integrated seminaries, are more critical of segregation in the church and more anxious to end it than the laity. Clerical opposition to desegregation comes mainly from Fundamentalist ministers who justify racial segregation on scriptural grounds, whereas ministers of the major denominations usually reject such interpretations and theologizing.

In some areas, lay opposition to desegregation is very strong, and organizations have been formed to resist it. This lay opposition has prevented many ministers from taking a public stand or expressing

---

[2] John Wicklein, "The Church in the South and Segregation," *The New York Times*, July 5–8, 1959.

their opposition to continued segregation. In Birmingham, a Methodist Laymen's Union was formed for the specific purpose of preventing the merger of the Central Jurisdiction (Negro) with the white conference. Wicklein reports that at the meeting which organized this Lay Union, 1800 laymen were in attendance.

The situation whereby only a few churches permit an individual Negro to even occasionally attend services; where interracial churches are practically nonexistent; where white ministers do not participate with Negro ministers in local denominational associations, has not escaped the attention of most Protestant leaders. Their increasing awareness has caused a problem of conscience and, from time to time, there have been official denunciations of segregation in church and demands for its cessation. Protestant theologians, seminary professors, and many other ministers have become increasingly articulate and critical in their accusations of failure of the church to alleviate the racial situation. T. B. Maston, in condemning segregation practiced in the churches, expressed fear that the churches may be the last to desegregate:

> Segregation in the church violates something that is basic in the nature of the church. How can a church exclude from "the church of God" those who are children of God? How can it, as "the body of Christ," withhold the privilege of worship from those who have been brought into union with Christ. . . .We must confess that there are churches, and they are not all in the South, that are thoroughly committed to the continuance of segregation in society and also within the church. We believe that such an attitude, which is the epitome of racial pride, cuts the very heart out of the Christian gospel and the Christian ethic. It imperils the soul of the church itself. How tragic it would be if the churches became "the last bulwark of racial segregation!" What a paradox if secularism and secular institutions "out-christianize Christianity!" It has frequently been said that eleven o'clock on Sunday morning is the most segregated hour of the week. It is close enough to the truth to embarrass many of our churches and to give to many Christians an uneasy conscience.[3]

And Waldo Beach, professor of Christian Ethics at Duke University, has also given a strong indictment of the racial attitude of the churches:

---

[3] T. B. Maston, *Segregation and Desegregation: A Christian Approach* (New York: The Macmillan Co., 1959), pp. 135–136.

The Christian will also be alert to the presence of the divine judgment in the failure of the churches, at this point in their life, to be the conscience of the community, to stand in clear Christian witness for the unity in Christ against the world's divisions which they have taken into their own life. No denial of their Lord is more poignant than this, where the churches have become social clubs, complacent mixtures of pietism and Rotarianism. Out of comfort, fear, and blindness the churches have for the most part capitulated to the segregation and prejudices of the world, and have become salt without savor.[4]

A study of racial practices in Protestant churches was made by Frank Loescher in 1948. He concluded that as a social institution they were making no contributions to the solution of the racial problem, but were merely retaining and enforcing the *status quo*:

> Protestantism, by its policies and practices, far from helping to integrate the Negro in American life, is actually contributing to the segregation of Negro Americans. . . . The churches in their denominational policies avoid making public their position on crucial types of relationships with Negroes. Finally, and most telling of all, the churches in their congregations and educational institutions adhere to a pattern of segregation.[5]

Practically the same charge is made by R. M. Miller, as a conclusion to an historical survey of racial attitudes manifested by Protestantism during the twenty years previous to 1939. He condemns the attitude prevalent during that time in Protestantism, especially the acceptance of and contentment with the existing state of affairs. He finds that it is only at the end of that period that Protestant consciences started to become uneasy about their complacency.[6]

For various reasons, it is impossible to determine the actual number of Negro Protestants who attend racially mixed congregations. The surveys made only indicate general situations or trends, and do not give actual representative statistics. Loescher has estimated that

---

[4] Waldo Beach, "A Theological Analysis of Race Relations," *loc. cit.*, pp. 217–218.

[5] Frank Loescher, *The Protestant Church and the Negro: A Pattern of Segregation* (New York: Association Press, 1948), pp. 15–16.

[6] Robert M. Miller, "The Attitudes of American Protestantism toward the Negro, 1919–1939," *Journal of Negro History*, 41 (July, 1956), 215–240; cf. also Robert M. Miller, "The Protestant Churches and Lynching, 1919–1939," *Journal of Negro History*, 42 (April, 1957), 118–131, which shows that although their concern over lynchings is irregular, it was deeper and more widespread than is commonly believed.

approximately eight million Negroes are affiliated with various Protestant denominations, seven and a half million of whom are members of separate Negro denominations such as the African Methodist Episcopal Church with over one million members, and the National Baptist Convention, U.S.A., with five million members. The remaining half million belong to predominantly white denominations, but he estimates that 99 percent of these are worshiping in segregated congregations and associate with the white members of their denomination only at assemblies or conventions. Of the others he says:

> There remains a handful of Negro members in local "white" churches. How many? Call it one-tenth of one per cent of all the Negro Protestant Christians in the United States — 8,000 souls — the figure is probably much too large. Whatever the figure actually is, the number of white and Negro persons who ever gather together for worship under the auspices of Protestant Christianity is almost microscopic.[7]

It must be remembered that this is an estimate and subject to all the objections and imperfections of any estimate. It was made in 1948, and indications are that the situation has improved because of the increasing awareness of the moral aspects involved. How great this improvement has been cannot be stated. Social and statistical studies along this line are needed to acquire any degree of certitude or points of comparison.

Proclamations condemning segregation and policy decisions which have been made at the national assemblies, as well as statements of Protestant leaders and theologians, have neither filtered down to any great degree to the individual churches, nor impressed or motivated the rank-and-file members. But this should not be a cause of wonderment. Papal social teaching also evidences tardiness in filtering down to Catholic laity and even occasionally to priests by whom it should be implemented and put into practice, to say nothing of actual resistance and opposition as was evidenced by the reception of *Mater et Magistra* in some quarters.

It is generally admitted that the Catholic record is better. Father John T. Gillard, S.S.J., writing in 1941, stated that there were 296,998 Negro Catholics in 1940, and that 63.7 percent of these were parishioners in "colored churches"; the remaining 36.3 percent were

---

[7] Frank Loescher, op. cit., p. 77.

regular parishioners in territorial churches together with white Catholics in the area.[8] This did not include Negro Catholics who occasionally attend a "white" church to hear Mass or receive the sacraments, but only actual parish members. Since the time of the survey, the number of Negro Catholics has more than doubled, and the percentage attending mixed parishes has also increased.

Higher incidence of integration within Catholic churches has not passed unnoticed by sociologists, as well as by Protestant leaders. Myrdal states that in southern Louisiana, the Catholic Church is the only one which allows Negroes to attend white churches, but that they try to keep Negroes in their own churches and discourage them from joining interchurch meetings, etc., and that it provides "a separate set of white priests — who seldom mingle with the other priests — for the Negroes."[9]

Various explanations have been offered for this difference. Some point to the small number of Negro Catholics (664,230 according to the 1962 Annual Report of the Secretary of the Commission for the Catholic Missions among the Colored People and Indians). This, they maintain, makes segregation relatively easy since there is a ratio of 62 white Catholics to every 1 Negro Catholic, compared to the Protestant ratio of 4 to 1. This difference and the larger numbers to be integrated create a greater problem for the Protestant churches.

It is claimed, too, that the hierarchical character of the Catholic Church, with authority over church policies and practices residing in the Pope and bishops, compared with the structure of Protestant denominations, where lay members exercise a high degree of control of policies and practices, enables the Catholic Church more easily to put into practice its official teachings.

Still others have explained that individual Protestants look upon their parish church as a social organization as well as a place of worship, whereas in the Catholic Church the emphasis is on the church as a place of worship, with the altar and tabernacle established as the center, and worship its prime function. They indicate that the congregation in the Catholic Church is usually not homogeneous, but is more likely to be composed of a cross section of all social classes

[8] John T. Gillard, S.S.J., *Colored Catholics in the United States* (Baltimore: Josephite Press, 1941), pp. 138–143.

[9] G. Myrdal, *op. cit.*, p. 871.

in the community. This, they believe, produces a greater toleration and realization of equality than obtains in the Protestant churches where the parishioners are usually drawn from the same social and economic levels.

It is impossible to assert with any degree of certainty the fundamental reason for this difference. Perhaps, it would be closer to the truth to say that all these factors influence the situation. But, whatever the explanation, the difference which does exist should not become an occasion to Catholics for pointing their finger in accusation or assuming a "holier-than-thou" attitude or resting in contented smugness. Considered by itself, the Catholic record has outstanding and mighty deficiencies. Father LaFarge speaks of the contributions of the Protestant churches to the Negro cause and their influence on Negro culture. He also stresses the religious instruction they provided to the Negro during slavery. Nor should one overlook the Protestant contribution to help end slavery in this country. The Abolitionist movement was supported and directed chiefly by Protestants, many of them ministers. The underground railway, a system of organized aid for fugitive slaves, had its origin in the complete reliance of the slaves on the Quakers whom they knew would never refuse food or shelter to them while they were escaping from slavery. Dwight Lowell Dumond, an expert on the history of the antislavery movement, writes this about the underground railway and its dangers:

> The risks involved on the part of those who joined in the work [the underground railway] were great. It had to be done in secret. Only those who were resourceful and courageous participated, and they did it because they were making a tangible stroke against slavery, aiding the oppressed, and engaging in a highly romantic enterprise. Most of them were Quakers and Presbyterians, but there were some Baptists, Methodists, Episcopalians, and Catholics. . . . Nearly all of them were Liberty-Free-Soil Republican party members.[10]

We have previously indicated how the Protestant division over slavery resulted in permanent schisms. On the other hand, the attitude of the Catholics, both clergy and lay, toward abolition was not what one would expect from a group largely composed of recent

---

[10] Dwight Lowell Dumond, *Antislavery: The Crusade for Freedom in America* (Ann Arbor: The University of Michigan Press, 1961), p. 313.

immigrants who had come in search of liberty and freedom, economic opportunities, and advancement. Evidence of their attitude can be seen in the contemporary Catholic press, which, with the exception of the *Catholic Telegraph* of Cincinnati, was strongly antiabolitionist. The *United States Catholic Miscellany* of Charleston, South Carolina, claimed that the treatment of slaves in the South was better than that of free Negroes or poor whites in the North, and that slaves represented legitimate property. The *Catholic Advocate* of Kentucky not only opposed abolitionism, but also accepted advertisements for slave sales and rewards for runaways — an indication of how Southern Catholics had accepted the fact of slavery.

This, however, should not be considered an indication that all Catholics were proslavery. The position of most Catholics, especially in the North, was that slavery should be ended, but that it should be done gradually and many could not see how it could be done legally since there were serious constitutional objections, and it would involve alienation of property which had been recognized by law and by the Constitution. Most Southern Catholics joined their Protestant neighbors in a defense of slavery, and believed that the evils connected with it could be removed, or at least mitigated by the universal acceptance and adoption of Catholic teaching on the spirituality of all men. The hierarchy and clergy of the South, because of the Church's precarious position in that area, tried to remain aloof from the problem even to a greater degree than the Northern clergy. In general, their attitude was that the matter being a strictly political issue, they would not commit themselves to a single position since they did not consider that a fundamental tenet of Catholicism was at stake. They believed that slavery was not *in se* opposed to the natural law, and therefore permissible if the conditions of a just servitude were observed and recognition made of the spiritual worth of the slave. In addition, they were occupied with the problems of a nascent church in a hostile environment which presented not only problems of the care of thousands of Catholic immigrants arriving each year, but also pressures from religious opposition and persecution. This was the period of church and convent burnings; riots and street fights; a virulent anti-Catholic literature; the Nativist and

Know-Nothing campaigns. In addition, the prominent role played by Protestants in the Abolitionist movement caused them to regard the entire movement as Protestant.[11]

This position is reflected in the *Theologiae Moralis* of Francis Patrick Kenrick which was intended to aid American priests to handle moral problems which were peculiar to this country and therefore not treated by the European theologians. He reaffirmed that slavery was not contrary to the natural law, and could be permitted to continue in the United States for the sake of the common good, even though, at the same time, he recognized that the slaves were originally unjustly captured and enslaved. Father Brokhage judges that Kenrick failed in his attempt to give a proper theological solution because he was talking about slavery in the abstract, and not as it was practiced in the country at that time. When Kenrick talked about slavery he was speaking about slavery as the theologians defined it, and not chattel slavery as practiced here. Thus, the word "slavery" became an equivocal term as he applied his theological principles to the actual situation. He also failed by neglecting to stress and indicate the obligation of the state to constantly work toward abolition of slavery.[12]

It should be indicated here that Jewish opinion on the question of abolition was similarly divided. There were some zealous Jewish abolitionists, as well as some staunch defenders of slavery, but for the most part, the majority of the Jews in the United States at that time adopted a middle ground position which would approximate that of the majority of Catholics. Bertram Korn explains the middle-ground position of the Jews as the result of their interest, as immigrants, in social and economic problems of personal adjustment to their new surroundings rather than in sectional political issues.[13]

Contemporary attitudes toward the slavery question are, of course, mainly of historical interest today. But in the years following emancipation, the actions of Catholics did not indicate a significant change

---

[11] Madeleine Hooke Rice, *American Catholic Opinion in the Slavery Controversy* (New York: Columbia University Press, 1944), p. 72; cf. also Carl Wittke, *The Irish in America* (Baton Rouge: Louisiana State University Press, 1956), pp. 125-134.

[12] Joseph D. Brokhage, *op. cit.*, p. 36 ff.

[13] Bertram W. Korn, *American Jewry and the Civil War* (Cleveland and Philadelphia: Meridian Books and the Jewish Publication Society of America, 1961), Chapter II, "The Rabbis and the Slavery Question."

or advance of attitude. Catholic Negroes were often compelled, long after the period of slavery, to sit in designated sections of the church, or in special pews, and could not associate with white parishioners or participate with them in parish activities. Occasionally, they were refused admittance to church and informed that they must hear Mass and receive the sacraments at the "colored church" as the laity, and some of the clergy, began to consider the existence of a special church as justification for enforcing segregation. In some instances, fortunately not too common, Negroes were refused admittance to the parish church even when there was no "colored church," and only baptism, matrimony, and extreme unction were available for them, with occasional opportunities for confession.

Jesuit Bend, Erath, New Orleans, and Newton Grove, all of which have relatively large Catholic populations, come to mind as synonyms for the shameful actions of Catholics who insisted on enforcing segregation in the church even when their bishops ordered them to cease their attempts.

At the Church of Our Lady of Lourdes in Erath, Louisiana, on November 27, 1955, Bishop Jules Jeanmard of Lafayette, in a decree read at every Mass, excommunicated several white women of the parish who had set upon and beat a white catechism teacher who had been instructing white and Negro children at the parish catechism school. By order of the Bishop, the decree of excommunication was attached to the doors of the church after the last Mass on November 27, to remain there until he ordered its removal. An automatic excommunication was to be incurred by anyone who attempted to prevent publication of the excommunication or dared to remove it from the church door. He also threatened to close the church if there was a repetition of such violence within the parish.

On October 2, 1955, a Negro priest was sent as a "supply priest" to say Sunday Mass for a mixed congregation at St. Cecilia's Mission in Jesuit Bend. On arriving, he found a police car parked in the driveway and two men, armed and in uniform, in front of the church. Three of the parishioners told him that a Negro priest could not say Mass in a white church. Informed of the incident, Archbishop Rummel suspended all services at St. Cecilia's and reduced the number of Masses to one at nearby churches in Myrtle

Grove and Belle Chasse until the members of the congregation were willing to accept "for service in these churches whatever priest or priests we find it possible to send them." On October 17, the *Osservatore Romano* published a front-page editorial entitled "Touches of Color" in which it supported the Archbishop's action and termed racial exclusiveness a sin against the nature of Catholicism and a negation of it.

In New Orleans, resistance to the order of Archbishop Rummel to desegregate parochial schools became so bitter that it amounted to an interference with the Church's exercise of its mission. After his warning that such interference was punishable in Canon Law with excommunication was disregarded, the Archbishop declared that three of the leaders of the resistance had incurred the penalty of excommunication.

At Newton Grove, when Bishop Waters of Raleigh ordered the closing of a Negro mission church, located a few yards from the main parish church and attended by eighty Negroes, and decreed that they were to attend the parish church, white parishioners were indignant. Parishioners angrily surrounded the Bishop during his visit to Newton Grove and protested his action. Finally they boycotted their parish church, some traveling as far as 60 miles to attend an "all-white" church. The order to consolidate the mission church had been given on May 31, 1953. After two weeks of protests and the beginning of the boycott, the Bishop again acted, and decreed that racial segregation in the churches of the diocese, either in seating arrangements or the reception of the sacraments, would not be tolerated.

Incidents such as these have caused some to regard the separate church established for Negroes as causing and perpetuating an injustice within the Church, and they claim that these churches merely make segregation in church possible. Some go even further and censure the action of the Church in establishing these parishes, and accuse priests and religious communities who staff them of being prosegregationist. This deprecation is not only uncritical and ununderstanding; it is unjust and unfair. Education in the faith and the preservation of that faith for many Negroes have been achieved through these parishes and the work of these priests when there had been neglect of the spiritual care of the Negro, voluntarily or involuntarily. Without these efforts, many would have been left completely without instructions and even without the sacraments. In Mississippi, the religious situation for Negro Catholics was described by Father Dutto in 1888. There Negroes were tolerated in the white churches, but seldom welcomed, and had to remain separate from the whites. In the entire state at that time there were two orphan asylums, one for boys and one for girls, but in neither would a Negro child be accepted. There were a total of 125 religious Sisters teaching, only one of whom taught colored children. In the entire state, there was not a single Catholic church or charitable organization organized for the Negro.[14] In 1898, Father William Teurlings became pastor at Washington, Louisiana. During his pastorate, he enlarged the church at Grand Prairie, and added a wing on it for the Negro Catholics when he learned that the spiritual care of the Negroes had been neglected for thirty years because "the chapel was too small, and the priests had been overworked or incapacitated by illness."[15]

The full story remains to be told of the heroic struggles and hardships of these early priests, secular as well as members of communities, who, working against unbelievable odds and under great handicaps, were entirely devoted to the care of the Negro Catholics and the conversion of others. The fact that they were engaged in this work made them sharers and partakers of the scorn and contempt shown to the Negroes themselves. Nor is this mere oversensitiveness or imagination. When the bishops of Louisiana, shortly after the Second Council of Baltimore in 1866, requested several religious communities to undertake missions among the Negroes of that state, the communities refused because they feared that their work among white Catholics would suffer when it became known that members of the community were working among the Negroes. The reality of this fear is verified by Father Dutto who remarks that even a priest working among the Negroes loses caste and is ostracized.

In Protestant denominations, separate churches are much older than in the Catholic. One of the first began in Philadelphia in 1787, when Negroes attending St. George's Methodist Episcopal Church

---

[14] L. A. Dutto, "Negroes in Mississippi," Catholic World, 46 (Feb., 1888), 583.
[15] William J. Teurlings, "One Mile an Hour: Priestly Memories," adapted by Rosalind Foley, unpublished manuscript, Chancery of Lafayette, Louisiana.

were required, as their numbers increased, to sit in the rear pews of the gallery. In protest they left and established their own church. From this group the independent Negro Protestant church in the North took its origin. Negro Catholics attended the regular parish church before separate churches were provided; although in the South, perhaps as a carry-over from slavery, they were usually in the gallery or in a special section. Segregated seating does not seem to have been the custom in Northern Catholic churches. Father Gillard cites a report of the U. S. Commissioner in 1871 which indicates that in Washington there was no segregated seating in the Catholic churches.

French-speaking San Dominican refugees in Baltimore formed a small congregation using the *chapelle basse* of St. Mary's Seminary until 1836, when the chapel of the then recently founded Oblate Sisters was used for services. This chapel, according to Father Gillard, is the first Catholic edifice in the country for the exclusive use of Negroes. As the congregation grew, larger quarters were required, and, in 1857, the basement of St. Ignatius' Church was dedicated, under the patronage of St. Peter Claver, and used by them. Later, a Universalist church nearby was purchased and renovated, and, in 1864, was dedicated as the Church of St. Francis Xavier, the first Catholic Church in the United States for Negroes. Previous to this, in 1844, the Chapel of the Nativity in Pittsburgh had been dedicated for the use of Negro Catholics, but within a year had to be closed and those who attended went to St. Paul's Cathedral. They continued to attend St. Paul's until 1865 when another church was opened for them.[16]

Following this beginning, a few churches or chapels were opened, e.g., in Charleston, South Carolina, in 1867; Louisville, 1870; Washington, 1874. Most of these were in border states rather than in the deep South. The opening of Negro churches there did not occur with any degree of frequency until almost the beginning of the twentieth century, which incidentally seems to agree with Woodward's theory of the late arrival of Jim Crow in the South. The reaction of Negro Catholics to the establishment of these churches was mixed. Some saw in them the opportunity to participate fully in all parish activi-

---

[16] Timothy J. Holland, S.S.J., "The Catholic Church and the Negro in the United States Prior to the Civil War," unpublished doctoral dissertation, Fordham University, 1950, pp. 87–88.

ties and to attend church without being compelled to sit in a separate place. Others rejected them completely, considered them as segregationist, and either continued to attend church with the whites, as in the past, or ceased attending altogether.

The intention and purpose in establishing these parishes was not to bring about segregation in the Church. Permission was granted to the various bishops to establish these parishes by the Second Plenary Council of Baltimore in 1866. Cardinal Barnabò, Prefect of the Sacred Congregation for the Propagation of the Faith, in the official instruction of that congregation to Archbishop Spalding, included consideration of means for taking care of the spiritual needs of the newly emancipated slaves as part of the council agenda. In its deliberations, the council made a plea for priests who would devote themselves to the care and conversion of the Negroes, and pleaded with Catholic Europe, where there was an ample supply of priests, to come to their aid. To implement the obligation, the council approved of the establishment of separate churches for Negroes where this was judged necessary. The actual words of the decree indicate that the intention was to procure the best means of advancing the spiritual welfare and Christian education of the Negroes. The bishops sought means of educating and converting the vast number of newly freed slaves and not of forcing Negro Catholics into segregated churches. The decree states:

> . . . it seems better to leave it to the zeal and prudence of the Ordinary to determine what should be done in different places for the good of the Negroes. Therefore, if, after having carefully considered the matter, it appears to the Bishop that the salvation of the Negroes will be advanced by building separate churches for them, anyone undertaking this endeavor, with the proper permission, will be most deserving of praise. But if, in other places, it is judged wiser to invite them to attend, with others, the already existing churches, let the Ordinary see that it is done so that the Church will not be further subjected to accusations. For it is a grave obligation binding us in conscience that the door be open for all who wish to come to Christ; that priests be on hand for all who seek the sacraments; that by all means a place be provided in which all who wish may attend the august sacrifice of the Mass on Sundays and holy days.[17]

In no way does the council indicate an intention to discriminate

---

[17] Acta et Decreta Concilii Baltimorensis II, Titulus X, Cap. IV, nn. 202–203.

or compel Negroes to attend segregated churches. In no way does it indicate any intention to appease prejudices and antagonisms of white Catholics, nor is there any mention of a fear that white Catholics might cease to attend church if Negroes were to continue to attend. It was, of course, recognized that many Catholics, especially after 1840, had absorbed and adopted the current attitude toward the Negro. This attitude was to permit him to attend church, but in special sections, and to receive the sacraments, usually after the white parishioners, while manifesting little or no concern about education or the improvement of environment or social conditions. But the prejudices and feelings of white Catholics did not motivate the conciliar decision. Recognition was made of these prejudices as hindrances and obstacles to the spiritual care of the Negro and this, in addition to the problems created by the neglect of education and social training of the former slaves, brought the council to the conclusion that, in some places, the best solution was a separate church. The Church looked upon these parishes as counterparts and equivalents to national parishes. The diocesan Synod of Baltimore in 1875 stated that Negro churches were to operate under the same regulations that had been established for German parishes.[18] The Second Synod of Richmond, in 1886, decreed that pastors of Negro parishes had the same obligations and rights as pastors of German parishes. It further provided that Negro Catholics should be encouraged to have recourse to their own pastors for the administration of the sacraments, for the sake of good order, but that Negro Catholics must be received with charity in any church or cemetery. At the same time, it stated that it was also desirable for the Germans to attend churches established for them, and that they should be advised to do so, but that, if they decided to rent a pew in the territorial parish, they were free to do so.[19]

---

[18] Synodus Diocesana Baltimorensis Octava quae Antecedentium etiam complectitur Constitutiones, n. 24. This also provided that if the territorial pastor was called to a sick Negro Catholic, living within his parochial territory, he must be available to him if it is feared that the sick man's own pastor cannot come to him in an opportune time. A similar provision permitting the territorial pastor to attend the sick call of a German Catholic was also made. But at the same time, it imposed a strict prohibition against the national pastor witnessing a marriage when at least one of the contracting parties was not German, or of baptizing a child if neither of the parents were German (n. 22).

[19] Acta et Statuta Synodi Richmondensis Secundae. n. 15.

It may be that these early synods considered it more desirable for the Negroes to attend their own church than for the Germans or other nationals, but it cannot be claimed that they intended to draw a line of demarcation between white and Negro parishes or to exclude the Negro from the white church. The present Code of Canon Law does not provide explicitly for parishes established on racial grounds, although it does for language or nationality differences but only by special indult. It is, however, the common teaching of canonists that the Negro parish is to be equated with the national or language parish:

> A parish established for Negroes within the confines of a territorial parish should be regarded as the equivalent of a national parish, but not a territorial parish even though all its parishioners reside entirely in a compact neighborhood inhabited solely by Negroes.[20]

The law permitting national parishes has always regarded them as temporary institutions, whose purpose was to provide for the spiritual necessities of those unable to understand the local language. Abbo and Hannan state that the purpose of the national parish is not the perpetuation of foreign elements and the disruption of national unity.[21]

Conclusive proof of the temporary and transitory character of the national parish is seen in a reply of the Sacred Congregation for the Propagation of the Faith on April 26, 1897, to a question proposed by the Apostolic Delegate to the United States, Archbishop Sebastian Martinelli, in which it was stated that children of foreign-born parents were not obliged to remain parishioners of national parishes after they reached adulthood, and that foreign-born adults, who could understand English, were not obliged to attend a national parish.[22]

The same transitory character must be attributed to Negro parishes. Laity and priests err in regarding them as permanent establishments to which Negro Catholics are obliged to belong. This has been pointed out several times in recent episcopal statements and pastoral letters, particularly those of Archbishop Rummel of New Orleans and of

---

[20] John Abbo and Jerome D. Hannan, *The Sacred Canons* (St. Louis: B. Herder Book Co., 1957), I, p. 278.

[21] *Ibid.*, p. 279 .

[22] *American Ecclesiastical Review*, 17 (July, 1897), 87.

Bishop Waters of Raleigh. Archbishop Rummel, stating that when separate facilities for the Negroes were established they were never intended to be permanent, recalled the reluctance and fear of Archbishop Francis Janssens, who dedicated St. Katherine's, the first Negro parish in New Orleans, in 1895, that it might become divisive but hoped that it would soon be possible to have all Catholics worship under the same roof. In the dedicatory sermon preached by Archbishop Janssens at the opening of St. Katherine's, he reaffirmed the freedom of the Negroes to continue to attend other churches. A New Orleans newspaper on the following day reported:

> Archbishop Francis Janssens preached an excellent sermon, and he perhaps never had a more attentive audience. . . . The archbishop said he was glad that the colored people had a church of their own, where they could come and take any seat in the house that they chose. . . . The archbishop stated that the church was not built to exclude the colored people from other churches, but on the contrary they were just as welcome to come to worship in the other churches as they had always been.[23]

The Negro Catholic, just as the Italian, or Polish, or German Catholic, has no obligation or duty to become or remain a parishioner in the church established for his nationality or race. Those who attempt to restrict them to such parishes sin by violating a right which they as Catholics have. It would seem that even local ecclesiastical authorities would not have the right to force attendance at a racial or national parish, except perhaps if there were grave danger of a loss of faith or other serious spiritual harm. Obviously these exceptions would be extremely rare today, and each case would have to be judged separately. The right to attend his territorial parish is given to him by the general law of the Church and this right cannot be suppressed without an apostolic indult if there were not a grave danger of spiritual harm and an obligation to avoid that danger. It cannot be suppressed because prejudices of white parishioners might lead them to abandon church attendance if Negroes are admitted. The harm they would undergo in this instance would, it is true, be scandal, but it would be pharisaical scandal. To prevent this type of scandal, no one is obliged to give up important

---

[23] *Times-Democrat* (New Orleans), May 20, 1895. Quoted in Charles B. Rousseve, *The Negro in Louisiana* (New Orleans: Xavier University Press, 1937), p. 139.

rights, or to suffer humiliation and embarrassment by being considered unworthy to associate with others, or to be permanently excluded from association with large segments of his fellow Catholics, or to permit himself to be scandalized as the Church is considered to be catering to racial hatred and prejudice and denying in practice what it teaches officially.

Father Francis Connell, C.Ss.R., describes this right of a Catholic to attend his territorial parish:

> Any Catholic living within boundaries of a parish of his rite is entitled to regard the local parish church as his church and to receive the normal pastoral services from the priests of that church. If a church of his nationality or race has been erected in the vicinity, he has a right, but no obligation, to accept it as his parish church and to receive the care of its clergy.[24]

Unfortunately, it frequently happens that when a parish has Negro members, the white parishioners are reluctant to associate with them in various parochial organizations and societies, or to admit them to parish entertainments and meetings. If they are unable to keep the Negro members out of these affairs, they make their displeasure known in their treatment, and in this way, attempt to discourage their returning. Parish priests in these circumstances often remain silent for fear of antagonizing the white parishioners or causing them to attend another parish. They are satisfied in making Mass and the sacraments available to their Negro parishioners, but do little else, if anything, to try to open the way to full participation in parish life. Condemnation of such parishes which afford only a partial participation to Negro members was made by Father LaFarge, who says that such a parish is not really a Catholic parish in spirit.[25]

Many Negro Catholics are converts. When they became Catholic they had to give up membership in their former church, which, it should be remembered, provides for Negroes not only a form and place of worship, but also their sole means of social and recreational association. Conversion to the Catholic Church and membership in a white parish where they are treated as pariahs means a great sacrifice for them. Too often the isolation of their new parish, the

[24] Francis J. Connell, C.Ss.R., "The Rights of the Catholic Negro," *American Ecclesiastical Review*, 114 (1946), 459–462.

[25] John LaFarge, S.J., *Catholic Viewpoint on Race Relations* (New York: Hanover House, 1956), p. 107.

irreplaceable loss of former associations, and the "cold-shoulder" treatment prove too much and they abandon Catholicism and return to their former church and associations.

Because of this rejection, often the Negro Catholic can find only in the Negro church an opportunity to share fully in parish life, to attend parish and sodality functions without being made to feel unwelcome, being pushed aside or ignored. And he continues to attend that church long after the territorial parish is not only willing to receive him, but anxious to have him. He realizes his freedom to attend the territorial parish, but elects to exercise his right of attending the specially provided church.

The practice of requiring Negroes to sit in certain sections, usually the balcony or gallery, or to have a few pews in the back saved for their use and to prohibit their sitting elsewhere in the church has, fortunately, been specifically prohibited in most dioceses. Many bishops have ordered pastors to remove from their churches signs designating colored seating. Wherever this practice is continued it is usually done through individual initiative, with or without the knowledge and approval of the pastor. But usually if this is brought to the attention of the Ordinary, it will not be tolerated. Another practice which has the same status today, is that of requiring Negroes to wait until all white communicants have received Holy Communion before they may approach the altar rail. In Southern churches, this practice as well as separate seating apparently began during slavery days when slaves were seated in a different section than their masters, and waited until they had received Communion. Whether these practices originated because of race or social position in a slave-master relationship is difficult to determine. Even if it started because of social differences, racial considerations soon became important, gradually displacing social distinction as the reason for it.

Segregated seating in Catholic churches has no right to exist today. Prescinding from the sin of disobedience involved in disregarding the bishop's order where he has commanded a discontinuation of the practice, the insult, degradation, and shame felt by the Negro subjected to such treatment are sufficient to constitute the sin of contumely. The federal government has ordered the end of Jim Crow seating on buses, trains, and airplanes; the courts have prohibited the states from enforcing segregation on municipal golf courses and beaches. Bus and train terminals, as well as air terminals, have been ordered to stop segregation within their waiting rooms, restaurants, lunch counters, and rest rooms. White Catholics using these facilities must do so on a nonsegregated basis. The law does not consider their feelings or any uneasiness they may claim to feel from the presence of a Negro. Nor does the law consider the possibility that the white person may cease to utilize these facilities. Yet, many Catholics expect that they can enforce such segregation within the Church. The freedom of a citizen to use public facilities and transportation without discrimination and without being insulted is certainly not more sacred than the right of a Catholic to worship God and receive the sacraments without being insulted or degraded.

The practical application of these facts was made by Bishop Waters of Raleigh when, in a pastoral letter, he reminded the Catholics of his diocese that separate churches were of very recent origin in North Carolina, and that previously white and Negro had attended the same Catholic church. He emphasized that their establishment did not mean that Negro Catholics were to be forbidden to attend any other Catholic church. Their purpose was to afford special care for Negro Catholics, and that all Catholics had the right to worship God together, a universal right in the Church. Having explained these points, he continued:

> Therefore, so that in the future there can be no misunderstanding on the part of anyone, let me state here as emphatically as I can: There is no segregation of races to be tolerated in any Catholic Church in the Diocese of Raleigh. The pastors are charged with the carrying out of this teaching and shall tolerate nothing to the contrary. Otherwise, all special churches for Negroes will be abolished immediately as lending weight to the false notion that the Catholic Church, the Mystical Body of Christ, is divided. Equal rights are accorded, therefore, to every race and every nationality as is proper in any Catholic Church and within the Church building itself everyone is given the privilege to sit or kneel wherever he desires and to approach the Sacraments without any regard to race or nationality. This doctrine is to be fully explained to each convert who enters the church from henceforth in the Diocese of Raleigh.[26]

Attempts of Catholics to drive Negro Catholics from their church through the manifestation of contempt or hatred, either by act or

---

[26] *Interracial Review*, 26 (July 2, 1953), 11.

word, are not only sins against justice because they are trying to
deprive them of a right given by the general law of the Church to
attend territorial parishes, they are also sins against charity, because
of the hatred involved, and sins of scandal. Obviously, those who
attempt to drive them out through threats of violence, or actual use
of force or fear, sin mortally through the use of unjust means or
physical harm. Father Gerald Kelly speaks of this sin of scandal
which is involved when a Catholic practices discrimination in
any way:

> Theologically, scandal is an occasion of spiritual harm to the neighbor.
> Scandal is very seriously involved when white Catholics practice segre-
> gation and discrimination; because their conduct makes it very diffi-
> cult for Negro Catholics to preserve their faith and well-nigh impossi-
> ble to convert Negroes to the faith. There can scarcely be greater
> scandal than this.[27]

Fides Documentation Service, an agency of the Sacred Congregation for the Propagation of the Faith, in a report in 1950 on the work
of the Church among the Negroes in the United States, stated:

> The major obstacle to the conversion of the American Negro is the
> attitude of white Catholics themselves. As the Negroes have become
> more educated, they have grown aware of the extreme discrepancy
> which exists between such an attitude and the real spirit of the
> Catholic Church. They read of the great pronouncements of the Holy
> Father, the Head of Christendom, and contrast his words of friend-
> ship and affection with the unfriendly attitude of the people next
> door. They are particularly sensitive when they find Catholics practic-
> ing such discrimination in the church itself.[28]

It should not be thought that these observations are made only
by a handful of Negroes, and that the vast majority, having little
contact with the Church or Catholics, know or hear little of this. The
great majority of the Negro population is keenly aware of the difference between the actions of many Catholics and the teaching of
their Church; between the commands of the bishop and the obedience which he is given. The Negro press often carries stories and
articles on this discrepancy, as the report in a nationally circulated
Negro magazine shows. It was written some months after the Jesuit

---

[27] Gerald Kelly, S.J., *Guidance for Religious* (Westminster: Newman Press,
1957), p. 307.
[28] *America*, 94 (Feb. 4, 1956), 505.

Bend incident when Archbishop Rummel ordered the church there closed because of the parishioners' refusal to permit a Negro priest to say Mass there:

> And, with a courage often rumored, but seldom seen in our time, the graying bishop closed the chapel at Jesuit Bend when the whites refused to accept a Negro priest. He called upon the whites to show charity; they answered him with a call for 50,000 members to join the White Citizens Councils to oppose him and signed a resolution saying they would never accept a Negro priest. Although he had stood like a rock, it soon appeared to many that even a rock could be crushed. Heart-wounded and sad, the bishop soon discovered he was a voice crying in the wilderness, a prophet without honor, a brave general whose sunshine and summer soldiers seemed to obey only the commands that pleased them.[29]

Incidents which receive national publicity in the Negro press, and which, in addition, are circulated verbally, go far to convince any Negro contemplating further investigation of the Church that he might as well stay in the church he now belongs to, or continue without any church affiliation — that there is no difference between the conduct of the white members of his denomination and the Catholic whites — that there is no difference between his denomination and the Catholic Church — both preach brotherhood, but do not practice it.

If the prejudices and discriminations of Catholic laity are causes of scandal, it goes without saying that these same attitudes and actions when manifested and performed by the clergy and religious are even greater scandals. Likewise, priests who deal brusquely or impatiently with a Negro should realize that even though their mode of acting does not spring from prejudice, frequently the Negro will consider it as such. The average white person receiving such treatment will be vexed or angered, will consider such actions and treatment as boorish and discourteous. But often a Negro treated this way will judge the priest prejudiced because from experience he has learned that this is usually the way prejudiced people treat him.

The refusal of a priest to permit a Negro Catholic to attend Mass or receive the sacraments, insisting that he must go to the colored parish for these is a source of scandal not only to the one who is

---

[29] Marc Crawford, "Negroes Still Segregated in Chapel Despite Prelate's Vows," *Jet*, 14 (May 15, 1958), 24–29.

rejected, but also to the white parishioners, who, seeing this, are confirmed and strengthened in their prejudices; become more convinced that the territorial parish is closed to Negroes; and become insistent in drawing the color line in other facilities. Not only does the priest have an obligation to avoid giving such scandal, but he has a positive obligation to instruct his parishioners and to try to form proper racial attitudes in them so that they will be able to recognize and fulfill the moral obligations that are incumbent upon them. Monsignor Gilligan stressed this obligation and made several suggestions for methods of fulfilling it. He suggested that at least once a year, the Sunday sermon should be on the rights of the Negro and the obligations of charity toward him; that specific injustices and wrongs should be denounced from the pulpit during the year; that parochial schools and Sunday schools should dedicate a week each year to the study and explanation of interracial matters and the obligations entailed; that textbooks which are used for religious instructions should be more explicit in their treatment of duties and obligations in racial matters.[30]

---

[30] Francis J. Gilligan, Morality of the Color Line, p. 207.

CHAPTER 17

THE RIGHT
TO ATTEND CATHOLIC SCHOOLS

There is a close relationship between the question of segregation in churches and segregation in Catholic schools. Frequently we look upon the parochial school as a private school. Parochial schools are private in one sense, that is, in relation to the general public; they are institutions operated by a religious denomination. But, in another sense, they are not private schools, that is, in relation to Catholics they are not private schools. Schools supported and operated by the state are commonly called "public schools," and, by common acceptance, this term is reserved to them in this country.

The Catholic Church, as a perfect society, has the right and the obligation to teach. The establishment and operation of diocesan and parochial schools is one way in which she fulfills this duty. Nor is her right to teach restricted to matters of religion, but extends beyond these and embraces all things helpful and conducive to the welfare of souls. Pius XI, in his encyclical on Christian education, makes this clear:

> Therefore, with full right the Church promotes letters, science, and the arts, in so far as necessary or helpful to Christian education, in addition to her work for the salvation of souls, founding and maintaining schools and institutions adapted to every branch of learning and degree of culture. Nor may even physical culture, as it is called, be considered outside the range of her maternal supervision, for the reason that it is also a means which may help or harm Christian education.[1]

[1] *Divini Illius Magistri*, Eng. translation, Terence P. McLaughlin, *op. cit.*, p. 81.

Diocesan and parochial schools are not private schools so far as Catholics are concerned. They are the public schools of the Church, established, operated, and controlled by the Church, as a perfect society, for the education of her members. The parochial and diocesan schools stand in the same relation to the Church and Catholics as the public schools do to the state and the citizens.

Even though there is cooperation with the legitimate requirements and regulations of the state concerning curriculum, teacher qualifications, and physical standards for health or sanitation, these schools are still media of the Church's teaching her members. It is interesting to note that the Code of Canon Law treats of the right to establish schools and legislates concerning them under the title, *The Ecclesiastical Magisterium*. The parochial school is a segment or part of the parish. It is built, supported, and maintained with parish funds or donations to the parish. The parishioners' obligation of contributing to its support is incumbent not only on parents who have children attending the school, but, as in all public endeavors and operations, on the entire community, which in this case is the entire parish. Diocesan schools have the same status as the parochial schools, proper allowance being made for their more communal nature as diocesan rather than parochial facilities.

In view of what has been said regarding the right of a Catholic to be a parishioner of his territorial parish, it follows that the right to utilize the various public facilities maintained by that parish is included. If we say that a Negro Catholic has the right to attend the territorial parish if he elects to do so in preference to the racial parish, it is only logical to say that he has the right to send his children to the parish school. The same conclusion should be drawn regarding the right to attend a diocesan school or college.

Obviously, if a family decides to exercise its right to attend a national or racial parish, it cannot claim the right to utilize facilities maintained and supported by the territorial parish. A Negro family, attending and supporting a Negro parish, could not claim the right to send the children to the territorial parish school. However, it should be indicated that even though, in this instance, a right cannot be claimed, charity and social justice may require that these children be accepted, particularly when their own parish does not have a school.

The order of charity demands that they be admitted to Catholic schools before non-Catholic white students. It is a distortion of the nature and purpose of the Catholic school to have situations in which white non-Catholics attend parochial schools while at the same time Catholic Negro children, living within the limits of the parish, are not accepted and have to attend the public school, or, as happens at times, travel as much as sixty or seventy miles daily to attend a Catholic school which will accept them. Catholic school authorities and administrators should also remember that it is possible for the school to lose its nature as a Catholic school when an excessive proportion of non-Catholic students are enrolled.

Speaking of the right of Negro children to attend the school of their parish, Father Connell calls it the same right as that possessed by the white children of the parish, but if the parish were operating two schools, which provided satisfactory facilities, teachers, etc., their right would not include designation of the school:

> The Negro parent of Catholic children has just as much right as the white parent to have his child receive the benefit of the Catholic education provided by the Church. Hence, in the event that there is only one parochial school available, the Negro child of the parish has the same right to be admitted as the white child, with the same qualifications as far as the principles and laws of the Catholic Church are concerned. If, however, the Church authorities have provided a separate school with satisfactory educational facilities for the colored children, it would seem that the Negro parents could not claim a strict right to send their children to the white school. Their right to procure a Catholic education for their children would not seem to contain the right to choose the particular institution in which that education is to be given. As far as justice is concerned, the ecclesiastical authorities have done their duty in providing a school in which a Negro child can receive an adequate Catholic education.[2]

Increasingly higher costs of operating schools, teacher shortages, and similar factors have resulted in the rapid diminution of the number of parishes with two schools. Today most of the schools for Negro Catholic children are operated by Negro parishes, and the pupils and their parents regularly attend that parish. But in those few instances where a parish does operate two schools, one for white children and the other for Negro children, I do not believe that the pastor has the right to designate, solely on the basis of race, which

---

[2] Francis J. Connell, "Rights of the Catholic Negro," loc. cit., p. 461.

of the two schools a child must attend. (It should not be thought that all such dual school parishes are in the Southern states. As late as 1961, a parish in a Northern diocese operated a Negro mission and school several blocks from the main church, located in a downtown area. Two communities of Sisters were engaged in the two schools, and the total enrollment of both schools did not exceed 225 pupils.)

If a pastor should decide to determine pupil assignment on the basis of sex, age, or intellectual ability, these would be legitimate criteria for selectivity, and parishioners would have no legitimate complaint because one school was for boys, the other for girls; or one of the schools was for those below a certain age, or grade, and the other for those above; or one was for those meeting a high IQ test rating requirement. These are criteria which can have a relationship to the purpose of Catholic education, at least indirectly. But the criterion of race does not have any apparent relationship, direct or indirect, with that purpose.

Therefore, even if the facilities were equal in every way, which would seem to be impossible because of the stigma and contumely necessarily implied by compulsory segregation, it does not seem that the authorities can consider themselves discharged of their obligation of providing a school for the Negro child. If the parents are parishioners, their rights include the use of parish facilities according to their needs, without being subjected to arbitrary restrictions having no relationship with the purpose of that facility, and which restrictions are enacted for one class only. If we say that the authorities have fulfilled their obligation by providing a "school in which a Negro child can receive an adequate Catholic education," it could also be said that they have fulfilled their duty when they provide a place in which a Negro Catholic can worship. But if a parish decides to erect a separate mission church for its Negro parishioners, no one can say that these parishioners have a right to attend only the place provided and not the parish church. As parishioners, they have not only the right to attend the territorial parish church, but also to attend the school which it provides. A parish which establishes an out mission or chapel of ease for the convenience of those living at a distance may urge and advise those, for whose convenience it was established, to attend it. But they cannot be compelled to do so as long as it retains its status as a mission church or chapel, and is not canonically erected as a territorial parish. If and when it receives canonical status as a territorial parish, then all who live within the limits will be its parishioners, unless they have elected to exercise their right to attend a national or racial parish. The same applies to Negro mission churches operated by so-called "white parishes," which de iure are missions of the parish, but de facto are separate parishes with distinct parish organizations, parish books and records, and financial structures. Until such time as they are legitimately established as either territorial parishes or racial parishes, separate from the other parish and with their own pastor, those who attend these missions are parishioners of the territorial parish and enjoy all the rights of parishioners.

Obviously, difficulties can arise when a Negro parent wants to exercise this right and send his child to the parochial school. The atmosphere of the community in some instances might be so hostile to the presence of the child in what it considers a "white school" that he would find it difficult to study or learn while in school; rejection by classmates and isolation from general activities in some cases can cause such great discontent to the child that school attendance becomes a daily source of misery and unhappiness. This is particularly so in a school in which there would be few, if any, other Negro children to afford some form of mutual support. Great prudence would have to be used by a parent exercising his rights when such conditions prevail. Recent newspaper pictures of jeering crowds, showing ridicule and abuse heaped by whites on a few Negro students who began attending a newly desegregated public school, can only lead to the conclusion that the Negro child who must withstand such treatment, especially if it is long-lasting, will have to possess great moral stamina, patience, and humility. Even where such violent reactions are not present, the daily and common rejection and avoidance which may be his experience will demand that consideration be taken of the emotional and temperamental dispositions of the child, as well as his motivation, training, and preparation, before subjecting him to such an ordeal. The same can be said for parents who, in order that their children may attend territorial parish schools, become members of that parish. An atmosphere of hostility and resentment to their presence could be a potential source of danger to their faith. In these instances, the virtue of prudence will have to be exercised so that the proper and best method of action will be guaranteed. All this, however, does not by any means work to the prejudice of the basic right which remains intact, even though in some instances prudence may counsel its nonexercise.

In addition to parochial or diocesan schools, there are other Catholic schools usually maintained and operated by religious communities. These may be grammar schools, secondary schools, or colleges, although the greatest number of these are at the college level. In fact, most of the Catholic colleges in this country are operated by religious communities rather than by dioceses. Some exceptions are the Catholic University of America which is conducted by the American hierarchy; Seton Hall University conducted by the Archdiocese of Newark; the University of Dallas operated by the Diocese of Dallas-Fort Worth. There are also a few secondary schools conducted by Catholic laymen, usually under the direction of the Ordinary, e.g., Canterbury School, New Milford, Conn., conducted by Catholic laymen under the direction of the Archbishop of Hartford.

These Catholic schools do not have the same status as the diocesan or parochial school. Strictly speaking, they cannot be considered as ecclesiastical public schools, but, on the other hand, neither are they strictly private schools. No school designating itself a Catholic school is a private school as against the Church. The fact that most of these schools are operated by religious communities and represent themselves as Catholic institutions indicate a relationship to the Church and its teaching office. This relationship is recognized in the Code of Canon Law which provides that the bishop has the right of visitation of all schools in matters concerning religion and moral instruction, and that the schools of religious communities are not exempt from this right.

While control of administrative detail and policy may not be within the direct power of the local ecclesiastical authorities, nevertheless, the school does have an ecclesiastical public character by reason of its claim to be a Catholic institution and to provide a Catholic education, and its recognition as such by the Church.

The public character of all "private schools," whether Church related or not, was indicated in the report of the President's Committee on Civil Rights which admitted the right of private citizens to establish and operate schools and to determine their policies. But the Committee held that these schools have a public responsibility to society at large because in their actual operation they have acquired a public character. They enjoy a degree of indirect government support, even when this only includes exemptions from taxation on property and facilities, as well as on profit. Benefactors are granted tax deductions and credits for contributions to these schools which often induce them to make donations so that they are thereby put in a more favorable tax position. In addition, these schools are engaged in the training and education of young citizens who will eventually take their place in society, and the state cannot be indifferent and unconcerned about the training they receive.[3]

The Committee also indicated that there was much racial discrimination in private schools whether these were vocational schools, colleges, or graduate schools. It discovered that many of these institutions in the North had established a fixed quota for the admission of Jewish students and allowed a mere token enrollment of Negro students. It did not indicate whether religious schools were included among those which discriminated on racial grounds, but the fact that some Catholic colleges do so was revealed in a study published in 1948 by Father Richard J. Roche. This revealed that of 154 Catholic colleges checked, 24 frankly admitted that they had restrictive policies concerning Negro applicants, and another 18 either did not answer that question or gave ambiguous replies. The survey also showed that there were only 17 resident Negro students in all these Catholic colleges, although there was a larger number of nonresident Negroes. The author estimated that the total number of Negro students enrolled at Catholic colleges at less than 500.[4]

Though not immediately under the control of the diocese, the public character of these schools as Catholic institutions obliges

---

[3] *To Secure these Rights*, p. 66; cf. Arthur S. Miller, *Racial Discrimination and Private Education: A Legal Analysis* (Chapel Hill: University of North Carolina Press, 1957), pp. 68–96, regarding the public nature of private schools.

[4] Richard J. Roche, *Catholic Colleges and the Negro Student* (Washington, D. C.: The Catholic University of America Press, 1948), pp. 54–59.

them to provide Catholic education to qualified Catholic applicants. This obligation, according to Father Roche, besides being one of charity to one's neighbor, is also one of distributive justice. He explains the immorality of the actions of officials of Catholic colleges in refusing to admit Negro Catholic applicants thus:

> The rights involved in a case such as the one under consideration, are the most general rights classified under *distributive* justice. While a Catholic institution of higher learning is a private institution as regards the state, no Catholic institution is private as against the Catholic Church. A Catholic educational institution is allowed to exist by the Church only for the purpose of fulfilling the educational aims of the Church, and those aims . . . allow no discriminations as to race. . . . Thus, any Catholic college which refuses to supply such opportunity because of racial considerations, takes part in a general denial of rights possessed under distributive justice by the Negro Catholic group. Such a college does not become just in its actions because there are some other Catholic colleges in the country which will supply the opportunity needed by the Negro applicant.[5]

It is difficult to see how a particular college and its officers incur an obligation in distributive justice through the free decision of a student to apply to that specific school for admission. There is a relationship between the individual and his parochial or diocesan institutions which can serve as a foundation for a right in distributive justice. But such a relationship seems to be lacking with a school operated by a religious community. Nor does the fact that such schools have a public character and are not strictly private seem to render availability of their services and use a right in distributive justice. If this public character were to beget this right, it would appear that there would be few things which would not be obligations of distributive justice since in the modern world of business all corporations are chartered by the state and even associations and partnerships are registered by the state and thereby acquire a public character. Exclusion of an obligation in distributive justice in this matter seems to be more consonant with the statement of Pius XII in which he depicted the difference between economic society and other societies whose obligations were chiefly under distributive justice:

It would be a mistake to claim that every particular enterprise is by

---

[5] *Ibid.*, p. 97 n.

its nature a society in such a way that relationships between those engaged in it are regulated by distributive justice . . . such a view is based on the hypothesis that every enterprise is by its nature within the purview of public law. The hypothesis is bad.[6]

Businesses, which are privately owned, but which are licensed by public authority, such as restaurants, hotels, etc., are not strictly private because of their licensing and the direct control exercised by the municipal or state government. Yet it does not seem that a claim to utilize these services can be founded on a right of distributive justice. An interesting point regarding the public character of such licensed establishments, and which through analogy is illustrative of the point here, was made by Justice Douglas in a separate concurring opinion in which he stated that restaurants were part of the public life of the various communities, and that, even though private enterprises, they were public facilities in which the state may not enforce racial segregation. He distinguishes between what is completely private and what is public even though privately owned:

One can close the doors of his home to anyone he desires. But one who operates an enterprise under a license from the government enjoys a privilege that derives from the people. Whether retail stores, not licensed by the municipality, stand on a different footing is not presented here. But the necessity of a license shows that the public has rights in respect to those premises. The business is not a matter of mere private concern. Those who license enterprises for public use should not have under our Constitution the power to license it for the use of only one race.[7]

It would seem that in addition to obligations of charity which are definitely involved in this situation, it would be better to describe the obligation of justice as one of social justice rather than distributive justice, despite the public character of these privately operated schools

---

[6] Pius XII, "Avec une égale," address to the 9th Congress of International Union of Catholic Employers, May 7, 1949, Eng. translation, Catholic Mind, 47 (July, 1949), 445–448. The Pope treats specifically of the opinion held by some that distributive justice demands that a company pay a living wage even though this would result in no profits remaining. The Pope insists that the relationship of the company to its employees is rather of social and commutative justice. Although the statement of the Pope can be applied with certainty only to the case described, nevertheless, there seems to be an analogous situation in the instance of these schools. Cf. also J.-Y. Calvez and J. Perrin, op. cit., p. 160, and John F. Cronin, Social Principles and Economic Life, p. 72.

[7] Garner v. State of Louisiana, Race Relations Law Reporter, Vol. 6 (Winter, 1961), 943–962.

in relation to the Church. Nor is this public character prejudicial
to the obligations of social justice. This is not to be understood as
a minimizing of an obligation of justice, but it would seem that
there is an important distinction between the obligations in justice
for the "official" Catholic schools, i.e., parochial or diocesan, and
those which are privately operated and controlled. Parallel would be
the situation where the state operates stores for the sale of alcoholic
beverages. In other states, these stores are licensed by the state, but
are privately owned. Both have a public nature, but the state store
is an actual operation of the government and such services should
be available to all qualified citizens, whose rights in relation to these
state stores would fall under distributive justice.

All Catholic schools have a dual public character. The first and
more important comes to them through the relationship to the
Church and their commitment to provide a Catholic education in
accord with the aims, ideals, beliefs, and teaching of the Church.
The second public character comes to them from the state through
their commitment to educate and train citizens. Under this civic
responsibility, the state exercises various controls over these schools.
In some states it stipulates subject and curriculum requirements;
establishes teacher qualifications and sets training standards and thus
in reality can determine who can and who cannot teach in these
schools; and exercises a degree of control of the actual administration
of the school, e.g., it sets standards for fire protection and sanitation;
or may require records and reports to be maintained and submitted
to various public agencies.

These responsibilities obligate Catholic schools to a double conformity; one to the requirements of the Church and the other to
the requirements of the state. In the matter of race relations, the
Church makes no demand for segregation — in fact, the practice is
alien to her concept of her members as being united by supernatural
bonds in the Mystical Body. She recognizes no superiority or preference predicated on race or any other material considerations. On
the other hand, the state has often legislated and required segregation
not only in the public schools, but also in Catholic schools. These
statutes prohibit interracial school attendance and provide penalties
for violations. In Tennessee, if white and Negro children were al-

lowed to attend the same school, there was provision for a fine of $50 for each offense and imprisonment for not less than 30 days or more than six months. These penalties applied to any teacher or administrator allowing interracial attendance or teaching such a class in any kind of school.[8] Oklahoma had a similar statute and in addition penalized the white students attending such a school.[9] In Florida, an individual, corporation, or association was prohibited from conducting schools of any kind (public, private, or parochial) in which both races were taught.[10] Kentucky also prohibited integrated schools,[11] and Georgia, by statute and by Constitution, provided that any private school accepting Negro and white pupils should lose its tax exemptions.[12]

In addition to penalties of fines or imprisonment, other pressures have been threatened if private schools attempt to desegregate. When Archbishop Rummel first announced that the parochial schools in the archdiocese would be desegregated, bills were introduced in the Louisiana legislature to withdraw tax exemptions from any denominational school which integrated, and to cease all state benefits to such a school. The benefits which would have been lost included free school books and writing materials, lunches, and bus transportation. The Mississippi legislature considered a similar law. But in both instances the bills were defeated.

In view of the Supreme Court's decision in the school cases, it is most probable that penalties and fines, as well as deprivation of benefits because these schools attempt to desegregate, would be declared unconstitutional as deprivations of the equal protection of the law. It is also likely that they could be considered as violations of the First Amendment guaranteeing religious liberty since they interfere with the free exercise and practice of religion. Several law experts have expressed the opinion that the state cannot apply such sanctions to compel private schools to segregate:

> It is fair to say that it is seriously doubtful that such sanctions are constitutional. Should they receive a judicial test, it can be forecast

---

[8] Tennessee Code Annotated, (1955), 49–3701, 49–3702, 49–3703.

[9] Oklahoma Statutes, Title 70, 5–7 (1951).

[10] Florida Statutes Annotated, 228.09 (1943).

[11] Kentucky Revised Statutes, 158.020 (1953).

[12] Georgia Constitution, Art. VII, E-1; Para. IV; Georgia Code Annotated, 92–201.

with some confidence that the Supreme Court would . . . strike down attempts to compel private groups to maintain policies of racial segregation.[13]

Apparently this legal opinion is based chiefly on the 1954 school decision so that previously it was not so strong an opinion. However, despite the probability that such laws would not be upheld, private school authorities have been reluctant to test them or to act openly against them. Under the circumstances, reluctance to do so is understandable. Speaking of the hardships which would follow from loss of tax exemption during the long period before final adjudication and disposition of the case, Miller explains:

> The interim difficulties would be considerable; it would take a brave administrator to undertake an attack on the statute or go ahead without regard to consequences. Severe deprivations could be the result, for the tax exemption amounts to a considerable subsidy — so much so that it could be of crucial importance to the financial viability of the organization.[14]

In addition, there is also the problem of harassment of private schools which integrate against the desire of the local government, carried on under the guise of enforcement of public order and health laws. Probability that such harassment could be enjoined successfully is not too great because of the difficulty of proving that there is actually harassment and revenge — it is extremely difficult to prove evil intent juridically, especially when it is cleverly masked as law enforcement for public order.

> . . . action taken by law enforcement officials to insure the most meticulous adherence to the exact letter of all statutes by private school personnel would undoubtedly be entirely valid; at least it would be impossible to prove an improper motive. The regulations relative to sanitation and fire protection are an example of such statutes. While ostensibly only carrying out the law or regulation, state officials conceivably could so harass a private school as to cause a great deal of annoyance and expense. . . . The point is that law enforcement officials do have the power, if not the right, to pursue policies and to take action that would result in disturbance and otherwise molest private school personnel. The abstract constitutional

---

[13] A similar opinion was expressed by Dean William Hepburn of Lamar School of Law of Emory University, Atlanta, at a meeting of the Commission on Human Rights of the Catholic Committee of the South. Cf. The Times Picayune (New Orleans), April 9, 1956.

[14] Arthur Miller, op. cit., p. 30.

principle of protection may be clear enough, but difficulties of proof and the probability of protracted litigation may go far to nullify that protection.[15]

A realistic picture of the problems of many Catholic educators must include recognition of the fact that such penalties exist and that enforcement of them is possible, and awareness of the more insidious harassment and molestation, as well as sanctions which could be applied by private individuals. Yet despite all these deterrents, some have acted. And, without fanfare, in some places where actual legal penalties were established, Catholic schools have desegregated. Done without publicity, the state is apparently unwilling to risk a test case of these laws and has not acted to apply the sanctions.

The greatest degree of successful desegregation without application of penalties or extreme opposition from either officials or private individuals has been secured when there was a minimum of publicity. This can be seen in the actions not only of individual schools, but also in diocesan action, e.g., Washington, Little Rock, Dallas-Fort Worth, etc. The president of Spring Hill College, a Jesuit institution in Alabama, said that integration had been accomplished there without publicity. He described the action: "We simply performed a quiet surgical operation on current prejudices by admitting Negroes."

Miller notes the advantage of a minimum of publicity and lack of fanfare and explains its relation to successful desegregation. This, he believes, gives the officials the opportunity to close their eyes to the occurrence even though it involves a violation of the law. Lack of publicity means that no pressure is being put on them to act. The situation would be different if there was wide publicity — then they would have to act either by upholding the law or opposing the integration policy in some way.[16]

Despite the progress that has been made and the desegregation of more schools, many Catholics, both lay and clerical, fear that it is not enough and that the Church is falling behind the government in her actions. They feel that the Church is following the lead of

---

[15] *Ibid.*, pp. 45–46.
[16] *Ibid.*, p. 127.

secular institutions rather than pointing the way and leading them
by her good example in this area of basic rights. They fear that
faltering or delay will result in a situation where, in some places,
the Catholic schools are the only segregated schools.

The fear that the Church will be outstripped by the government
and secular organizations in the field of race relations is also expressed
by non-Catholics who are critical of their denomination's record.
We have previously mentioned the statement of Maston that it
would be a tragedy if the churches were to be the last bastion of
segregation, and if secularism "out-Christianized Christianity."

Concern over the reluctance of Catholic colleges to accept Negro
students and fear of tardiness by Catholics were expressed some time
ago by Father Gerald Kelly. Speaking of Father Roche's study in
which a gradual and cautious acceptance of Negro students by
Catholic colleges is shown, Father Kelly remarked that many saw
this as an indication of great social progress and achievement, but
that he regarded it in a different light: "To me it merely shows
how little we have done; and it makes me wonder how late we shall
be in doing the remainder."

It is regrettable that his concern was not more widely heeded,
both by Catholics and non-Catholics. It might have softened the
blow and spared the embarrassment and need of explanations arising
from charges such as these:

a) Against Protestant Churches: "Although the Protestant churches
stress the dignity and worth of the individual and the brotherhood
of man, the racial behavior patterns of most church members have
not been affected by these principles."[17]

b) Against Christian churches in general: "But few Christian
churches have ever been, whether in America or elsewhere, the spear-
heads of reform."[18]

c) Against Catholic and Protestant churches (on the occasion of
the Archbishop of Atlanta's announcement that the parochial schools
would be integrated as of September 1, 1962): "The Roman Church
is an old one. It is wise in the techniques of timing and action. . . .
Actually, neither it nor the Protestant churches in the South can be

---

[17] George Simpson and Milton Yinger, op. cit., p. 546.
[18] G. Myrdal, op. cit., p. 877.

too proud of their record. The Christian church should lead, not follow. But everywhere it has left it to secular and lay persons to make the initial fight."[19]

Because of the prevalence of the opinion that the Church contributes little for the betterment and correction of the social order, we are led to seek not only assurance that it is contributing, but also the ideals and standards which it strives to obtain in making this contribution. In 1956, Pius XII, speaking of secular doubts of the contribution of the Church to social reform, said:

> . . . a church which says of herself that she is a standard towering over the nations may, today, expect to be asked about her contribution to the creation of social order. Without being presumptuous, the Catholic Church can point to the fact that, in the course of her history, she has contributed mightily to the building and betterment of social life. Historical research has long substantiated this. Nor did the Church by any means close her eyes to the profound social disorders which were brought on by the age of technology and capitalism. She has never presumed that she would be able to solve the social question by herself. She may, however, point with pride to the values, necessary for such a solution, which she maintained and still maintains. . . . The Church has always strongly emphasized that the building of a durable social order requires besides the reform of external conditions, the cultivation of conscience: the orientation of conscience by unequivocal principles and the development of the moral strength to act always in accord with this conscience. The Church claims, and has proven the claim, that she knows how to mold men to such character.[20]

This is the challenge facing the Church in this country — to bring the weight of her moral power to bear not only to help reform the actual social institutions and conditions which produce and are produced by segregation, but also to develop and form right consciences in her children and an awareness of their moral obligations, and through her powers to bestow grace to enable them to act in accord with the principles of justice and charity. Father LaFarge calls this task of the Church in the area of race relations "a ringing challenge" to the Church to give witness to charity and integrity.[21]

[19] Ralph McGill, columnist and publisher of the *Constitution* (Atlanta), quoted in *Newsweek*, June 25, 1962, p. 82.

[20] Pius XII, "Mit freudiger Erregung," radio address to the 77th National German Catholic Congress, September 2, 1956. English translation, *The Pope Speaks*, 3 (Winter, 1956–1957), 233–237.

[21] John La Farge, S.J., "Decision on Segregation," *Catholic Mind*, 52 (1954), 577–587.

But this challenge to the Church will not be fully or properly met if it is merely approached in terms of the obligatory. It cannot merely be a question of: "*What are we obliged to do in charity or in the various forms of justice?*" The challenge will only be met properly when we seek to find out how far we can go to bring about desegregation. If we wait for judicial backing for all our decisions or are limited to what is obligatory, we shall soon find ourselves outdistanced by everyone else. The Church should not and cannot wait for the courts to clear the path before she proclaims her moral teachings, nor can she permit government agencies and secular institutions to proclaim and practice the truths which it is her duty and right to proclaim. In the field of morality, the Church must lead the way — and not be led.

CHAPTER 18

PAPAL AND EPISCOPAL TEACHING

No papal allocution or encyclical is concerned solely and directly with racial prejudice and discrimination. However, in the body of papal social teaching, from Leo XIII to Pope John XXIII, there is much which concerns this subject indirectly. This social teaching falls into three general categories — statements on minority rights; on the dignity of man; and on racism.

It is impossible to attempt to show in detail the development and interrelation of these categories in the papal documents. We must be limited to a general outline or broad sketch of this. The difficulty involved in a detailed development can be understood in the case of Pope Leo XIII, whose pontificate extended over a period of twenty-five years, and who left a large corpus of documents containing his social teaching. In these writings, he taught, on various occasions and at different times, the dignity of man based on his personality and social nature; on man's free will; on his redemption by Christ and his call to membership in the Mystical Body; his sacredness by reason of grace and the indwelling of the Holy Trinity; and his ultimate supernatural end and the obligation to strive toward it.

Leo's teaching, together with that of his successors, especially Pius XI and Pius XII, form a unified theology of the social relationships and obligations based on the personal dignity of man; the spirituality of his soul; his possession of liberty protected by the moral law; his responsibilities to God, to society, and to himself; and his possession of basic and essential human rights.[1]

Regarding the teaching on the dignity of man, Father Giles Staab states that Leo XIII made explicit the Church's doctrine on this, and that previously, back through the Middle Ages, it was only implicit. The reason why Leo made this explicit, Father Staab believes, was that the world had returned to the condition of paganism such as had been prevalent at the time of St. Peter and St. Leo the Great, and which had caused St. Peter to appeal to the Christians: "You, however, are a chosen race, a royal priesthood, a holy nation, a purchased people; that you may proclaim the perfections of Him who has called you out of darkness into His marvellous light" (1 Pet 2:9).

In the writings of Pope Pius XII, the teaching of his predecessors on man's dignity is repeated but with a stronger emphasis on the principle of human solidarity in its physical, spiritual, and supernatural aspects. Continuity in papal teaching on man's dignity can be seen by a comparison of this statement of St. Pius X, made in 1904, with statements of his successors:

> The truly remarkable dignity of man as a son of the heavenly Father, in whose image he is formed, and with whom he is destined to live in eternal happiness, is also revealed only by the doctrine of Jesus Christ. From this very dignity, and from man's knowledge of it, Christ showed that men should love one another as brothers, and should live here as becomes children of light.[2]

Pius XII, in 1956, repeated this same doctrine, stressing more strongly the brotherhood of man:

> . . . Christians realize that every man is really the "neighbor" of his fellow-man; even more — that they are brothers. And this for two reasons: they have the same Father, Creator and Lord of Life, and they have the same Savior and Guide, the Son of God made man, a divine worker among workers, the model of true charity. He has made love of neighbor the second commandment, like unto the first. He

---

[1] Giles J. Staab, O.F.M.Cap., *The Dignity of Man in Modern Papal Doctrine: Leo XIII to Pius XII, 1878–1955* (Washington, D. C.: The Catholic University of America Press, 1957), pp. 8–11. Cf. also James F. Lover, C.Ss.R., "A Study of Significant Papal Statements from Leo XIII to Pius XII against Racial Discrimination," unpublished master's dissertation, School of Social Science, The Catholic University of America, 1944.

[2] Pius X, encyclical, *Acerbo nimis*. English trans., Vincent Yzermans, *All Things in Christ* (Westminster: Newman Press, 1954), p. 49.

is the source of man's respect for his fellow-man and of the ever greater protection afforded to individual liberties.[3]

On the occasion of the bestowal of the red hat on the newly created cardinals in 1946, Pius XII described the ideal which the Church was seeking for men, and stated that it was the Church's aim to form men who would be:

> . . . established in their inviolable integrity as images of God; men proud of their personal dignity and their salutary freedom; men rightly jealous of equality with their fellows in all that touches the most intimate roots of human dignity.[4]

Several years later, the Pope mentioned this goal again and added that the Church was convinced that she could not labor more effectively than in the continued endeavor to form men in conformity with this ideal.[5]

The brotherhood of man, which is established through human solidarity in its various aspects, imposes on each individual the responsibility and obligation to recognize the natural and supernatural dignity of his fellowman:

> Each of you, each of those who are dependent upon you, is called, as a son of the Church and a member of the Body of Christ, to the fullness of human and divine life. It is your responsibility to see to it that the treasures of this life are henceforth increased, not only in you, but equally well, in each of your brothers over whom Providence has granted you partial authority. Be increasingly sensitive to the presence and the call of Christ in all human beings, even the poorest, the most helpless. May your professional work contribute to the amelioration of their lot![6]

Papal teaching on personal dignity and the brotherhood of all men, which transcends national and racial barriers, was most succintly stated by Pius XII:

---

[3] Pius XII, allocution to the Organization for the Improvement of the Fucino, May 25, 1956. Eng. trans., The Pope Speaks, 3 (Autumn, 1956), 183.

[4] Pius XII, allocution, La elevatezza, February 20, 1946. English trans., Catholic Mind, 44 (April, 1946), 193–203.

[5] Pius XII, allocution, Vous avez voulu, September 7, 1955, to Tenth International Congress of Historical Sciences. English trans., American Ecclesiastical Review, 133 (Nov., 1955), 340–351; Catholic Mind, 53 (Dec., 1955), 742–750.

[6] Pius XII, allocution, Soyez les bienvenus, October 8, 1956, to Catholic Association of Small and Medium-sized Businesses. English trans., The Pope Speaks, 3 (Spring, 1957), 408–409.

Then, too, the Church has since the time of its inception instilled in humanity definite principles which, little by little, silently and unobtrusively, but in an all the more permanent manner, influenced cultural life and modified it profoundly from within. Let us single out in particular the following: the orientation of all human existence toward a personal God before Whom man stands as a child before his father; respect for the personal dignity of the individual; men are all equal insofar as nature, origin, and destiny are concerned, without distinction of caste or nationality; they are all brothers and sisters in Jesus Christ; likewise, the union of men among themselves and the establishment of social life, not as a result of the instinctive impulses of the masses or through the will of a dictator, but under the influence of Christ. One could also include due consideration of manual labor, compatible with the dignity of free man. It is thus, let us add in passing, that the ancient practice of slavery was cut down at its roots long before it was possible to suppress it as an economic and social institution. Read the brief letter of the Apostle Paul to Philemon. Considered from this point of view, it is a cultural document of primary importance.[7]

It should not be considered that our application of papal social teachings, which are directly concerned with the general social order, to the racial problem represents a distortion of those teachings or that it is a mere theological lucubration. The validity of such application of these teachings to racial prejudice and segregation appears to be confirmed in one of the last public statements of Pius XII, made about two months before his death. In an address to members of the International Society for Blood Transfusion, he mentioned the various moral problems involved in genetics, hereditary illnesses, and the Rh factor, and then, extending his remarks on heredity, he applied them to racism, saying:

> What we say about heredity could be applied in a wide sense to the communities which are constituted by the races of mankind. But the danger here comes more from an exaggerated insistence on the meaning and value of the racial factor. We know only too well the excesses to which pride of race and racial hatred can lead. *The Church has always been actively opposed to attempts at genocide and to practices arising from what is called the "color bar."* (Italics added.)[8]

---

[7] Pius XII, allocution, *C'est bièn volontiers*, March 9, 1956, to International Union of Archaeological Institutes. English trans., *The Pope Speaks*, 3 (Autumn, 1956), 162.

[8] Pius XII, allocution, *Le Congrès International*, September 5, 1958, to International Society for Blood Transfusion. English trans., *The Pope Speaks*, 6 (1960), 386–391.

There are two startling things in this statement. First, is the linking and inclusion of genocide with practices of the "color bar," indicating not their similarity in effect, but rather their affinity in cause, since both spring from racial pride and racial hatred. The opposition of the Church to the Nazi and Fascist attempts to exterminate the Jews is well known. This opposition was made effective in the protection and various aids which the Holy See attempted to give to the Jews who were being sought out and persecuted at that time. These efforts extended even to melting down religious vessels in order to obtain gold to avert a Nazi threat to "disperse" the Jews of Rome.[9] However, since the opposition to the "practices arising from what is called the 'color bar,'" mentioned by Pius XII is not explicit in the previous papal documents, it must be contained there implicitly.

The second surprising feature of this statement is the use of the term "color bar." The address was given in French, but this expression was used in an English form (. . . tentatives de genocide, ou des pratiques inspirées par ce qu'on appelle le "colour-bar"). While this word is more common in continental and British usage than in America, it is, nevertheless, used here. It is more inclusive than the more common expressions, e.g., racial segregation, and it embraces the various patterns of racial restrictions. Webster's Third New International defines it as:

> A bar or barrier hindering or preventing colored persons from participating with whites in various activities and ranging in severity from social discrimination and conventional debarring from some occupations to a strict legally enforced exclusion from any skilled occupations (as in the Union of South Africa).

This, I believe, represents the most far-reaching of papal statements on racial prejudice and segregation, and is especially important since it is probable that the Pope intended to apply principles enunciated in previous social teachings, especially those on racism, to the present-day patterns of racial segregation. The encyclicals and allocutions of a Pope who has enjoyed a long reign usually show a development and a continuity from previous statements. This is particularly true in the statements of Leo XIII and Pius XII. To properly understand a later papal document, this continuity and

---

[9] Joseph L. Lichten, "Pius XII and the Jews," Catholic Mind, 57 (March, 1959), 159–162.

relationship with previous teachings should be taken into consideration.[10]

Pope John, in his *Pacem in terris*, included two significant passages relating to racial relations. In the first, he castigated attempts to establish "watertight compartments" in which members of one group are prevented from associating with members of another racial group:

> There are groupings of people of more or less different racial backgrounds. However, the elements which characterize an ethnic group must not be transformed into a watertight compartment in which human beings are prevented from communicating with their fellowmen belonging to different ethnic groups. That would contrast with our contemporary situation, in which the distances separating peoples have been almost wiped out. Nor can one overlook the fact that, even though human beings differ from one another by virtue of their ethnic peculiarities, they all possess certain essential common elements and are inclined by nature to meet each other in the world of spiritual values, whose progressive assimilation, opens to them the possibility of perfection without limits. They have the right and duty, therefore, to live in communion with one another.[11]

In the other passage, he clearly denies the possibility of any theoretic justification for racial discrimination. And it is also important to notice that the Pope speaks of the basic human rights which are possessed by all men, and that *they have an obligation, as well as the right, to claim these as marks of personal dignity:*

> On the contrary, the conviction that all men are equal by reason of their natural dignity has been generally accepted. Hence *racial discrimination can in no way be justified, at least doctrinally or in theory.* And this is of fundamental importance and significance for the formation of human society according to those principles which We have outlined above. For, if a man becomes conscious of his rights, he must become equally aware of his duties. Thus he who possesses certain rights has likewise the duty to claim those rights as marks of his dignity, while all others have the obligation to acknowledge those rights and respect them.[12]

The bishops of the United States and of South Africa, either as individuals or as national groups, have issued explicit statements on racial segregation and prejudice. The most important of these re-

---

[10] W. J. Smith, S.J., "How to Interpret Papal Documents," *Catholic Mind*, 60 (Feb., 1962), 21.

[11] John XXIII, encyclical, *Pacem in terris*. English trans., St. Paul Editions, pp. 35–36.

[12] *Ibid.*, p. 18.

garding the American racial problem is the 1958 statement of the American hierarchy, *Discrimination and the Christian Conscience*, issued in the name of the bishops of the United States. This statement represents the culmination of a gradual progression from a concern for the spiritual care only to an explicit statement of the immorality of racial segregation and prejudice. Briefly, we shall try to outline the development of this explicitness. The Second Plenary Council of Baltimore, in 1866, expressed solicitude only for the spiritual care of the recently emancipated Negroes, and appealed for priests and religious who would devote their entire energy to their care. The Third Plenary Council of Baltimore, in 1884, ordered that a mission collection be taken up annually to help finance the care and instruction of both the Negroes and the Indians in the United States. The development toward the explicitness of the 1958 statement may be considered to start with the 1884 Pastoral Letter issued during the Third Plenary Council, when it had been realized that the appeal of the previous council for priests and religious was generally unheeded in Europe, while at home, few of the religious communities were able to help since they were experiencing great difficulty caring for the various national groups of Catholics arriving from Europe each year in increasing numbers. In this pastoral letter, the bishops were primarily concerned with the problem of providing instruction for the Negroes, and in accord with their decision to establish an annual mission collection, were anxious that it be done efficiently and that Catholics be motivated and encouraged to contribute generously to it.

> . . . Out of the six millions of our colored population there is a very large multitude who stand sorely in need of Christian instruction and missionary labor; and it is evident that in the poor dioceses in which they are mostly found, it is most difficult to bestow on them the care they need, without the generous cooperation of our Catholic people in more prosperous localities.[13]

When peace had returned at the end of World War I, the bishops of the country issued an outstanding pastoral letter. In addition to their solicitude for the religious care and instruction of the Negro, there is in it a reproval of those who were attempting to stir up

---

[13] *The National Pastorals of the American Hierarchy (1792-1919)*, Peter Guilday (ed.) (Westminster: Newman Press, 1954), p. 263.

racial hatred, and a declaration of the equality of all races in the eyes of the Church; but although it condemns racial hatred, it makes no reference to segregation:

> The lot of the Negro and Indian, though latterly much improved, is far from being what the Church would desire. Both have been hampered by adverse conditions, yet both are responsive to religious ministration. In the eyes of the Church there is no distinction of race or of nation; there are human souls, and these have all alike been purchased at the same great price, the blood of Jesus Christ. . . . In the name of justice and charity, we deprecate most earnestly all attempts at stirring up racial hatred; for this, while it hinders the progress of all our people, and especially of the Negro, in the sphere of temporal welfare, places serious obstacles to the advance of religion among them.[14]

Twenty years later, in 1939, in a letter addressed to the president of the Federated Colored Catholics of the United States, sent in the name of the American hierarchy, the bishops spoke of segregation patterns as causing *social injustices* to the Negroes. Citing the encyclical, *Sertum Laetitiae*, of Pius XII, in which the Pope mentions his paternal love and affection for the Negroes of the United States, the bishops express the hope that all Christians will emulate the example of charity given them by the Pope:

> Indeed your activities foster the hope in us that you will be a great force, gathering strength with the years, to break down customs and practices, born of selfish individualism and arrogant false assumptions, which have placed on our colored brothers the ugly burden of crushing social injustices. . . . When the father of the whole Church holds our colored brothers in special affection, surely the Christian family will emulate his charity. It were a sham Christianity were we to try to exclude from the embrace of justice any man, or to make our charity narrower than the outstretched arms of Christ on Calvary.[15]

In 1942, the bishops ask that the rights of the Negro be recognized, and that economic opportunities be made available to him.

---

[14] *Ibid.*, pp. 286–287; *Our Bishops Speak: National Pastorals and Annual Statements of the Hierarchy of the United States*, Raphael M. Huber, O.F.M.Conv. (ed.) (Milwaukee: The Bruce Publishing Co., 1952), p. 20.

[15] Letter of Most Rev. Samuel A. Stritch, Archbishop of Milwaukee, and Most Rev. Emmet M. Walsh, Bishop of Charleston, in the name of the Hierarchy of the United States, to Dr. Thomas W. Turner, Hampton Institute, President of Federated Colored Catholics of the United States, November, 1939, Raphael M. Huber, *op. cit.*, p. 178.

The full benefits of our free institutions and the rights of our minorities must be openly acknowledged and honestly respected. We ask this acknowledgment and respect particularly for our colored fellow citizens. They should enjoy the full measure of economic opportunities and advantages which will enable them to realize their hope and ambition to join with us in preserving and expanding in changed and changing social conditions our national heritage.[16]

The following year, 1943, the most forthright, up until that time, of episcopal statements on the rights of the Negro was made. The bishops recognized the contradiction and inconsistency in the United States' attempting to achieve world peace and to secure freedom for other nations when, at the same time, these same benefits and opportunities were denied to certain groups of their own citizens at home. They indicated Negro contributions to the development of the country and the difficulties which he was experiencing in obtaining and exercising his constitutional rights. They point out that it is an obligation of justice to see that constitutional rights are extended to Negroes:

We owe to these fellow citizens, who have contributed so largely to the development of our country, and for whose welfare history imposes on us a special obligation of justice, to see that they have in fact the rights which are given them in our Constitution. This means not only political equality, but also fair economic and educational opportunities, a just share in public welfare projects, good housing without exploitation, and a full chance for the social advancement of their race. When given their rights in fact as in law, they will prize with us our national heritage and not lend ear to agitators whose real objective is not to improve but to destroy our way of living. In many of our great industrial centers acute racial tensions exist. It is the duty of every good citizen to do everything in his power to relieve them. To create a neighborhood spirit of justice and conciliation will be particularly helpful to this end.[17]

For fifteen years after this, the bishops' annual statements made no mention of the race problem. They later explained this silence as being occasioned by the fact that during that period progress was being made in healing racial prejudice and removing discrimination. But by 1958, the fifteen year period of progress had halted, and instead of a continuing advance, it merely marked time. "It appears," the bishops stated, "that in recent years the issues have become

---
[16] Raphael M. Huber, op. cit., p. 113.
[17] Ibid., p. 119.

confused and the march toward justice and equality has been slowed, if not halted in some areas. The transcendent moral issues involved have become obscured, and possibly forgotten." Recognizing the essential character of the racial problem as a moral and religious issue, they explained the essential equality of all men, despite personal, cultural, or educational differences between individuals, and indicated the obligations of Christian charity. Having presented this background, the statement then concerned itself with the problem of racial segregation in the United States. It forthrightly posed the question whether compulsory racial segregation was compatible with Christian teaching, and the answer was given that it was not compatible for two reasons: (a) all compulsory segregation marks the segregated person as inferior; (b) segregation has resulted in a widespread denial of basic human rights:

> Legal segregation, or any form of compulsory segregation, in itself and by its very nature imposes a stigma of inferiority upon the segregated people. Even if the now obsolete Court doctrine of "separate but equal" had been carried out to the fullest extent, so that all public and semipublic facilities were in fact equal, there is, nonetheless, the judgment that an entire race, by the sole fact of race and regardless of individual qualities is not fit to associate on equal terms with members of another race. We cannot reconcile such a judgment with the Christian view of man's nature and rights. . . . (2) It is a matter of historical fact that segregation in our country has led to oppressive conditions and the denial of basic human rights for the Negro.[18]

The statement that all forms of compulsory segregation stigmatize those segregated as inferior is tantamount to saying that all forms of compulsory segregation are discriminatory because they deprive the individual of the respect, honor, and recognition of his human dignity which is due. We have also seen that it is implicit in the Supreme Court decision in the school cases that all forms of racial segregation are discriminatory, and, therefore, unconstitutional. We have also seen that the courts have subsequently so interpreted the school decision.

It is interesting to note the statement of the Apostolic Delegate,

---

[18] Eugene McManus, S.S.J., *Studies in Race Relations* (Baltimore: Josephite Press, 1961), pp. 62–72, and *Catholic Mind*, 57 (Jan., 1959), 82–87, both reprint the statement of the hierarchy, "Discrimination and the Christian Conscience."

Archbishop Egidio Vagnozzi, who while visiting the Archbishop of New Orleans, on May 4, 1961, declared that the statement of the American hierarchy represented the position of the Church on racial segregation:

> On the question of integration, the Bishops of the United States, in 1958, issued a statement, *Discrimination and the Christian Conscience.* That is the position of the Church, a position to which every good, right-thinking Catholic must subscribe.[19]

The Catholic hierarchy of South Africa has been equally frank in its condemnations of *apartheid.* They spoke out against it in 1952, 1957, and again in 1960. In the first of these statements, which was read in all the Catholic churches, they declared:

> Discrimination based exclusively on grounds of color is an offense against the right of non-Europeans to their natural dignity as human persons. Though most of the basic rights of non-Europeans are in theory respected, conditions arising out of discriminatory legislation (such as laws restricting employment), social conventions and inefficient administration seriously impair the exercise of these fundamental rights. The disruption of family life is a case in point.[20]

Again at a meeting of the hierarchy in 1957, they issued another statement and condemned the doctrine of white supremacy which is implicit in the practice of *apartheid:*

> Apartheid is sometimes described as separate development, a term which suggests that under apartheid different races are given the opportunity of pursuing their respective and distinctive social and cultural evolutions. It is argued that only in this manner will these races be doing the will of God, lending themselves to the fulfillment of His providential designs. The contention sounds plausible as long as we overlook an important qualification, namely, that separate development, here, is subordinate to white supremacy. The white man makes himself the agent of God's will and the interpreter of His providence in assigning the range and determining the bounds of non-white development. One trembles at the blasphemy of thus attributing to God the offences against charity and justice that are apartheid's necessary accompaniment.[21]

---

[19] "Apostolic Delegate on Race," *America,* 105 (June 3, 1961), 387; "Voice of Authority on Race Relations," *Liguorian,* 49 (Sept., 1961), 54.

[20] Statement of the Archbishops and Bishops of South Africa, June 29, 1952, *Catholic Mind,* 50 (Sept., 1952), 572–576; *Irish Ecclesiastical Record,* 79 (Jan., 1953), 71–75.

[21] Statement of Catholic Bishops of South Africa, Pretoria, July, 1957, Eugene McManus, *op. cit.,* pp. 84–86; *The Shield-Collegian,* 37 (March, 1958), 14–16.

In less than three years, it was again necessary for the South African bishops to speak out even more forcefully against *apartheid* because of their growing concern over the harm which *apartheid* was inflicting on the future of the country and its citizens. They repeated their teaching on the physical and spiritual unity of the human race, and on the existence of natural rights possessed by all men. They condemned legislation which prohibited free associations of the races and banned interracial marriage, stating that such laws were opposed to the principles of Christianity and violated the fundamental rights of man. They declared that it was immoral to refuse to associate with other persons solely because of race:

> In the social sphere the same essential unity, on which the following pronouncements have been based, holds. The opportunity must be provided for those who attain to the recognized standard of education, whether formal or informal, and have a community of interests, to associate with others. Nor may a person refuse to associate with other persons of equal educational standing solely on the grounds of color, for such a refusal is a denial of human dignity and man's essential unity. The introduction of legislation limiting this free association and social intercourse is a contradiction of Christian principles, as well as a refusal to acknowledge the essential unity of the human person. Such legislation has, in fact, gone to the extent of denying certain fundamental rights, as in the case of the Mixed Marriages Act, which has deprived individuals of the free choice of their partner in marriage solely on the grounds of color, a prohibition which the divine law and the natural moral law do not impose.[22]

The hierarchy of Northern Rhodesia also found it necessary to speak out on racial matters in 1958. They asserted in their statement their authority to teach in the field of social affairs based on the mission of the Church to preach the Gospel to the whole world. This mandate of Christ gave to the Church the right to teach not only on purely religious matters, but also on social, political, and economic questions insofar as they have a relation to morality. They reaffirmed the physical and spiritual unity of the human race and enumerated basic natural rights, including the right to associate with one's fellowmen, and warned Catholics of the immorality involved in suppression of any of these rights:

---

[22] Statement of Catholic Bishops of South Africa, Pretoria, January 25–February 2, 1960, Eugene McManus, *op. cit.*, pp. 73–83; *Catholic Mind*, 58 (July, 1960), 375–383.

We warn all Catholics that they cannot reconcile with their Catholic conscience any tendency to introduce legislation which would secure the rights of one section of the community by curtailing the rights of others, especially those rights which we enumerated previously.[23]

It would require a separate study to examine in detail even representative statements of individual bishops of the United States and South Africa, so we will be limited to mentioning some of these. Archbishop Denis Hurley, O.M.I., of Durban, South Africa, has made several statements on the color bar in South Africa. In a statement, made in May, 1959, he warned that if the color bar were not abolished within ten years, the Union of South Africa would find itself the only advocate of white supremacy in a continent composed, for the most part, of self-governing African states, and subject to the moral and political pressures in the United Nations, as well as actual economic sanctions and boycotts applied by neighbor nations.[24]

Among the American bishops, the names of Bishop Albert Fletcher of Little Rock; Archbishop Paul J. Hallinan of Atlanta; Bishop Victor Reed of Oklahoma City-Tulsa; Archbishop Joseph Rummel of New Orleans; and Bishop Vincent Waters of Raleigh represent some of the Southern bishops who have spoken on race prejudice and segregation. Cardinal Meyer of Chicago, Bishop Wright of Pittsburgh, and Bishop William Connare of Greensburg represent some of the Northern bishops who have spoken on this matter. However, it can be said that Archbishop Joseph Rummel's pastoral letter to the clergy and laity of the New Orleans diocese, when he was the Ordinary, is the most representative of all the statements of individual bishops and is outstanding in its clearness and explicitness, as well as being the one which aroused the greatest opposition. Archbishop Rummel makes it quite clear that he is exercising his teaching authority as bishop of the diocese when he cites the statement of Pius XII that bishops share in the papal teaching authority. He further cites Pius XII that canonists and theologians can, under the guidance of the Pope and bishops, apply the principles of their

---

[23] Pastoral letter of the Hierarchy of Northern Rhodesia, January 6, 1958, Catholic Mind, 57 (Jan., 1959), 88–95.

[24] La Documentation Catholique, 56 (July 5, 1959), 858–861; cf. also pastoral letter of the Bishops of Tanganyika, "The Church in a Pluralistic Society," Catholic Mind, 60 (Jan., 1962), 59–63.

sciences to dogmatic, moral, or social questions, and that when the higher authority gives approval to their conclusions, they can be considered safe norms of moral conduct. Archbishop Rummel then states: "This is precisely the procedure which we must apply to the problem of race segregation." He declares that racial segregation, as such, is morally wrong and sinful for three reasons:

1. It denies the physical unity of the human race.

2. It denies the supernatural unity of men and the universality of the Redemption.

3. It violates justice and charity.[25]

Bishop Albert Fletcher of Little Rock has prepared a Catechism on the morality of segregation and discrimination for use in Confraternity of Christian Doctrine discussion clubs.[26] In this catechism, he condemns segregation as immoral and considers compulsory segregation as discrimination. He defines segregation, as practiced in the state of Arkansas, as "a permanent condition or state, imposed by law or custom on the members of the Negro race, isolating them to a greater or lesser extent from white fellow citizens and limiting them in the exercise of their freedom as compared with other citizens, principally in the fields of job opportunity, education, housing, and public services" (q. 1). He then states that segregation as enforced in Arkansas is "immoral because it discriminates unjustly and uncharitably against human beings on the basis of race alone" (q. 12).

Moral theologians who have written on the question of racial segregation have maintained that it is immoral because of the violations of charity and justice and the affront to human dignity which is necessarily involved in segregation. There are some differences of theological opinion as to whether a certain action violates commutative or social justice; or whether certain matters are obligations of charity or of justice; or if certain forms of protest, such as Sit-Ins, are morally justifiable, but there is not, to the writer's knowledge, a single Catholic theologian who has written a defense of enforced racial segregation or claimed that it is morally unobjectionable.

In view of all these facts — the papal statements, the pastorals

---

[25] Pastoral letter of Archbishop Rummel, *Catholic Mind*, 54 (May, 1956), 296–300.

[26] Most Rev. Albert L. Fletcher, *An Elementary Catholic Catechism on the Morality of Segregation and Racial Discrimination*, 1960.

and statements of the hierarchy, both individually and as a group, and the writings of the theologians, I believe that we can say that *all enforced racial segregation, such as we know it in the United States, is discriminatory, and that it is immoral because it violates charity or justice, or occasionally both.*

CHAPTER 19

OBJECTIONS OF
CATHOLICS TO EPISCOPAL STATEMENTS

The American hierarchy's statement, *Discrimination
and the Christian Conscience,* and the pastoral letters of individual
bishops, particularly that of Archbishop Rummel, asserting that racial
segregation was sinful, were received with mixed reactions by Catholics. Many hailed them, rejoicing that the Church was making her
position and teaching clearer and more explicit. Others resented them,
considering them to be statements which exceeded episcopal authority.
In New Orleans, an association of Catholic laymen, opposed to integration in Catholic schools as well as in public schools, appealed
to the Holy See for an official declaration of the morality of segregation and for a reply to certain questions they posed regarding the
right of a bishop to define questions of morality.

Nor was this criticism limited to American Catholics. *The Tablet*
(London), in an editorial, criticized the school integration policies
of Archbishop Rummel and attempted to justify the action of the
Catholics of New Orleans who had appealed to Rome, and based
their justification on the toleration of slavery by the American hierarchy. They asked how a bishop could declare something "to be
immoral which was not and would not have been declared morally
wrong at an earlier date."[1]

Arguments and objections brought forth at different times to support such opposition and criticism of the episcopal statements include
the charge that in medieval times various conciliar decrees, as well

[1] *The Tablet* (London), August 17, 1957. Cf. "British Critics of Archbishop
Rummel," *America,* 98 (Oct. 19, 1957), 63.

270

as papal letters, enforced segregation of the Jews. The Third Lateran Council in 1179, Paul IV's *Cum nimis absurdum* of 1555, and the decree of Pius V in 1569, are given as examples of segregation enacted and enforced by the Councils and the Popes. These papal and conciliar decrees compelled the Jews to live in certain sections of town — the ghettos; forbade their exercise of certain professions, e.g., medicine or holding public office; and required distinctive clothing or emblems to be worn by Jews to facilitate their recognition as Jews. Segregationists draw a parallel between these decrees and the segregation of Negroes. They indicate that both forms of segregation have been practiced for many years, even in churches, without ever having been declared immoral, and ask: "How can a practice, about which there has been silence for a long time, suddenly become sinful and immoral?" They conclude that episcopal statements, such as that of Archbishop Rummel, indicating that racial segregation is sinful, imply that the medieval papal and conciliar decrees regarding the Jews are likewise immoral.

Erroneously, they take these statements to be episcopal "definitions of morality" in the sense that they represent arbitrary infallible declarations of morality, extending beyond that contained in the universal *magisterium*, rather than in the true sense of a moral teaching by the bishop, i.e., a declaration protecting and defending matters already explicitly defined by the Church or universally accepted, and interpretations and applications of the moral teaching of the Church. Infallibility, they say, can be exercised by the bishops gathered in ecumenical council with the Pope or by the Pope alone, speaking *ex cathedra*, but that neither individual bishops nor local synods nor councils enjoy infallibility. None of these, they conclude, can issue a "definition of morality," especially when it implies that former decrees of ecumenical councils and papal enactments and practices were immoral and sinful.

These objections have raised doubts and created questions of conscience for Catholics who live in a society where racial segregation has been practiced for a long time, and who are reluctant, for various reasons, to abandon practices which have become customs, but who, at the same time, are uneasy of conscience because of the conflict between the statements of their bishops and their own practices.

Therefore, it will be necessary to say a few words about the question of the Jews during the medieval period; about the authority of the bishop to teach; and finally, about the previous silence of the Church in reference to the morality of segregation.

Jews in Medieval Christendom: This is not the first time that the attitude and treatment of medieval Christendom toward the Jews has been used as, at least, a partial justification of a modern racial practice. During the 1930's, some Italian Fascists, advocating anti-Semitism, cited the conciliar and papal restrictions of the Jews as an ecclesiastical precedent. Maritain took note of this and rejected their claim, stating that the medieval Jewish situation was no proof that anti-Semitism represents a constant ecclesiastical policy as was claimed by these Italian Fascists, as well as some American anti-Fascists:

> If we avoid a unilateral selection of texts, and if there were sufficient acquaintance with the philosophy of history, it would be understood that neither the policy adopted at certain periods regarding the Jews by medieval Christendom, nor the supervening mistakes and abuses which may have occurred, prove that the Catholic Church is bound to antisemitism. I mention this for the benefit of certain Italian Fascist writers, as well as for certain American anti-Fascist writers.[2]

It is impossible to present here an adequate historical survey of the various stages and events in the development of medieval anti-Jewish attitudes and restrictions which occurred, not only in the Papal States, but also in other European countries. But it is necessary to indicate that the basis of these restrictions enacted by conciliar decree or papal letter was *always religion and not race*. There is an essential difference between these decrees and the Nazi anti-Semitism, where the fact of blood or race was the sole consideration — Aryan versus Semitic. Nazi anti-Semitic laws were applied whether or not the person practiced or professed the Jewish religion. His religion made no difference — his subjection to the penalties of the law was established by the fact of blood or race. The Aryan clause of the Law of April 7, 1933, and the Nuremberg Laws of September 15, 1935, barred Jews from the practice of medicine, law, and other professions. It defined a Jew as one who had at least one Jewish grandparent. The children

---

[2] J. Maritain, *Anti-Semitism* (London: Geoffrey Bles: The Centenary Press, 1939), p. 26 n.

of a Jewish convert must attend a Jewish school and could not be admitted to a Christian school. An outstanding victim of these anti-Semitic laws was Edith Stein, who, even though a convert to Catholicism and a Carmelite nun, was executed as a Jew in the concentration camp at Auschwitz.

On the other hand, the medieval restrictions were based solely on religion, and were removed when a Jew accepted Christianity. The element of race or blood was not considered, and the Jew, as soon as he had been baptized, was admitted to full participation in society. Realization of this fact moved some to accept baptism and profess Christianity insincerely, while secretly they remained Jewish believers. It was not, however, unheard of for converted Jews to rise to high positions in the ecclesiastical and civil government of the Church; and in several Italian dioceses, the bishops were Jewish converts.

It is difficult to see a parity between this type of segregation, based on the fact of religion, and that practiced in the United States which is based on the fact of blood or race. A similarity could be asserted if a Negro, who is intelligent, capable, well educated, and politically gifted, could become governor or senator in a Southern state, which, under present conditions, does not seem imminent.

According to Grayzel, a Jewish scholar, papal policy toward the Jews was founded on several religious principles. First, and most important, was the desire to convert the Jews to Catholicism. It would be the crowning success of the Church if the conversion of the Jews could be accomplished as they represented the only non-Christian element in Western Europe. The second principle, and almost equally important in the eyes of contemporary Christians, was the desire to defend Christianity from any possibility of error and to prevent proselytization of the faithful by Jews. He also maintains that Innocent III expressed, in theological terms, the status Jews should have in an otherwise totally Christian society. Essentially, this involved a consecrational concept of temporal society in which the fullness of citizenship and participation would be available to Christians only. Perpetual servitude and subservient social position were the lot of the Jews because of guilt incurred by participation in the crucifixion. Like Cain, the Jew was to be a wanderer and a fugitive on the face of the earth. The social status of the Jew was expressed in terms of the Church-Synagogue symbol. The Church was the Bride, the Synagogue was the rejected wife; the Synagogue and its members were Hagar, the slave girl, and her children, but the Church was the freewoman and her members were the children of the freewoman. Seen in the light of a consecrational conception of society, restrictions against the Jews (and Saracens) seemed to flow logically and necessarily. Christians must be kept away from the Jews lest their faith or morals be corrupted by the example or teaching of the Jews; and the Jews must be excluded from holding positions of authority or jurisdiction since this would mean that the slave was superior to the freeman, and in addition, they could misuse this power and authority to induce Christians to abandon their religion.

Dr. Grayzel concludes that by mid-thirteenth century, the European Jews were well on the way to complete exclusion from Christian society, but that this exclusion would have been accomplished even without the enactments of the Church since, in addition to the religious reasons, there were other factors involved which would have sufficed to effect it. The rise of national states was one of these factors, since the reluctance of the Jews to associate or intermarry with Christians, at a time when interracial intermingling was laying the foundations of the various modern nations, set the Jews apart and outside the bonds of a national unity. A new economic order, emphasizing industry and commerce, was beginning to replace the agrarian economy. This constituted another factor since it made the Jew expendable and no longer necessary for the role of banker and money-lender which he held when the Church had strict prohibitions against Christians taking interest. Dr. Grayzel admits that the desire of the Church to convert the Jews and the fear of Jewish proselytizing, more or less, justified some of these restrictions in view of the circumstances and the rivalry between the two religions. But he avers that the attack on the foundations of Jewish economic, political, and social life exceeded a legitimate self-defense and were enacted because of the notion that the life of the Jew, in its daily events and circumstances, must give constant proof to all that God has rejected the Jews.[3]

Dispassionate and nonpartisan study by historians is needed in the

---

[3] Solomon Grayzel, The Church and the Jews in the XIIIth Century (Philadelphia: Dropsie College for Hebrew and Cognate Learning, 1933).

question of the Jews in medieval Europe. Such a study would be most helpful in determining the relationship between a justifiable self-defense by the Church and the enactment of these restrictions. But it is beyond the scope of this work to attempt to make such a judgment. If the conclusion is reached by historians that in some instances these limits were exceeded, it would not indicate any change in moral teaching on the part of the Church in condemning racial segregation today. Administrative and disciplinary decrees, whether conciliar or papal, do not enjoy a guarantee of infallibility, nor do civil laws and statutes enacted for the administration of ecclesiastical territories.

These enactments involve no exercise of infallibility of either an ecumenical Council or the Pope since they are not concerned with dogmatic or moral teachings. Rather they are social, political, and disciplinary measures enacted to solve the problem of a religious minority which existed within the confines of an otherwise politically, religiously, and socially homogeneous entity, and in which the consecrational concept of the temporal and social order, as described above, was prevalent. Speaking of these restrictions, Charles Journet has denied that the theologian has any obligation to attempt to present a justification of them, when the Pope is acting as the ruler of the pontifical states, and that there is even less necessity to attempt a defense of all that was done in the various Christian states against the Jews:

> The measures the Popes adopted to regulate the activities of the Jews and to limit their influence, were dictated by the need to maintain the basic principle of the political constitution of the West. They belonged to the logic of a consecrational conception of the temporal order which, by definition, granted the quality of citizenship to Christians alone. Doubtless they did not amount to the solution of the Jewish problem. They were but a solution, a political and provisional compromise.[4]

The statement by a bishop or group of bishops that racial segregation is immoral does not mean a condemnation of conciliar acts and decrees enacted several centuries ago. Such statements made today are not made with any intention of referring to or passing judgment

---

[4] Charles Journet, *The Church of the Word Incarnate*, translated by A. H. C. Downes, Vol. I (London: Sheed and Ward, 1955), pp. 231–240.

on the disciplinary decrees or civil statutes enacted for the pontifical states. Who would say that Pope Pius was passing judgment on the actions of his predecessors and the councils and declaring their actions immoral when, citing the words of the Mass: ". . . sicuti accepta habere dignatus es munera pueri tui justi Abel, et sacrificium Patriarchae nostri Abrahae," he pointed out that here Abraham is called our patriarch and our ancestor, and stated that anti-Semitism is un-Christian:

> Notice that Abraham is called our Patriarch, our ancestor. Anti-Semitism is incompatible with the thought and sublime reality expressed in this text. It is a movement in which we Christians can have no part whatsoever. . . . Anti-Semitism is unacceptable. Spiritually we are Semites.[5]

These medieval enactments must be considered within the religious-political-social situation in which they arose, and within the framework of the prevalent concept of temporal society as a chosen, elected, and consecrated society. The Church was the sole unifying principle of the whole of Western Europe, and the Jewish community was the only segment not a member of the Church. In the zeal to bring Jews within the Church, we know that excesses did take place. St. Thomas Aquinas was most emphatic in condemning the forcing of Jews to be baptized, and many contemporary Popes enacted legislation prohibiting such forced baptisms. In fear that the faith of its members be corrupted and lost, or in its concept that the rejection of Christ by the Jews and their continued refusal to believe in Him deserved punishment, it is possible that excesses took place and unjustifiable prescriptions were enacted. This appears to be the conclusion of Father Van der Ploeg, who, in his work on the Jews and the Church, wrote:

> Regrettable things have been done by Christians, members of the Catholic Church, and sometimes even by the authorities of that Church. . . . Murdering Jews, robbing them of their lawful possessions, accusing them of committing frightful crimes while the Black Death was ravaging Europe, using force to convert them . . . banishment by hundreds of thousands, all these are dark pages in the history of Christendom. They prove that the spirit of the Gospel, especially the commandment of fraternal charity, to say nothing of justice, was

---

[5] Pius XI, allocution to Directors of the Belgian Catholic Radio Agency, September, 1938, quoted by J. Maritain, *Anti-Semitism*, p. 27.

never understood. However necessary it is to reduce all that happened to its true proportions and to look at it in the light of the ideas, social and political conditions, etc., of its own time, the evil cannot be argued away or condoned.[6]

Peril and danger to the Church also had an influence in the enactment of these laws as a part of the self-defense of the Church. This can be seen in the enactments of the Popes during the Reformation period when the Church was threatened with the loss of vast numbers of its members, and when it was attempting to stem the tide of the Reformation. The Papacy apparently feared the activity of the Jews, and it was then that it enacted its most stringent restrictions, e.g., Paul IV, in 1555, required that the Jews in the Papal States be restricted to the ghetto, and compelled them to sell their real estate holdings; in 1569, Pius V extended this restriction to the ghetto to all Christian lands, and finally expelled the Jews from the papal territories, except Rome and Ancona; Gregory XIII, in 1581, subjected the Jews to the jurisdiction and penal inflictions of the Inquisition for certain offenses.

As we have stated, a judgment as to whether limits of legitimate self-defense were exceeded must be left to the historians. But, at any rate, the existence of these enactments cannot be construed as a justification of racial segregation as we know it today. Strangely enough, the nature of these medieval restrictions and their relation to the *magisterium* of the Church has been understood better by a rabbi than by some Catholics. Rabbi Arthur Gilbert, in writing on the relation of the Jews to the Ecumenical Council called by Pope John, mentions these anti-Jewish enactments of previous councils, and while he regrets the harm that they inflicted on the Jewish community, he recognizes that there is no question of an involvement of either dogmatic or moral teaching:

> It must be recognized that the decrees were disciplinary, rather than dogmatic, i.e., they were considered an aspect of the Church's pastoral concern rather than a clearly pronounced teaching on the Jews to become part of Catholic theology for all time. Disciplinary actions — not given the weight of dogma — can at any time be revoked or changed; and as we note from Church history, these enactments were

---

[6] J. Van der Ploeg, O.P., *The Church and Israel*, translated by a Religious of the Retreat of the Sacred Heart (Washington, D. C.: Catholic Distributors, 1956), p. 37.

not always so faithfully observed. Nevertheless, they were harmful enough for the Jews in those days.[7]

What has been said regarding the nonvalidity of objections to episcopal statements based on this medieval legislation can, I believe, be summarized in the following manner:

1. Present episcopal statements have no bearing on the old situation. They are not made within a frame of reference to the medieval situation and do not involve or imply any judgment on that situation.

2. The restrictions themselves represent either disciplinary decrees or civil enactments for the control and government of the pontifical states and cannot be considered as expressions of moral or dogmatic teaching.

3. The modern racial and the medieval Jewish situations are not parallel since in the medieval restrictions, the sole consideration was religion, not race.

4. It is possible that some of these restrictions were excessive and not justifiable, but they are explainable in view of the prevalent consecrational concept of temporal society, as well as the fear of harm coming to the faith of Christians through Jewish activities and influences.

Authority of the Bishop to Teach: Questioning the right of a bishop to teach in matters of faith and morals for his diocese stems from an erroneous or distorted notion of the role of the bishop in the *magisterium* of the Church.[8] Canon 1326 states that bishops, even when gathered in local council, are not infallible, but that they are true teachers and doctors under the authority of the Pope for the faithful committed to their charge. In 1954, Pope Pius XII, in two allocutions, explicitly affirmed that only the Pope for the universal Church and the bishops for their dioceses constitute the *magisterium* of the Church.[9] In the second of these allocutions, he condemned the attempt to restrict the function of the bishops to religious

---

[7] Arthur Gilbert, "A Jew Looks at the Ecumenical Council," *Ave Maria,* 94 (Dec. 9, 1961), 5–7.

[8] J. C. Ford, S.J., and Gerald Kelly, S.J., *Contemporary Moral Theology,* Vol. I: "Questions in Fundamental Theology" (Westminster: Newman Press, 1958), Chap. III.

[9] Pius XII, allocution, *Si diligis,* English trans., *The Pope Speaks,* I (2nd Quarter, 1954), 153–158, AER, 131 (1954), 127–137; and allocution, *Magnificate Dominum.* English trans., *Catholic Mind,* 53 (May, 1955), 311–320; AER, 132 (1955), 52–63.

matters, administration of the sacraments, and liturgical functions, and to exclude them from the sociopolitical field. In opposing this modern tendency, he reaffirmed the right of the *magisterium* to teach on the entire matter of the natural law and its applications insofar as they are related to morals. He said that when the Pope, for the entire Church, and the bishops, for their dioceses, publish instructions and propositions on matters falling within the ambit of the natural law, the faithful are bound by these and cannot "invoke that saying (which is wont to be employed with respect to opinions of individuals): 'the strength of the authority is no more than the strength of the arguments.'"

The *magisterium* of individual bishops is restricted to teaching and protecting truths already defined by the Church's universal *magisterium*, and does not extend to the closing of theological controversies. This does not mean that the teaching of an individual bishop is to be equated with the opinion of a theologian or a scientist. It carries greater weight than this, not because of the bishop's theological or scientific training and knowledge, nor because of the proofs and arguments he adduces to support his teaching, but because of his office and his role as part of the divinely constituted *magisterium* of the Church.

Applying these facts to the teachings of the individual bishops on racial segregation, we can draw these conclusions. In several instances, these statements represent examples of exercises of the teaching office of the bishop. This is, I believe, particularly true of the statement of Archbishop Rummel in 1956. However, some statements should be considered primarily moral exhortations or legislative decrees and orders, applicable to their dioceses. This is so in instances of statements made by individual bishops to government committees, and declarations that parochial schools in their diocese will be open to all Catholic children regardless of race.

We have previously mentioned that Archbishop Rummel specifically referred to the *Si diligis* of Pius XII, affirming the role of the bishop as part of the official *magisterium*, who enjoys the pledge of Christ of guidance when his teaching is under the direction of the Holy See. This explicit relation of the Archbishop's statement to the magisterial office, as well as the actual wording used, indicates that it is intended to be a presentation of teaching rather than a legislative decree or an exhortation:

> For months we have prayed, studied and consulted about the problem with a sense of our responsibility for the welfare of all souls that constitute the spiritual family for which in virtue of our office as Archbishop we are responsible before God. With an appeal to the Holy Spirit, we now submit for careful consideration the following results, especially regarding the moral difficulties which segregation presents.[10]

As a matter of fact, the letter offers no practical regulations in the matter of segregation in the archdiocesan schools, the key problem for which a solution was sought. Prayers are requested by the Archbishop that the decision on methods, which would be made later, after further consideration and study, would be in conformity with the will of Christ, advantageous for the salvation of souls, and accepted by all in a spirit of justice and charity. Hence the letter could not be considered primarily an exhortation or a legislative decree since there was no command or prohibition of any action, except that implied in any declaration of the moral perversity and sinfulness of a socioeconomic system.

That the letter falls within the scope of the *magisterium* in protecting and teaching defined doctrine is apparent in the reasons which the Archbishop gives for the sinfulness of segregation, viz., it denies the solidarity of the human race; it denies the universality of the Redemption; and it violates the virtues of justice and charity. The first two of these are defined truths for whose protection the bishop has a responsibility. Further, it cannot be considered as closing a theological controversy, which would be beyond the scope of the individual bishop's *magisterium*. We have already mentioned the practical unanimity of the theologians who have discussed or written on segregation. It cannot be said that there was any *theological* controversy for the Archbishop to attempt to close.

This, of course, is but one of the many statements made by various bishops regarding segregation, although it is probably one of the more important and explicit statements. There are also others which can be considered primarily as exercises of the teaching office of the bishop, and secondarily as exhortative or legislative. Bishop Fletcher's

---

[10] *Catholic Mind*, 54 (1956), 296.

catechism on segregation, the pastorals and statements of the South African bishops are examples of pronouncements containing all three elements: teaching, legislative, and exhortative, but in which, I believe, the teaching element is primary.

That the statements of the bishops are reflective of true Catholic teaching is confirmed by the words of Pius XII: "The Church has always been actively opposed to attempts at genocide and to practices arising from what is called the 'color bar.'" In fact, these words were quoted in the statement of the American hierarchy, *Discrimination and the Christian Conscience*, where it is suggested that the denial of human rights which results from segregation as practiced in the United States must surely have been in the mind of Pope Pius when he made this remark. The identification of *Discrimination and the Christian Conscience* as representative of the "position of the Church," by the Apostolic Delegate, Archbishop Egidio Vagnozzi, on May 4, 1961, is further evidence of the conformity of such declarations with Catholic doctrine and of the unreasonableness of claims that they are abuses of the episcopal office and powers and of the request for an *ex cathedra* papal definition.

Previous Silence Regarding the Immorality of Segregation: It is relatively easy to appreciate the quandary and dilemma faced by some Catholics, particularly when they are led to view the statements of the bishop as representing definitions of new morality initiated by the bishop and, therefore, an overextension of his authority and teaching power. They have heard it argued that bishops and priests in this country have remained silent for many years and have said nothing on the morality of segregation. In fact the Church practiced it by providing separate schools, separate seating in churches, by segregating diocesan conventions and sodality meetings, etc. In view of such silence and the actual practice of segregation for such a long time, a dilemma arises: either the statements made by the bishops declaring segregation sinful represent a change in the moral doctrine taught by the Church, or else the silence and practices of the Church and the bishops and priests in the past were sinful. Many Catholics who have heard this argumentation have been disturbed and perplexed by it. There can be no doubt that, presented in this manner, it is a forceful argument and as such deserves some consideration and examination in the light of theological principles.

It is the writer's belief that these practices and the silence in the matter of racial segregation in years past can only be explained adequately by the admission that *the sinfulness of enforced racial segregation was not recognized either by ecclesiastical authorities or by the theologians of that time.* It is important to note here that we are speaking of the lack of recognition of the sinfulness of segregation. At no time was there lacking an awareness of the sinfulness of rash judgment and injustice against the Negro. This was recognized, and taught, not only after emancipation, but also during slavery. Bishop Augustine Verot, while Vicar Apostolic of Florida, in a famous sermon preached at the Cathedral in St. Augustine, on January 4, 1861, spoke against claims of the abolitionists, but also, in the latter part of the sermon, spoke of the duties and obligations of slaveholders to provide for the physical, spiritual, and moral needs of their slaves. He mentioned the rights of free Negroes and condemned as unjust the laws which some states had enacted against them. He declared that it was equally "unjust to vex the free colored as the white because they are Irish or German," or, on account of their religion. Bishop Verot calls unjust those state laws which attempt to enslave the free Negro, or to expel him from the state, or to molest or harass him.[11]

What was lacking was a realization that enforced racial segregation is discriminatory and unjust. For that moral judgment to be made, it required time, experience, and proof. It was only after the weight of evidence had been accumulated that the judgment could be made by the theologians and the bishops, that compulsory racial segregation was morally wrong. Indeed, the practices and prejudices of many years are actually barriers to the recognition and acceptance of this judgment by many Catholics, and this includes some priests. Father Gerald Kelly, S.J., spoke of this reluctance of some priests to recognize and admit the immorality of segregation, and he lamented that for some of them, death alone would solve the problem.[12]

We have already seen the solicitude of the Church to provide for

---

[11] *Freemans Journal* (New York), June 18, 1864, and July 9, 1864.

[12] *Proceedings of the 13th Annual Convention, The Catholic Theological Society of America,* (1958), p. 64.

the spiritual care and education of the Negro. The situation of the young Church in America must be realized in order to appreciate properly the problems she faced in order to provide care for the Catholics. Archbishop Eccleston of Baltimore, in 1838, in his report to the Society for the Propagation of the Faith, mentions the need of spiritual care to be given to the slaves in his diocese. He is convinced, from experience, that there is no class in the entire country among whom it would be possible to work more fruitfully, but is unable to do all that he would like for their salvation. At that time, his diocese comprised the entire state of Maryland and the District of Columbia, and the administration of the Diocese of Richmond: an area of over 74,000 square miles, in which there were just sixty-one churches and chapels, and seventy-four diocesan priests. Over one half the population consisted of Negro slaves.[13]

In 1858, Bishop William Elder of Natchez reported that his diocese covered 47,000 square miles with a total of twelve priests for the entire territory.[14] Over half the population consisted of Negroes — 309,878 slaves and 930 free Negroes. In a letter to the Society for the Propagation of the Faith, which Monsignor John Tracy Ellis states gives a picture of every Southern diocese at that time, he appeals for help in providing for the spiritual care and instruction of these slaves:

> What a harvest of souls among these 310,000 Negroes, every one of them immortal, made to the image and likeness of God, redeemed by the Precious Blood of the Son of God! Oh, what a frightful havoc Satan is making among them! What numbers of children die without baptism! how many grown persons live and die in ignorance of God, and still worse, buried in miserable sins and habits of sins, which they neither know nor care to free themselves from. . . . They need instructions and the Sacraments. . . . Are there not Priests of God — at least in the generous Apostolic land of France — are there not still some there, who are ready to put the sickle into this abundant field?[15]

In 1888, the problems facing the Church in caring for souls were still great. The work of converting the Negro had made very little progress. In the Diocese of Wilmington there were 100,000 Negroes, only 100 of whom were Catholic; in the Diocese of Richmond there were approximately 300 Negro Catholics in the entire state when

---

[13] *Documents of American Catholic History*, John Tracy Ellis (ed.), 2 ed. (Milwaukee: The Bruce Publishing Co., 1962), pp. 246–251.

[14] *Freemans Journal* (New York), June 5, 1858.

[15] John Tracy Ellis, *op. cit.*, pp. 325–329.

Bishop Keane began personally to instruct them in his cathedral at Richmond in 1878.[16] The coming of the Josephite Fathers in 1871, when the first four missionary priests from the newly founded Mill Hill were sent from England by Herbert Vaughan (later Cardinal-Archbishop of Westminster), represented the first organized effort to convert and care for the souls of the Negro in this country. By 1893, there were no more than twenty Catholic churches in the United States for the Negroes. The Josephite Fathers staffed eight of these twenty, the Benedictines were in charge of several others, while the Jesuits were caring for Negro Catholics throughout southern Maryland, St. Louis, and Macon and Augusta, Georgia.[17]

During the post-Civil War period, the efforts of the Church toward the Negroes were concentrated on an attempt to provide a religious education and to train them in various occupations and to be useful citizens. In fact, a school was usually the first section of a mission to be built and from this the Negro church and parish would develop. The problems were such that there was apparently little time for concern over social or political aspects or considerations. The suddenness of emancipation had resulted in thousands of former slaves being given full citizenship without previous preparation, education, or training. For the most part, these ex-slaves were illiterate, as many states had laws which prohibited teaching them to read or write. A lifetime of suppression, ignorance, and lack of social, political, and cultural training which had been their common lot for generations under slavery left deep marks. The training, education, and absorption of these vast numbers of former slaves represented the Negro problem facing the country immediately after the Civil War. The Constitution gave certain rights to its citizens and the Fourteenth, Fifteenth, and Sixteenth Amendments were enacted to protect and guarantee these rights for the Negro.

To solve the problem of how to bestow the rights of citizens on the Negroes in view of the widespread lack of education and training among them, as well as the prejudices against a race which still

---

[16] John R. Slattery, S.S.J., "The Seminary for the Colored Missions," *Catholic World*, 46 (Jan., 1888), 541–550.
[17] John Gillard, S.S.J., *The Catholic Church and the American Negro* (Baltimore: St. Joseph's Society Press, 1929), pp. 39–45; Edward D. Reynolds, S.J., *Jesuits for the Negro* (New York: America Press, 1949).

bore the stigma of slavery, a compromise was made. This compromise was summed up in the "separate but equal" principle. In this way, the rights of the Negroes, it was believed, would be safeguarded, while, at the same time, association with them or any idea of social equality would be prevented. This appeared to be the perfect compromise. All the legal and political rights of the Negro would be protected and preserved, and white citizens would not have to associate with members of a group who were mostly illiterate, uneducated, and uncultured. No injustice could be seen in this solution. In theory, it seemed fine and it found legal sanction in the court decisions for over a half century.

But it required almost the entire half century before it was realized that "separate but equal" was only an abstraction. In practice it was impossible, without injustice, to enforce the principle of "separate but equal" on racial grounds.

A few notable exceptions were able to recognize immediately the discrimination and injustice of racial segregation. Probably the most articulate and most prominent was Archbishop John Ireland of St. Paul. His recognition of the immorality of segregation, as early as 1890, and his open declarations against it are remarkable and probably unparalleled. In April, 1890, in a sermon at St. Augustine's Church in Washington, D. C., a Negro Catholic church, Archbishop Ireland declared that to make a man sit in a corner reserved for his race was a contradiction of justice. Again in January, 1891, on the twenty-eighth anniversary of the Emancipation Proclamation, he advocated the removal of all color lines and the opening of industrial jobs and all professions to the Negro. He realized that his statements had met with almost universal rejection, and his reply to those who considered his position and stand untimely is a prophecy still to be fulfilled:

> Aye, untimely today, my words will be timely tomorrow. My fault, if there be a fault, would be that I am ahead of my day. The time is not distant when Americans and all other Christians will wonder that there ever was a race problem.[18]

Unfortunately, his views were rejected and disregarded, not only by

---

[18] James H. Moynihan, *The Life of Archbishop John Ireland* (New York: Harper & Bros., 1953), pp. 228–229; cf. also Eugene McManus, *op. cit.*, pp. 64–65.

the laity but also by his fellow bishops. Archbishop Ryan of Philadelphia is reported to have remarked to Archbishop Corrigan of New York that Ireland had caused a sensation in saying that Negroes should have social equality, and that his enthusiasm had led him too far, but his intentions were good.[19]

One of the few who openly approved of Archbishop Ireland's views at that time was Father John R. Slattery, S.S.J., who said that the rejection of the Archbishop's stand by so many Catholics was the product of ignorance. They should have recognized that it was merely the application of sound Catholic principles to the Negro problem:

> It is no surprise to meet with negrophobia among the ignorant, but very painful is it to find intelligent people subject to the same mania. Just here stands out the boundless distance between the Catholic Church and many of her children. How narrow the views of some Catholics about the Negro are plainly appeared (sic) last spring when Archbishop Ireland in a sermon delivered in the colored church in Washington, laid down the very A B C of civil and religious, political and manhood equality. What he said is but the expression of the Catholic faith applied to the Negro problem. Yet his words were received with scorn by some Catholics, yet they were men who should have known better. And it is far less wonder that an archbishop felt obliged to teach such fundamental truth than that Catholics were found who refused to hearken to them. The cry of "No Social Equality" was raised — a mere subterfuge to throw dust in our eyes.[20]

John Boyle O'Reilly was an outstanding lay Catholic who pleaded for the cause of justice for the Negro in his "Speech in Behalf of the Negro," delivered on December 7, 1885, in which he speaks out against segregation practices.[21] It is also interesting to note that in France, Henri Gregoire, Bishop of Blois in the schismatic French Constitutional Church, 1790–1801, also opposed racial prejudices which were apparently common in the French possessions and colonies. He sought particularly the extinction of racial prejudice through the enactment of laws recognizing interracial marriage; admission of

---

[19] James H. Moynihan, op. cit., p. 228.
[20] John R. Slattery, S.S.J., "The Catholic Negro's Complaint," Catholic World, 52 (Dec., 1890), 348.
[21] John Tracy Ellis, op. cit., pp. 428–432.

Negroes to public office; and providing for a liberal education of Negro children.[22]

However, it should not be considered that the long delay in the recognition of the violation of morality in racial segregation is a singular instance. There are other questions of moral theology where the application and pertinence of general and universal principles of morality to certain areas of human behavior are not apparent for some time. One instance of this is the rapidly growing opinion regarding the immorality of prizefighting. In fact, with recent ring injuries and deaths, many of the sports writers are predicting and even demanding legal bans or restrictions by the state legislatures. Yet it was only in 1950 that Father Francis Connell, C.Ss.R., was one of the first American theologians to question the morality of prizefighting, asserting that "it is difficult to reconcile prizefighting, as we have it today with Catholic principles of morality." Before this time, however, some European theologians had briefly treated of the morality of boxing. Opinions varied from that of Iorio, who considered it merely a national sport in America, to that of Ubach, who apparently considered the gloves as lethal weapons, and termed boxing a form of duel, prohibited by the law against dueling.

Since 1950, many medical men have made studies of the injuries to the brain, sight, and hearing inflicted in the ring, and concur that prizefighting as it is today should be condemned as immoral. Today, the cumulative weight of theological and medical opinion has become so great that the immorality of prizefighting is rapidly becoming common theological teaching.[23]

A similar pattern can be discerned in the realization of the immorality of segregation. One of the first American theologians to

[22] Henri Gregoire, *Essay on the Nobility of the Skin,* translated by Charlotte Nooth (Paris: printed by Setier, 1826), p. 65.

[23] Francis J. Connell, "Prizefighting and Boxing," *AER,* 122 (Jan., 1950), 58–59; Eugene Hillman, C.S.Sp., "The Morality of Boxing," *Theological Studies,* 12 (1951), 301–319; G. C. Bernard, C.S.C., *The Morality of Prizefighting* (Washington, D. C.: The Catholic University of America Press, 1952); "Ring Requiem," *America,* 107 (April 21, 1962), 73; "Professional Boxing Condemned (by Vatican Radio)," *The Tablet* (London), April 7, 1962; John C. Ford, S.J., "Notes on Moral Theology, 1945," *Theological Studies,* 6 (1945), 540; Gerald Kelly, S. J., "Notes on Moral Theology, 1950," *Theological Studies* 12 (1951), 75–78.

raise various questions on the morality of the color line was Monsignor Francis Gilligan, who in 1929 declared that many of these practices could not be reconciled with justice and charity. Father Gerald Kelly, S.J., has called *The Morality of the Color Line* by Monsignor Gilligan a real pioneer study and a capable application of theological principles to race relations.[24]

In 1937, Father John LaFarge, S.J., said that enforced segregation was *theoretically* indifferent, but when put into practice tended to injustice since it could not avoid the imputation of an essential inferiority.[25] In 1946, Father John E. Coogan, S.J., wrote that segregation was unjust because it robbed the Negro of his self-respect.[26] The San Antonio (Texas) Archdiocesan Committee on Interracial Relations, in their report, declared that segregation without injustice can exist only in the abstract, and that in practice there is no racial segregation without discrimination, and no discrimination without violation of justice.[27]

In the application of general moral principles to concrete and specific practices, the virtue of prudence plays a vital role. Its increase as an active virtue will be aided and advanced not only by the experiences of individuals, but also by the social experiences of the entire community, and, in this way, the gap between abstract truth and practical applications of that truth can be lessened. Speaking of this function of the virtue of prudence, Father John Connery, S.J., has indicated that through it, moral science can benefit from long social experience in formulating its more remote conclusions:

> The cumulative experience of a generation will contribute to moral science itself. While it is true that prudence must work from the general principles of moral science, and hence supposes them, it is also true that prudence must play an important part in formulating the more remote conclusions of the moral law. Such conclusions, it is true, are virtually contained in the principles themselves and might, at least in theory, be deduced from them. But in practice metaphysical relations are often obscure. They are brought to the surface often

---

[24] Gerald Kelly, S.J., *Guidance for Religious,* p. 310 n.

[25] John LaFarge, S.J., *Interracial Justice* (New York: America Press, 1937), pp. 107–124.

[26] John E. Coogan, S.J., "Christian Untouchables?" *Review for Religious,* 5 (1946), 107–113; John P. Markoe, S.J., "A Moral Appraisal of the Color Line," *Homiletic and Pastoral Review,* 48 (1948), 834.

[27] Daniel M. Cantwell, *The Challenge of Interracial Justice,* pp. 41–42.

enough only as the result of experience. The prudential judgment of an individual in one generation may well become established as a moral conclusion in the next. Thus prudence has a function not only in regard to individual acts, but also, though more remotely, in regard to moral science itself. . . . In moral science its function will be merely to bring to the surface the relations between moral principles and the more remote conclusions that are frequently hidden from the speculative intellect.[28]

This function of prudence, described by Father Connery, has, I believe, been operative in the formulation of the moral judgments on racial segregation. The experiences of these several generations have shown, under the guidance of prudence, that in the concrete, racial segregation is not the morally indifferent act that it appears to be when regarded abstractly and speculatively. These experiences have shown that a moral judgment must be made against segregation, as it is practiced, and that the principles of charity and justice are violated by it. It does not represent any new morality in the sense that moral principles have been altered. It merely means that these moral principles have been shown, through experience, to be violated under such practices of racial segregation.

---

[28] John R. Connery, S.J., "Prudence and Morality," *Theological Studies*, 13 (1952), 582.

CHAPTER 20

PERSONAL RESPONSIBILITY

Inevitably, in discussing a socioeconomic problem which is fundamentally a moral one, the problem of personal responsibilities will arise. When such a social system is judged morally objectionable, the question of the liceity of cooperation with that system or toleration of it by an individual becomes important. This is particularly true in the case of racial segregation. The morality of tolerating or cooperating with segregation practices and the responsibility of the individual frequently present a serious problem of conscience. However, it is impossible to attempt an exhaustive casuistic enumeration of obligations incumbent on individuals according to their abilities and state in life, or even to describe the variations of circumstances which might affect an obligation. Instead, we must contain the statement regarding personal responsibility within the broad framework of general principles, admitting the possible existence of factors which may prevent formal guilt and culpability, as well as the existence of excusing causes which may justify the toleration of objectionable acts or the postponement and delay of required acts.

There can be no doubt that in practicing or approving racial segregation, many seriously sin against various virtues, although they are not aware of the immorality of their acts. Social and environmental influences, education, training, prejudices, and other influences have resulted in a complete unconsciousness and unawareness of the morality involved in their actions, tantamount to invincible ignorance, excusing from formal guilt.

Father Donald Miller, C.Ss.R., speaking of the subjective or formal guilt of the actions of some people in their relations with Negroes, says that this guilt can only be judged by God since in these instances their ability to make proper judgments of right or wrong has been impaired by improper training and education.[1] Thus, in the various actions relating to different areas of racial interrelations, material and, granting the necessary conditions, formal sins against justice and charity are committed.

A similar situation may obtain in reference to the toleration of the objectionable system of segregation or particular practices within the system. We do not have reference here to permitting a situation to continue in order to protect the *de facto* common good or in order to secure a greater or higher good. We should indicate, however, that this is not a question of ends justifying the means, but rather the permission and toleration of a lesser evil for the sake of a greater good. We have already spoken about the vital role of the virtue of prudence in determining a justifiable permission of segregation practices. Regarding such toleration, it is interesting to note that the bishops of South Africa, even though they condemned racial segregation as "intrinsically evil," at the same time, recognized that cultural and social differences of the races in South Africa may justify or actually require "differential legislation."

> This condemnation of apartheid as something intrinsically evil does not imply that perfect equality can be established in South Africa by a stroke of the pen. There is nothing more obvious than the existence of profound differences between sections of our population, which make immediate total integration impossible. . . . All social change must be gradual if it is not to be disastrous. Nor is it unjust for a state to make provision in its laws and administration for the differences that do exist. . . . It would be unreasonable, therefore, to condemn indiscriminately all South Africa's differential legislation.[2]

Father Gerald Kelly, speaking of a gradual plan tending toward full school desegregation as morally justified where necessary in order to avoid violence and bitterness, compares it to a delay in restoring stolen goods to their owner, or to an "installment plan" restitution:

---

[1] Donald F. Miller, C.Ss.R., "Questions about Racial Segregation," *Interracial Review*, 29 (August, 1956), 137.
[2] Eugene McManus, *op. cit.*, pp. 85–86.

It seems, however, that if the gradual plan is necessary in order to avoid such evils as physical violence and prolonged bitterness, it is morally justified, just as, for example, the duty of restoration may be fulfilled gradually when complete restitution cannot be made immediately without incurring proportionately great evils.[3]

Unfortunately, gradual plans are taken by many to indicate a do-nothing attitude in which no changes are accomplished by conscious or deliberate effort, and gradualism is understood as a euphemism for inactivity. The result has been that any mention of a gradual plan arouses immediate antagonism in many who have undergone a life-time of discrimination and are impatiently awaiting removal of all racial restrictions. C. Vann Woodward has indicated the views which have been taken of "gradualism," and insists that it has a legitimate and proper role in the solution of race problems.

The preponderant evidence points to the eventual doom of segregation in American life and the triumph of the Second Reconstruction — in the long run. But the "long run" implies "gradualism," and "gradual-ism" is a word that has acquired almost as evil associations as the word "appeasement" once had. Impatience with the word among people who have already waited nearly a hundred years for promised rights is readily understandable. The word is used here not to propose or define a policy, but to characterize a historic phenomenon. Undesirable or not gradualism is an unescapable fact and a basic characteristic of the New Reconstruction.[4]

Obviously when we speak of tolerating segregation, it is to be under-stood within the framework of a system of amelioration and correc-tion, culminating in a complete discontinuance of racial segregation. We do not intend to indicate an impassive and indifferent permission of these practices. The individual has a responsibility to work for the correction of defects in the social system, according to his oppor-tunities and abilities. Father Harold Cooper, S.J., indicates that obligation as having a negative as well as a positive aspect. Presented or considered negatively, he must refuse to support segregation either politically, financially, or morally, lest his action aid, strengthen, or enlarge it. Considered positively, he should, according to the gravity of the difficulties which will be encountered and his abilities, work to abolish segregation. This he can accomplish through prayers, by

---

[3] Gerald Kelly, "Notes on Moral Theology," *Theological Studies*, 15 (1954), 80.

[4] C. Vann Woodward, *The Strange Career of Jim Crow*, p. 178.

acquiring a deeper knowledge of the Church's social teaching for himself and then extending it to his family, and finally, by putting this teaching into practice so that his deeds and his words will afford a constant good example and encouragement for others.[5]

We should mention again the obligation to resist feelings of hatred or animosity or temptations to prejudice which spontaneously arise. These tendencies to rash judgment or uncharitableness should be resisted just as any other temptation. The personal responsibility to control and regulate one's actions and to resist temptations to racial hatred was summed up by Brother Gerald Schnepp, S.M., in a radio address on integration in the schools of St. Louis:

> . . . if you nourish the prejudice; if you try to influence others to be prejudiced; if you close your eyes to your moral obligations; if you convey race prejudice to your children — then I would say that it is time for a re-examination.[6]

Fulfillment of these obligations may mean that those who do so will be forced to act differently from the general and common practices of their neighbors. But this departure from prevalent ideals and actions, while it may render decisions and deeds more difficult for the individual, cannot always be used as a justifying reason for conformity. The requirements of Christian living will often demand nonconformity. Father LaFarge speaks of the obligation of Catholics to be nonconformists in matters of marriage, divorce, religious education, ecclesiastical laws of abstinence on Fridays, and other moral questions, and indicates a parallel obligation to be a nonconformist in the matter of race relations.[7]

Probably the most efficient natural impetus to action on both the personal level, through restraint of prejudice and of actions stemming from dislike and aversion, and on the social or community level, through endeavors to improve race relations in the community, is the ability to appreciate the feelings, emotions, and reactions that the individual Negro experiences when he is discriminated against. Father Gerald Kelly speaks of empathy, or the ability to imagine oneself in

[5] Harold L. Cooper, S.J., "Questions and Answers on Segregation," *Social Order*, 6 (1956), 432.

[6] Gerald J. Schnepp, S.M., "Integration in St. Louis Schools," *Catholic Mind*, 51 (Oct., 1953), 613–617.

[7] John LaFarge, *Catholic Viewpoint on Race Relations*, p. 119.

the place of another and stresses its value as a means of understanding the importance of increased efforts to improve race relations:

> . . . any white man with good will and a good imagination can learn much by using what psychologists call "empathy" — namely, by putting himself in the Negro's place, by trying to feel what the Negro feels in the various frustrating circumstances that make up the pattern of discrimination. Psychologically, this cultivation of a strong "fellow-feeling" is perhaps the best antidote for aversion, because one powerful emotion tends to neutralize the other. Besides, deep feeling for the Negro stimulates constructive action in his behalf. Some of the greatest strides towards interracial justice have been made by white men who had the power of sharing the hurt feelings of the Negro.[8]

Empathy, however, involves the ability to apprehend the internal emotions and reactions of another *as if you were that person.* It should not be confused with *identification.* The *as if* condition is essential for empathy, and, without it, the apprehension of another becomes identification.

An outstanding attempt to learn what the Negro experiences, and what his emotional reactions are to his daily contacts with whites, was made by a reporter who, through medication, temporarily changed his skin color and traveled through the deep South as a Negro. After approximately five weeks of travel, he allowed his skin to return to its normal color and reentered the white world. He described his experiences and feelings in a book which represents what is probably the most extensive documentation of racial empathy. The author, John Howard Griffin, gives a description of the hatred of some whites toward Negroes, manifested by what the Negroes call "a hate stare," and which Griffin indicates was one of the most profound and stirring emotional experiences he ever had:

> Once again a "hate stare" drew my attention like a magnet. It came from a middle-aged, heavy-set, well-dressed white man. He sat a few yards away, fixing his eyes on me. Nothing can describe the withering horror of this. You feel lost, sick at heart before such unmasked hatred, not so much because it threatens you as because it shows humans in such an inhuman light. You see a kind of insanity, something so obscene the very obscenity of it (rather than its threat) terrifies you. It was so new I could not take my eyes from the man's face. I felt like saying: "What in God's name are you doing to yourself?"[9]

[8] Gerald Kelly, "How to Think and Act about the Race Problem," *loc. cit.,* p. 311.
[9] John Howard Griffin, *Black Like Me* (New York: Signet Books, 1962), p. 53.

We have spoken of the twofold moral obligation of the white person to (1) control and regulate personal actions, thoughts, and dislikes, and to (2) make a personal contribution, according to circumstances and his abilities to help correct the social system, by acting according to the principles and obligations of social justice and social charity. A similar duplex obligation, mutatis mutandis, is incumbent on the Negro, namely to regulate and control his interior and exterior acts, and to contribute to the correction of the social system.

It is a recognized fact that frequently the Negro is prejudiced against the white person and bears hatred and rancor against all whites. This animosity is, of course, largely brought about by the abuses and mistreatment the Negro has undergone. While this may explain the existence of such hostility, it does not make it less undesirable or less harmful. Too frequently, because of inability to direct hatred and rancor against the white man, other minority groups are utilized as substitutes, e.g., Jews, or even distinguishable Negro groups such as darker Negroes or lower classes. Particularly harmful is the inner direction of frustrated hostility toward one's self, resulting in psychological complexes and self-hatred. Often such attitudes result in oversensitiveness and suspicion of whites who are sincerely attempting to effect social change, and a refusal to assist or cooperate with them in a common effort. Juan Comas has written on this oversensitiveness and suspicion which result from an inferiority complex:

> There are Negroes whose quite understandable inferiority complex leads them to read hostility to their race, and the wish to keep them down, into any painful or even disagreeable action or decision, even when it relates to an individual only and color prejudice does not enter into it in the slightest degree. The seething rancor and hatred born of past offenses, the mistrust of advances by white people, the bitter and sometimes overt loathing of anything white, must all be conquered, subdued and forgotten if a real spirit of understanding is to grow up between the two races.[10]

There is an obligation on the part of the educated, upper-class Negroes to play a responsible role as leaders in endeavors toward a betterment of the social, economic, and educational position of poorer and uneducated Negroes. Frazier, an outstanding Negro sociologist,

---

[10] Juan Comas, *Racial Myths*, p. 26.

has criticized the middle-class Negroes of this country for their failure
to assume the responsibility of leadership which is theirs by reason
of position and education and for their indifference toward the advancement of the Negro race, except insofar as they were personally
advanced by it or made more acceptable to the whites, and finally
for their exploitation of the lower classes, which exploitation, he
claims, is as bad as any inflicted by the whites.[11] However, it is
possible that the fact of partial or limited desegregation is responsible
for the existence of a "marginal person," that is, a Negro who has
special interests in both the white and the Negro community. This
phenomenon may explain some instances of what has been criticized
as self-interest or indifference.[12]

Recently, John Fischer, editor of Harper's, wrote that the most
pressing need of the Negro is Negro leadership which will assume
the task of training the lower classes to accept their responsibilities
as good citizens. He maintains that there are four general areas
where improvement must be made before fears of integration are
assuaged and prejudice lessened. These are: crime, neighborhood
deterioration, civic apathy, and moral irresponsibility. Only a few
Negro leaders, he writes, are squarely facing this problem.[13] His
article aroused a storm of controversy. There was an "extraordinary
outpouring" of letters to the editors and it was claimed that 60 percent
of these were in general agreement with the article, while the other
40 percent were in disagreement.

It may be debated whether Mr. Fischer's suggestion of an all-
Negro Citizen's Council is the best means of removing prejudice or
whether, as has been claimed, his demands are unrealistic in that he
expects the underprivileged and uneducated Negro groups to exhibit
social, moral, and civic conduct superior to that demanded of socially
and educationally superior white groups. Nevertheless, all will admit
the need of the continuation and expansion of aid and support to
groups or individuals endeavoring to advance the underprivileged

---

[11] E. Franklin Frazier, Black Bourgeoisie (Glencoe: Free Press & Falcon's
Wing Press, 1957), pp. 234–238.

[12] Hylan Lewis and Mozell Hill, "Desegregation, Integration, and the Negro
Community," Annals of the American Academy of Political and Social Science,
304 (March, 1956), 122.

[13] John Fischer, "What the Negro Needs Most," Harper's, 225 (July, 1962),
12–19.

groups. Frequently Negro leaders express the lack of support which they experience as representative of a handicap to the progress of their work. Whitney Young, Jr., of the National Urban League, has told of his difficulty in securing financial support for the operation of the National Office of the Urban League, as well as for its affiliates, and he has stressed the scarcity of white and Negro willingness to cooperate for meeting the problems specified by Mr. Fischer. This, he indicated, renders the suggestion of a new organization, made by Mr. Fischer, completely unrealistic.[14]

It is most likely that desegregation may mean for some upper-class Negroes an economic disadvantage. This is particularly so in instances where segregated facilities have caused a duplication of jobs, as in educational systems, where there is an almost completely re-duplicated administrative setup. Desegregation may well mean, in some of these instances, that jobs will be abolished and work consolidated. Negroes who are at present holding these jobs may fear that with the abolishment of positions they will be at a dis-advantage in competing against white incumbents for the jobs. Hence, some are not too anxious to see a complete end of segregation. Frazier has described their attitude:

> Because of their privileged position behind the walls of segregation members of the upper class generally do not contemplate without misgivings the complete integration of the Negro into American life. The Negro business and professional men who enjoy monopolies in the Negro community do not want to meet the competition of men and institutions in the larger community.[15]

Others, however, do not believe that desegregation will mean the end of racially distinct facilities. They believe that desegregated services and institutions will coexist with their racial counterparts, and that the patronization of these by Negroes will be irregular. For certain types of services, the desegregated facilities will be preferred; while for others, habit or other factors will lead to the utilization of the racially distinct facility.[16]

In view of the possibility of economic loss, it is understandable

---

[14] *Harper's*, 225 (Sept., 1962), 6.

[15] E. Franklin Frazier, *The Negro in the United States*, rev. ed., (New York: The Macmillan Co., 1958), pp. 298–299.

[16] Hylan Lewis and Mozell Hill, *loc. cit.*, 122.

298 THEOLOGY AND RACE RELATIONS

why there would be lack of enthusiasm, especially when great difficulties had to be overcome in order to secure the education and the training necessary to qualify for these positions. The Negro professional and business man who, even though he foresees a possible economic disadvantage to himself, works and struggles for the advancement of his neighbor and for the discontinuance of segregation must certainly be commended for his altruism and charity, particularly when his possible loss and disadvantage would most likely remove an *obligation* of charity, thereby making his act supererogatory.

The most extreme organized reaction of Negroes to segregation and the abuses they have suffered is found in the Black Muslims. Basically this is a religion, representing an ultimate in protest against injustice to the Negro. The Black Muslims, differing from such organizations as the Urban League or the NAACP, reject any idea of racial integration on any level with the whites. Social, religious, economic, educational, or political integration is discountenanced and rejected by them. Their goal is the absolute and complete separation of the races through the establishment of a separate territory or state to be given by the federal government to the Negroes as compensation for the centuries of free slave labor and as restitution for the theft of land from the Indians, who are also nonwhites. For the Black Muslims, Christianity is a white man's religion and has been the chief instrument used by them for the continued enslavement and degradation of the Negro. This was accomplished chiefly through the preaching of Negro ministers. It is impossible for the liberated Negro to continue to be a Christian — Christianity is incompatible with his welfare and his interests. The white man and his Christian religion must be completely rejected.[17]

An amazing feature of the Black Muslims is that, though the chief appeal is ordinarily to the social misfit, nevertheless, a strict and most rigid rule of morality, which is almost completely puritanical, is imposed on the members and apparently adhered to by them strictly. This code does not look forward to a reward in a future life nor is it

---

[17] Cf. C. Eric Lincoln, *The Black Muslims in America* (Boston: Beacon Press, 1961), pp. 84–97; James Baldwin, "Letter from a Region in My Mind," *New Yorker,* November 17, 1962, 59 ff.; E. U. Essien-Udom, *Black Nationalism: A Search for an Identity in America* (Chicago: University of Chicago Press, 1962); Haynes Johnson, *op. cit.,* Chap. IX, "Slaves of the Stars and Stripes," pp. 136–150.

based on any spiritual or supernatural motives. Its motivation is strictly natural — namely, that this is the proper way for the Negro, as the true ruler of the earth, to live. Certain foods (pork and cornbread) are forbidden by dietary laws. In general only one meal a day is permitted, and overweight, which is not corrected, is punished by a fine. Attendance at Black Muslim temples is required several times a week, and absenteeism is punished. Male members are required to seek converts, and failure to obtain them is penalized. This may well account for the interest and amazing success they have had with the rehabilitation of criminals, alcoholics, and dope addicts. There is a very strict code of sexual morality binding on both men and women members. Economy, self-reliance, and responsibility, as well as thrift and avoidance of credit buying and similar virtues are inculcated and practiced. In a word, the Black Muslims succeed in accomplishing improvement in at least three of the areas which Mr. Fischer claims need reform: crime, neighborhood deterioration, and moral responsibility. Regarding civic apathy, the refusal of the Muslims to associate with whites would preclude any mutual civic endeavors.

The success of a religion which is essentially anti-Christian and established on racial hatred in rehabilitating those who have at least been exposed to Christian instruction and training is an indication of the injuries done by Christians who are prejudiced. It is an indictment of the practices of the Christian denominations who have failed even though they possess the teachings of Christ on charity and brotherly love, while a religion lacking these and professing hatred is able to succeed.

But movements such as the Muslims, even though they are successful in the rehabilitation of the fallen and in imposing a high code of morality and inculcating economic virtues such as thrift and economy, nevertheless, are seriously harmful both to the individual and to society at large. The hatred which is generated and increased gradually poisons the heart of the member, and it is inevitable that the Black Muslim will eventually present himself as the Negro counterpart of the extreme white racist or anti-Semitic Nazi. "A man cannot hate his brother without being a murderer."

Even though membership and participation in such organizations by Negroes may appear to be reasonable and to have a foundation in the treatment they have received, nevertheless, this does not justify such acts. The obligation of charity to refrain from such hatred or cooperation with organizations fostering hate is incumbent on the Negro no less than on the white. Voluntary membership or cooperation with hate groups such as the Ku Klux Klan and similar organizations by whites cannot be justified and is morally reprehensible. So is voluntary membership and cooperation of Negroes with hate groups morally wrong. The fact that the whites have inflicted injuries and given occasion for hate does not eliminate the obligation to love all, even our enemies. The command "Love your enemies, do good to those that hate you, pray for those who persecute and insult you, that so you may be true sons of your Father in heaven" (Mt 5:44–45) binds all.

Finally, the very magnitude and complexity of the race problem can cause some who are well-intentioned and desirous of contributing and aiding in the resolution of the question to become discouraged. The intricacies of the problem and the opposition of some to change modes of action or to lessen prejudices have led to discouragement. They ask what their small contribution can do to effect a change in the social system in the face of such opposition. When such discouragement takes hold, they are led to abandon all efforts to reform social systems and, following the path of least resistance, drift along with general practices and customs. Internally disapproving of common modes of action, they maintain silence and offer no resistance. That such discouragement, with its resultant passive toleration, is an important factor in the continuance of an unjust social system has been recognized by the Catholic bishops of South Africa. In their 1962 Pastoral Letter they indicated this and tried to encourage their people to action, pointing out the great importance of even the smallest deed which has been transformed by the alchemy of charity. Their enheartening words, stressing the value of the simplest act of charity, and their exhortation to the greatest form of empathy, the ability to see Christ in the lowest and neediest of their fellowmen, as an important factor in a Christian solution of the race problem, should be pointed out to all, white or Negro, who are liable to become victims of a sense of futility and hopelessness because of the scope and size of the problem. Indicating the duty of all Christians to

work toward a peaceful relationship between the various races form-
ing society, the bishops state:

> Some people tend to let themselves be overawed by the immensity
> and complexity of the problems of our times. They lose heart and
> sink back into passive inactivity at the thought that they lack both
> the numbers and the power to influence national policy. Because they
> cannot perform great deeds, they sit back and do nothing. They forget
> Our Lord's assurance that the cup of cold water given in His name
> will have its reward before God.
>
> Christian charity always begins with little things, just as God the
> Son took the form of a little child to bring divine love to the world.
> Christian charity is concerned with human beings, with men and
> women of any and every kind. It is the love of God reflected in men's
> dealings with each other.
>
> The ordinary and seemingly insignificant kindly deeds and gentle cour-
> tesies of daily life are the signs that men love God above all else,
> and their neighbors as themselves for God's sake. It is these simple
> acts, multiplied a million times each day, which most certainly bring
> the healing influence of Christ's presence and of His teachings to bear
> upon the disorders and injustices which afflict us.
>
> If charity grows cold among men, it is because they do not want to
> take to heart all that is meant by seeing Christ in their neighbor.
> How can Christ be there in someone poor or needy or distressed?
> "Lord, when was it that we saw Thee hungry, or thirsty, or a stranger,
> or naked, or sick, or in prison, and did not minister to Thee? And
> the King will answer: 'Believe me, when you refused it to one of
> the least of my brethren, you refused it to me' " (Mt 25:44).
>
> Here, then, is the Christian test which must be applied to racial
> prejudice. As long as we have acted like that toward anyone who differs
> from us in color, so it is that we have acted toward Christ Himself.[18]

---

[18] "Christ in Our World," pastoral letter of the Archbishops and Bishops of
South Africa, Pretoria, January 30–February 2, 1962, *Catholic Mind*, 60 (1962),
60–61.

SELECTED BIBLIOGRAPHY

BOOKS

Abrams, Charles, *Forbidden Neighbors: A Study of Prejudice in Housing* (New York: Harper & Bros., 1955).

Ahmann, Mathew H. (ed.), *The New Negro* (Notre Dame: Fides Publishers, 1961).

Alphonsus Liguori, St., *Opera Moralia*, ed. by Leonard Gaudé, C.Ss.R., 4 vols. (Graz: Akademische Druck — U. Verlanganstalt, 1953).

Ariel (Buckner H. Payne), *The Negro: What is his ethnological status? Is he the progeny of Ham? Is he a descendant of Adam and Eve — What is his relation to the white race?* (Cincinnati: published for the proprietor, 1867).

Ashmore, Harry S., *The Other Side of Jordan* (New York: W. W. Norton & Co., 1960).

Barnett, Richard, and Garai, Joseph, *Where the States Stand on Civil Rights* (New York: Bold Face Books, 1962).

Becker, Gary S., *The Economics of Discrimination* (Chicago: University of Chicago Press, 1957).

Berrigan, Philip, S.S.J., *Catholic Church and the Negro* (St. Louis: The Queen's Work, 1962).

Blaustein, Albert P., and Ferguson, Clarence Clyde, Jr., *Desegregation and the Law: The Meaning and Effect of the School Segregation Cases* (New Brunswick: Rutgers University Press, 1957).

Bloch, J. M., *Miscegenation, Melaleukation, and Mr. Lincoln's Dog* (New York: Schaum Publishing Co., 1958).

Brokhage, Joseph D., *Francis Patrick Kenrick's Opinion on Slavery* (Washington, D. C.: The Catholic University of America Press, 1955).

Calvez, Jean Yves, S.J., and Perrin, Jacques, S.J., *The Church and Social Justice: The Social Teaching of the Popes from Leo XIII to Pius XII (1878–1958)*, tr. by J. R. Kirwan (Chicago: Henry Regnery Co., 1961).

Carmichael, Omer, and James, Weldon, *The Louisville Story* (New York: Simon and Schuster, 1957).

Carter, Gwendolen M., *The Politics of Inequality: South Africa since 1948* (London: Thames and Hudson, 1958).

Changing Patterns in the New South (Atlanta: Southern Regional Council, 1955).

Church and Race in South Africa: Papers from South Africa, 1952–1957, illustrating the Churches' Search for the Will of God, edited by David M. Paton (London: SCM Press Ltd., 1958).

Clark, Dennis, *The Ghetto Game: Racial Conflicts in the City* (New York: Sheed and Ward, 1962).

Comas, Juan, *Racial Myths* ("The Race Question in Modern Science Series") (Paris: UNESCO, 1951).

Congar, Yves M.-J., O.P., *The Catholic Church and the Race Question* ("The Race Question in Modern Science Series") (Paris:UNESCO, 1953).

Conway, Msgr. J. D., *What they ask about Morals* (Notre Dame: Fides, 1960).

Costello, Joseph A., S.M., *Moral Aspects of Segregation* (New Orleans, 1956).

Cotter, A. C., S.J., *The Encyclical "Humani Generis" with a Commentary* (Weston: Weston College Press, 1952).

Cronan, Edward P., *The Dignity of the Human Person* (New York: Philosophical Library, 1955).

Cronin, John F., S.S., *Catholic Social Principles: The Social Teaching of the Catholic Church Applied to American Economic Life* (Milwaukee: The Bruce Publishing Co., 1955).

————— *Social Principles and Economic Life* (Milwaukee: The Bruce Publishing Co., 1959).

DePloige, Rt. Rev. Simon, *The Conflict between Ethics and Sociology,* tr. by Charles C. Miltner, C.S.C. (St. Louis: Herder, 1938).

Doherty, Joseph F., *Moral Problems of Interracial Marriage* (Washington, D. C.: The Catholic University of America Press, 1949).

Dollard, John, *Caste and Class in a Southern Town,* 3 ed. (Garden City: Doubleday & Co., 1957).

Dumond, Dwight Lowell, *Antislavery: The Crusade for Freedom in America* (Ann Arbor: University of Michigan Press, 1961).

Dykeman, Wilma, and Stokely, James, *Neither Black Nor White* (New York: Rinehart & Co., 1957).

Essien-Udom, E. U., *Black Nationalism: A Search for an Identity in America* (Chicago: University of Chicago Press, 1962).

Fletcher, Most Rev. Albert, *Elementary Catholic Catechism on the Morality of Discrimination and Racial Segregation* (Little Rock, 1960).

Ford, John C., S.J., and Kelly, Gerald, S.J., *Contemporary Moral Theology.* Vol. 1: *Questions in Fundamental Moral Theology* (Westminster: Newman Press, 1958).

Frazier, E. Franklin, *Black Bourgeoisie.* (Glencoe: Free Press & Falcon's Wing Press, 1957).

————— *The Negro in the United States,* rev. ed. (New York: The Macmillan Co., 1958).

Giles, Harry H., *The Integrated Classroom* (New York: Basic Books, 1959).

Gillard, John T., S.S.J., *The Catholic Church and the American Negro* (Baltimore: St. Joseph's Society Press, 1929).

————— *Colored Catholics in the United States* (Baltimore: Josephite Press, 1941).

Gilligan, Francis J., *The Morality of the Color Line* (Washington, D. C.: The Catholic University of America Press, 1929).

Gilson, Etienne (ed.), *The Church Speaks to the Modern World: The Social Teachings of Leo XIII* (Garden City: Image Books, 1954).

Ginzberg, Eli, et al., *The Negro Potential* (New York: Columbia University Press, 1956).

Grayzel, Solomon, *The Church and the Jews in the XIIIth Century: A Study of their Relations during the years 1198–1254, Based on the*

Papal Letters and the Conciliar Decrees of the Period (Philadelphia: Dropsie College for Hebrew and Cognate Learning, 1933).

Greenberg, Jack, *Race Relations and American Law* (New York: Columbia University Press, 1959).

Guste, Robert, *For Men of Good Will* (New Orleans, 1957).

Hanke, Lewis, *Aristotle and the American Indians: A Study in Race Prejudice in the Modern World* (Chicago: Henry Regnery Co., 1959).

Huddleston, Trevor C. R., *Naught for your Comfort* (Garden City: Doubleday & Co., 1956).

Johnson, Charles S., *Patterns of Negro Segregation*, 2 ed. (New York: Harper & Bros., 1943).

Johnson, Haynes, *Dusk at the Mountain: The Negro, the Nation, and the Capital — A Report on Problems and Progress* (Garden City: Doubleday & Co., 1963).

Karon, Bertram P., *The Negro Personality: A Rigorous Investigation of the Effects of Culture* (New York: Springer Publishing Co., 1958).

Kelly, Gerald, S.J., *Guidance for Religious* (Westminster: Newman Press, 1957).

Kelly, Gerald, S.J., and Ford, John C., see Ford.

Kenrick, Francis P., *Theologiae Moralis*, 3 vols. (Philadelphia: Eugene Cummiskey, 1843).

King, Martin Luther, *Stride toward Freedom: The Montgomery Story* (New York: Harper & Bros., 1958).

Korn, Bertram W., *American Jewry and the Civil War* (Cleveland and Philadelphia: Meridian Books and the Jewish Publication Society of America, 1961).

LaFarge, John, S.J., *The Catholic Viewpoint on Race Relations* (New York: Hanover House, 1956).

―――― *Interracial Justice: A Study of the Catholic Doctrine of Race Relations* (New York: America Press, 1937).

―――― (ed.), *Sermons on Interracial Justice* (New York: Catholic Interracial Council, 1957).

Laurenti, Luigi, *Property Values and Race: Studies in Seven Cities. Special Research Report to the Commission on Race and Housing* (Berkeley: University of California Press, 1960).

Lincoln, C. Eric, *The Black Muslims in America* (Boston: Beacon Press, 1961).

Litwack, Leon F., *North of Slavery: The Negro in the Free States, 1790–1860* (Chicago: University of Chicago Press, 1961).

Loescher, Frank S., *The Protestant Church and the Negro: A Pattern of Segregation* (New York: Association Press, 1948).

McEntire, Davis, *Residence and Race: Final and Comprehensive Report to the Commission on Race and Housing* (Berkeley: University of California Press, 1960).

McLaughlin, Terence P., C.S.B. (ed.), *The Church and the Reconstruction of the Modern World: The Social Encyclicals of Pius XI* (Garden City: Image Books, 1957).

McManus, Eugene P., S.S.J., *Studies in Race Relations* (Baltimore: Josephite Press, 1961).

Man, Race, and Darwin: Papers Read at a Joint Conference of the Royal Anthropological Institute and the Institute of Race Relations (London: Oxford University Press, 1960).

Maritain, Jacques, Anti-Semitism (London: Geoffrey Bles: The Centenary Press, 1939).

——— The Person and the Common Good, tr. by John J. Fitzgerald (New York: Charles Scribner's Sons, 1947).

Maston, T. B., Segregation and Desegregation: A Christian Approach (New York: The Macmillan Co., 1959).

Messner, Josef, Social Ethics, tr. by J. J. Doherty (St. Louis: B. Herder Book Co., 1949).

Miller, Arthur S., Racial Discrimination and Private Education: A Legal Analysis (Chapel Hill: University of North Carolina Press, 1957).

Myrdal, Gunnar, An American Dilemma: The Negro Problem and Modern Democracy (New York: Harper & Bros., 1944).

Nelson, William Stuart (ed.), The Christian Way in Race Relations (New York: Harper & Bros., 1948).

O'Neill, Joseph E., S.J. (ed.), A Catholic Case Against Segregation (New York: Macmillan Co., 1961).

Proudfoot, Merrill, Diary of a Sit-in (Chapel Hill: University of North Carolina Press, 1962).

Ramsey, Paul (ed.), Faith and Ethics: The Theology of H. Richard Niebuhr (New York: Harper & Bros., 1957).

Rice, Madeleine Hooke, American Catholic Opinion in the Slavery Controversy (New York: Columbia University Press, 1944).

Roche, Richard J., O.M.I., Catholic Colleges and the Negro Student (Washington, D. C.: The Catholic University of America Press, 1948).

Rose, Arnold, The Roots of Prejudice ("The Race Question in Modern Science Series") (Paris: UNESCO, 1951).

Senser, Robert, Primer on Interracial Justice (Baltimore: Helicon, 1962).

Shuey, Audrey M., The Testing of Negro Intelligence (Lynchburg: J. P. Bell Co., 1958).

Staab, Giles J., O.F.M.Cap., The Dignity of Man in Modern Papal Doctrine: Leo XIII to Pius XII, 1878–1955 (Washington, D. C.: The Catholic University of America Press, 1957).

Stanton, William, The Leopard's Spots: Scientific Attitudes toward Race in America, 1815–1859 (Chicago: University of Chicago Press, 1960).

Tannenbaum, Frank, Slave and Citizen: The Negro in the Americas (New York: Alfred A. Knopf, 1947).

Weatherford, W. D., American Churches and the Negro: An Historical Study from Early Slave Days to the Present (Boston: Christopher Publishing House, 1957).

Weaver, Robert C., The Negro Ghetto (New York: Harcourt, Brace & Co., 1948).

Wittke, Carl, The Irish in America (Baton Rouge: Louisiana State University Press, 1956).

Woodward, C. Vann, The Strange Career of Jim Crow, new and rev. ed. (New York: Oxford University Press, 1957).

Wynes, Charles E., *Race Relations in Virginia, 1870–1902* (Charlottesville: University of Virginia Press, 1961).

ARTICLES AND PERIODICALS

Alberti, Ottorino, "L'Unita del Genere Umano nell'insegnamento del Magistero della Chiesa," *Divinitas*, 3 (1961), 735–797.

Baldwin, James, "Letter from a Region in My Mind," *The New Yorker* (November 17, 1962), 59 ff.

Bernard, Raymond, S.J., "Some Anthropological Implications of the Racial Admission Policy of the U.S. Sisterhoods," *The American Catholic Sociological Review*, 19 (June, 1958), 124–133.

Bernstein, Barton J., "Case Law in Plessy v. Ferguson," *Journal of Negro History*, 47 (July, 1960), 192–198.

Brodie, Sydney, "The Federally Secured Right to be Free from Bondage," *Georgetown Law Journal*, 40 (March, 1952), 367–398.

Brumley, Cal, "Segregation Costs," *The Wall Street Journal* (December 17, 1957).

Buckley, William F., Jr., "Desegregation, Will it Work? No." *Saturday Review*, 44 (November 11, 1961), 21–22.

Butsch, Joseph, S.S.J., "Negro Catholics in the United States," *Catholic Historical Review*, 3 (1917), 33–51.

Cantwell, Daniel M., "Race Relations — As seen by a Catholic," *The American Catholic Sociological Review*, 7 (December, 1946), 242.

Carter, Hodding, "Desegregation Does Not Mean Integration," *New York Times Magazine* (February 11, 1962), p. 21 ff.

Clinch, Mary, "A Freedom Rider Remembers," *Community*, 22 (October, 1962), 3 ff.

Connell, Francis J., C.Ss.R., "The Bishop's Teaching Authority," *American Ecclesiastical Review*, 134 (April, 1956), 272–274.

————— "Rights of the Catholic Negro," *American Ecclesiastical Review*, 114 (1946), 459–462.

Connery, John R., S.J., "Notes on Moral Theology," *Theological Studies*, 15 (Dec., 1954), 594–626.

————— "Prudence and Morality," *Theological Studies*, 13 (December, 1952), 564–582.

————— "Social Aspects of Catholic Dogma," *Catholic Mind*, 50 (1952), 484–493.

Coogan, John E., S.J., "Christian Untouchables?" *Review for Religious*, 5 (1946), 107–113.

Coonan, John L., "Catholics and Colour Prejudice," *Clergy Review*, 44 (May, 1959), 287–293.

Cooper, Harold L., S.J., "Priests, Prejudice, and Race," *Catholic Mind*, 57 (1959), 499–505.

————— "Questions and Answers on Segregation," *Social Order*, 6 (1956), 432–433.

Didas, James F., S.S.J., "Negro Challenge to the Church," *Catholic Mind*, 50 (1952), 257–262.

Dunn, James J., S.S.P., "Priests and Prejudice," *Pastoral Life*, 6 (March-April, 1958), 29–31.

Dunne, George H., S.J., "The Meaning of Racism," *Commonweal*, 69 (February 6, 1959), 492–494.

Dutto, L. A., "Negroes in Mississippi," *Catholic World*, 46 (February, 1888), 577–588.

Fischer, John, "What the Negro Needs Most: A First Class Citizens' Council," *Harpers*, 225 (July, 1962), 12–19.

Friedel, Lawrence M., S.V.D., "Is the Curse of Cham on the Negro Race?" *American Ecclesiastical Review*, 106 (1942), 447–453.

Gasnick, Roy M., O.F.M., "The Popes Speak on Racism," *The Homiletic and Pastoral Review*, 59 (June, 1959), 827–831.

Gilbert, Arthur, "A Jew Looks at the Ecumenical Council," *Ave Maria*, 94 (December 9, 1961), 5–7.

Gillard, John T., S.S.J., "Catholicism and the Negro," *Interracial Review*, 12 (June, 1939), 89–91.

Gilligan, Francis J., "The Color Line Considered Morally," *American Ecclesiastical Review*, 81 (1929), 482–491.

———— "Moral Aspects of Segregation in Education," *Proceedings of the 13th Annual Convention of the Catholic Theological Society of America* (1958), 51–64.

———— "Race Relations and Human Rights," *Interracial Review*, 19 (October, 1946), 150–153.

Gleason, Robert W., S.J., "The Immorality of Segregation," *Thought*, 35 (Autumn, 1960), 349–364.

Hayes, Charles L., "The Sit-in Demonstrations — In Retrospect," *Interracial Review*, 35 (June, 1962), 147–148.

Hyland, Philip, "The Field of Social Justice," *The Thomist*, 1 (1939). 295–330.

Janssens, Rt. Rev. Francis, "The Negro Problem and the Catholic Church," *Catholic World*, 44 (March, 1887), 721–726.

"Jim Crow, Librarian," *Interracial Review*, 27 (March, 1954), 40.

Jones, Virginia Lacy, "How Long? Oh, How Long?" *Library Journal*, 89 (December 15, 1962), 4504 ff.

Kaplan, Sidney, "The Miscegenation Issue in the Election of 1864," *Journal of Negro History*, 34 (July, 1949), 274–343.

Kelly, Gerald, S.J., "The Common Good and the Socio-Economic Order," *Proceedings of the 7th Annual Convention of the Catholic Theological Society of America* (1952), 83–110.

———— "How to Think and Act about the Race Problem," *Review for Religious*, 10 (1951), 316–324.

———— "Notes on Moral Theology, 1946," *Theological Studies* 8 (1947), 97–117.

———— "Notes on Moral Theology, 1950," *Theological Studies*, 12 (1951), 52–92.

———— "Notes on Moral Theology, 1951," *Theological Studies*, 13 1952, 59–100.

———— "Notes on Moral Theology, 1953," *Theological Studies*, 15 (1954), 52–102.

Kenealy, William J., S.J., "Desegregation: Challenge to Conservatives," *Social Order*, 12 (June, 1962), 249–256.
———— "The Legal Profession and Segregation," *Social Order*, 6 (1956), 483–490.
Lichten, Joseph L., "Pius XII and the Jews," *Catholic Mind*, 57 (March, 1959), 159–162.
McDermott, John, and Clark, Dennis, "Helping the Panic Neighborhood: A Philadelphia Approach," *Interracial Review*, 28 (1955), 131–135.
McGrath, Oswin, O.P., "The Theology of Racial Segregation," *Catholic Mind*, 55 (1957), 483–486.
Maritain, Jacques, "The Menace of Racialism," *Interracial Review*, 10, (1937), 70–71.
Markoe, John P., S.J., "A Moral Appraisal of the Color Line," *Homiletic and Pastoral Review*, 48 (1948), 828–836.
Meier, August, "Boycotts of Segregated Street Cars, 1894–1906: A Research Note," *The Phylon*, 18 (1957), 296–297.
Miller, Robert M., "The Attitudes of American Protestantism toward the Negro, 1919–1939," *Journal of Negro History*, 41 (1956), 215–240.
———— "The Protestant Churches and Lynching, 1919–1939," *Journal of Negro History*, 42 (1957), 118–131.
Rideau, E., S.J., "Charité Sociale," *Catholicisme*, II, 984–985.
Roberts, Gene, Jr., "Negro Education — For What?" *New York Times Magazine* (November 19, 1961), p. 26 ff.
Rorty, James, "What Segregationists Really Fear," *Ave Maria*, 88 (July 26, 1958), 5–7.
Slattery, John R., S.S.J., "The Catholic Negro's Complaint," *Catholic World*, 52 (December, 1890), 347–353.
———— "The Seminary for the Colored Missions," *Catholic World*, 46 (1888), 541–550.
Sullivan, Terry, "What is it like to be a Freedom Rider?" *Interracial Review*, 35 (June, 1962), 145.
Thorman, Donald J., "Catholic Approach to the Race Problem," *America*, 95 (May 5, 1956), 133–134.
Wicklein, John, "The Church in the South and Segregation," *New York Times*, July 5–8, 1959.
Woods, Sister Frances Jerome, C.D., "The Popes on Minority Rights," *Social Order*, 8 (1958), 465–472.
Woodson, Carter G., "The Beginnings of the Miscegenation of the Whites and Blacks," *Journal of Negro History*, 3 (October, 1918), 335–353.

INDEX

Abolition, attitude of Catholics, 223 f; Jewish attitude, 224

Abrams, Charles, on quota system, 179 f

Alphonsus Liguori, St., on common signs, 90

American Anthropological Association, resolution on Negro intelligence, 208

Anastasi, Anne, on Negro IQ, 207

Apartheid, 216; Catholic bishops on, 51, 265 f; condemnation, 291; immorality, 50 f

Ariel (pseud.), see Payne, Buckner H.

Association, right of, 47

Backbiting, 69 ff

Baltimore, II Council, authorizes Negro parishes, 229; III Council, Indian and Negro collection, 261

Beach, Waldo, on charity in race relations, 88; on racial attitude of churches, 218 f; on scarcity of theological literature, 2

Benevolent quota in housing, 179 ff

Bishops, right to teach, 278 ff

Bishops of Northern Rhodesia, on charity, 83

Bishops of South Africa, on apartheid, 51, 265 f, 291; on charity, 300 f; on prudence, 99 f

Bishops of Southern Rhodesia, on apartheid, 266 f

Bishops of U. S., 1958 statement, 51; development, 261 ff

Black Muslims, 298 ff

Blaustein, A., and Ferguson, Clarence C., Jr., on Brown decision, 189

Blood, mystique of, 14

Boycott, to prevent Negro employment, 141 f

Brotherhood of man, in papal documents, 256 ff

Brownson, Orestes, on Negro equality, 53

Brown v. Board of Education of Topeka, 187 ff

Buchanan v. Warley, 170

Calhoun, John C., defense of slavery, 55

Calvez, J.-Y., Perrin, J., on right to work, 132

Carter, Hodding, on school integration, 210 f

Casas, Bartolome de las, on "natural slaves," 9, 52

Catholic Church, establishing Negro parishes, 228 ff

Catholic colleges, Negro attendance, 245 f

Catholic newspapers, on abolition, 223

Catholics, Negro, in integrated parishes, 220 f; and racial prejudice, 9

Catholic schools, nonparochial, 244 f

Chamberlain, Houston Stewart, and racism, 15

Chambers, Robert, 29

Charity, common signs, 88 ff; in housing problems, 183 f; and justice, role in race relations, 62 ff; nature of, 83 ff; obligations of teachers and pupils, 211 ff; role in race relations, 87 f; social, 94 ff; South African bishops on, 300 f; violated in treatment of Negro co-worker, 145

Church, competence in social problems, 6 ff; conversion of Negro, 40; right to teach, 239 f

Churches, Catholic, segregated seating, 234 f; segregation in, 93, 216 ff

Ci torna sommamente (allocution), on obligation to strive toward end, 45 f

Civil Rights Cases of 1883, 196 ff, 211

Civil Rights Commission of 1961, on jury exclusion, 74 f

Color bar, 258 f; in South Africa, 267

Comas, Juan, on late appearance of racial prejudice, 8

Common good, 76 ff; and function of government, 45

Common signs of charity, 88 ff